WILDLY TOWARDS TRUTH

A SOUL-CENTERED GUIDE TO
FINDING AND LIVING YOUR PURPOSE

ALEXIS PIERCE

Copyright © 2025 Alexis Pierce

All rights reserved. This book may not be reproduced or transmitted in whole or in part, in any form or by any means, electronic or mechanical, including photocopying, recording, or by any information storage and retrieval system now known or hereafter invented, without permission in writing from the publisher.

ISBN: 978-1-7353477-0-7

Cover design by Jelena Mirkovic Jankovic
Visual harmonization by Santosh David

Library of Congress Control Number: 2025908444

Disclaimer: The information shared in this book is for educational and informational purposes only and is not intended to be viewed as medical or mental health advice. It is not designed to be a substitute for professional advice from your physician, therapist, attorney, accountant or any other health care practitioner or licensed professional. The Publisher and the Author do not make any guarantees as to the effectiveness of any of the techniques, suggestions, tips, ideas or strategies shared in this book as each situation differs. The Publisher and Author shall neither have liability nor responsibility with respect to any direct or indirect loss or damage caused or alleged by the information shared in this book related to your health, life or business or any other aspect of your situation. It's your responsibility to do your own due diligence and use your own judgment when applying any techniques or situations mentioned in or through this book. References to persons or situations in this book are fictional, though they may be based on real life situations. Some names and identifying details have been changed to protect privacy. Please be aware that any websites or references that were available during publication may not be available in the future.

Artificial Intelligence clause: This book was written by Alexis Pierce. OpenAI's ChatGPT was used to brainstorm sensory-inclusive language and assist in the glossary to summarize unique or original concepts mentioned in the text. All content decisions remain the sole work and responsibility of the author. The use of AI was guided by ethical standards to ensure originality, authenticity, and respect for intellectual property.

Published by Alexis Pierce LLC
Printed in Dallas, Texas

DEDICATION

To the truth within you.
May its ceaseless siren guide you
home to freedom.

TABLE OF CONTENTS

A Note from Alexis	*xiii*

Introduction

Your Soul's Clarion Call	1
My Promise to You	2
The How-To of "Just Be You!"	2
Pushing Through the "Yeah… But" Resistance	3
Who This Can Help	4
Self-Trust, Not Self-Help	4
Does the Word Soul Make Your Skin Crawl?	6
How to Use This Book	7
How This Book is Organized, AKA What to Expect	7
Little Ways I've Tried to Help You Win with the Book	8
What This Book Won't Do	10
A Beginning Prayer	13

PART I — BREAKING FREE

CHAPTER 1 — A NEW PURPOSE

Miserable in a Life You Love	17
15 Seconds to Remember Who You Are	18
Can You Want More Than Everything?	19
Rock Bottom at the Top	21
Consciousness Shifter — Imagine Purpose Like This	22
Without Truth, It's Just Guessing	23
What Do We Mean by Purpose?	24
Guiding and Leading at the Same Time	25
100 Words for Purpose	26
What Are You Hoping Purpose Will Give You?	27
Chapter 1 Summary	29

CHAPTER 2 — WHY YOUR PURPOSE ISN'T YOUR JOB

Set Up to Fail	31
The 3 Myths About Purpose That Mess with Your Head	32
Myth #1 — Your Purpose is Your Job or Work in the World	33
Danger Danger: 3 Ways You Lose When Your Purpose Is Your Career	34
Myth #2 — If You Achieve Success, You'll Be Happy	38
Myth #3 — Contentment and Meaning Are Your Rewards for Doing Well	40

Consciousness Shifter — A New Era of Being	42
Chapter 2 Summary	44

CHAPTER 3 — YOU'RE PLANNING FOR PURPOSE BACKWARD

This Recipe Doesn't Make Fulfillment	47
$100 Million in Vaccines Solves Global Peace, Right?	48
A Visionary Alternative	49
Shana & The Permaculture Massage Accounting Movement Center	51
Consciousness Shifter — You Can't Cobble Your Way into Purpose	52
Chapter 3 Summary	53

CHAPTER 4 — OTHER LIES ON PURPOSE

Dying of Good Ideas	55
Punishing Kids with Passion	56
Passion and the Anti-Force	59
Purpose Is Not Your "Why" or Motivation	60
Holding a Clear Channel — i.e. Opening Versus Controlling	62
When Your "Why" Leaves You Empty	63
Consciousness Shifter — Purpose Is Not Your Mission Or Life's "Work"	64
Strengths Tests Won't Help You Get Clear	67
Purpose Isn't About Meaning, Either	67
Service Is a Consequence, Not Your Purpose Itself	68
God's Work Doesn't Work as a Paradigm for Purpose	69
Chapter 4 Summary	70

CHAPTER 5 — WORKING WITH LIFE FOR TRUE PURPOSE

The Thorn in the Side of Your Otherwise Tolerable Life	73
Consciousness Shifter — Life Is You and You Are Life	75
Life Is Always for You	77
Square One and a Green Door	78
Endlessly Spiraling Green Doors	79
The Soul Doesn't Stop	81
Misreading the Soul's Signals	82
Two Ways the Soul Screams	83
The Easier Hard Road	87
The Metaphor that Saved Me	88
Excavating the Human Purpose	89
Living for the Fun of It	91
Being Whole and Always More	92
Chapter 5 Summary	94

PART II — CHARTING A NEW PATH

CHAPTER 6 — YOUR SOUL'S WORLD

Your Inner Truth	99
Real-World Roots	100
Impact of Your Vision	102
First Contact	102
Your Soul's World Makes You Unique	103
Your Soul's World is Just One Question Away	104
Let It be Simple	104
Creating Heaven on Earth	105
Going Beyond the Mind	106
The Soul's Goal	106
Consciousness Shifter — Becoming a Portal for Truth	107
Is Hate Truth Too?	108
What Your Soul Knows for Sure	109
But Aren't You Just Being Idealistic?	110
Does "Ideal" Mean Perfect?	111
Can Your Purpose and Vision Change?	112
Chapter 6 Summary	114

CHAPTER 7 — YOUR SOUL'S PURPOSE

Your Pathway to Liberation	117
Defining Purpose	118
Consciousness Shifter — On the Trail of Purpose	120
Disempowering Yourself out of Purpose	122
Beyond the Work Persona	122
Should You Quit Your Job?	123
Turning Obligations into Soul-Level Gifts	124
But Aren't You Meant to Serve?	126
The Inner Game	128
The Fight Between Truth and Thought	129
Abdicating Your Power and Claiming It Back	130
Chapter 7 Summary	132

CHAPTER 8 — YOUR DARK FUEL

The Duality of Wholeness	135
The Light and Shadow	137
Whole—and Polarized—Like the Globe	138
The Yin and Yang of Your Purpose	139

Consciousness Shifter — Finding Yourself on the Inner Map	139
Putting Purpose into Words	140
What Truth Feels Like	143
Bracing for Emotional Whiplash	144
Do You Have to Suffer to Expand?	145
Unraveling Cause and Effect	146
The Doing of Purpose	147
When Purpose Feels Good	148
The Seduction of Shadow	149
Chapter 8 Summary	152

CHAPTER 9 — LIVING YOUR PURPOSE WITH DARK FUEL ALCHEMY®

Consciousness Shifter — Sources of Power	155
The Unshakeable Truth of Finding Answers Within	157
The Hard Part of Change	158
Mistaken Humility	159
Wrestling with Arrogance	159
Trusting Your Deep Wisdom Within	161
Emptying Yourself and Choosing More	162
Taking the Wheel	163
Turning Miserable into Marvelous	163
Alchemy in Action	165
Running Away on the Fear Train	166
The Soul's Perspective on Timing	167
Invitations into Truth	168
Everything in Relation to Truth	169
Drama Tornadoes	170
Thresholds of Purpose	171
Consciousness Shifter — Love as a Way of Life	172
Remember the Green Doors?	173
Are You Doomed to Suffer Forever?	174
Favorite Static Stations	176
Building the Muscles of Soul Strength	177
Chapter 9 Summary	178

PART III — CONNECTING WITH YOUR SOUL

CHAPTER 10 — YOUR UNIQUE SOUL'S WORLD

Into the Impossible	184
Your Internal Operating System	185

But What If It Doesn't Work?	185
What If You Can't Visualize?	187
Honoring Your Wisdom and Abilities	187
Preparing to Tune In	192
Chapter 10 Summary	193

CHAPTER 11 — SOUL'S IDEAL WORLD EXPLORATION #1

Guided Exploration	195
Do This Right After	198
Take It Further	198
Michael's Example	200
Journaling Prompts	201

CHAPTER 12 — SOUL'S IDEAL WORLD EXPLORATION #2

Guided Exploration	203
Do This Right After	206
Take It Further	206
Michael's Example	207
Journaling Prompts	208
Sprinkle in Grace	210

CHAPTER 13 — SOUL'S IDEAL WORLD EXPLORATION #3

Guided Exploration	213
Do This Right After	216
Take It Further	216
Michael's Example	217
Journaling Prompts	219
Practices to Intentionally Live Your Soul's Ideal World	219
Example Manifesto of You	221

CHAPTER 14 — SOUL PURPOSE EXPLORATION #1

Slipping Through the Eye of the Needle	223
How Your Purpose Fits into the Bigger Picture	224
Guided Exploration — Your Soul's Truth	225
Do This Right After	227
Michael's Example	228
Troubleshooting — You Have Multiple Options for the Linchpin	230
Troubleshooting — Safety is Your Linchpin	230
Troubleshooting — You've Narrowed It Down to a Concept	231
Troubleshooting — You Can't Settle into Your Soul's Vision	232
Troubleshooting — You're Thinking More Than Feeling	234

Take It Further	234
Brainstorming Inspired Action	235
Michael's Example — Inspired Action	235
Your Turn	237
What If You Feel Sad or Grieve Once You Realize Your Purpose?	237
Should You Share Your New Discoveries?	238
Practices To Embody Your Soul's Purpose	239

CHAPTER 15 — SOUL PURPOSE EXPLORATION #2

The Flip Side	243
Guided Exploration — Your Dark Fuel	245
Do This Right After	246
Michael's Example	248
Troubleshooting Your Dark Fuel — Finding the Right Fear	250
Troubleshooting Your Dark Fuel — You Can't Feel an Answer	251
Troubleshooting Your Dark Fuel — You're Not Sure You Did it Right	252
Absolution & the Moment I Live For	254
Take It Further	255
You're becoming an emissary for your truth	257
Journaling Prompts	257
Practices to Embody Your Soul's Purpose Using Dark Fuel	258

CHAPTER 16 — YOUR SOUL PURPOSE STATEMENT

The Anti-Climax	265
What Your Statement Will and Won't Do	266
Your Statement's 3 Parts	267
Michael's Example	268
Your Turn	268
Example Purpose Statements	269
Troubleshooting Your Statement	272

PART IV — BECOMING YOU

CHAPTER 17 — LIVING YOUR TRUTH

Cost Of Admission into Purpose	279
Consciousness Shifter — Do You Have to Change Everything?	280
But You Still Have to Change, Right?	281
Is This Manifestation?	281
Your Ego Doesn't Need Transcending	282
Becoming a Vessel for Your Soul	284
Chapter 17 Summary	286

CHAPTER 18 — TRUSTING YOUR INNER IMPULSE

    Yielding in the Dance of Life   289
    Tripping Yourself Up Externalizing... Again!   290
    Signs You're in Your Dark Fuel Hemisphere   291
    Signs You're in Your Truth Hemisphere   292
    What If Truth Feels Confusing?   294
    Pulling Out the Rug from Under You   295
    Traversing the Neutral Zone   296
    Consciousness Shifter — Letting Go of Control   297
    Practicing Surrender   299
    Freeing Yourself Up for Your Future   299
    What If You Don't Know What Your Dream Is?   300
    Chapter 18 Summary   302

CHAPTER 19 — A CALL TO POWER

    Expanding Beyond You   305
    A Collective Calling   306
    Mindful Awakening   307
    Consciousness Shifter — Fierce Surrender   307
    A Glimpse into The Future   308
    Chapter 19 Summary   310

Fully Your Own   *313*

Glossary   *315*

Acknowledgments   *321*

About Alexis   *323*

A NOTE FROM ALEXIS

You have a purpose. This book will help you define what that is without the guesswork, aptitude tests, or advanced geometry required to triangulate your skills, passions, and values.

Because your purpose isn't what you do. It's you.

When you live from a place of embodied purpose within, everything you do becomes an expression of your purpose, including the actions you choose to take in the world.

You already have the answers within you, so this book won't tell you what to do. Instead, it will help you come home to your truth and work with life to expand into your full potential.

Then no matter what decisions you make, you'll have the tools to empower yourself to live your purpose and create a fulfilling, happy life.

(Because that's what really matters.)

In love,

Alexis.

p.s. A word on the consensus reality this book exists in… Life is filled with unjust, indiscriminate violence built on the backs of very real discrimination.

Still, no one can rob you of your purpose.

It's inherently you.

Your purpose is so intimately tied to who you are that it cannot be separated from you or denied to you—no matter your opportunity, ability, education, race, background, gender, or any other reason people have used to belittle and disadvantage others across time and space.

This book aims to liberate purpose from the grasp of careerism and productivity and redefine it as of you, for you, and by you.

This is the calling of your soul.

Purpose is not found in perfection or productivity—it lies in the radical act of being wholly you.

INTRODUCTION

"Be prepared to see your world in an entirely new light."

Your Soul's Clarion Call

There has never been a more urgent call for a revolution in purpose. Societies around the world are reviving beliefs and traditions that came before the individualistic, performance-based pressure of our current culture. Yet, spirituality has remained largely untouched.

We confuse purpose with productivity and fulfillment with full bank accounts. All the while, your soul keeps guiding you down paths you're actively avoiding because they don't look like the promise of endless ease you expected.

It's time for a soul awakening.

It's time to claim your truth.

Above all, it's time to live your purpose with everything you've got because our collective future depends on it.

This is your clarion call and pathway home.

My Promise to You

If you give this book an earnest chance, it will guide you through a process to understand your unique purpose and how you can live it more fully every day. I call this process Dark Fuel Alchemy®.

Dark Fuel Alchemy® is an invitation into a new way of being.

It is not prescriptive, meaning you won't learn the 21 steps to enlightenment that you have to follow exactly, or you'll never understand your purpose. This book is more of a love note from me to you about what I've discovered and explored over ten years of guiding myself and others into greater purpose, authenticity, and peace. It's a cheat sheet on how to approach life's big, gnarly questions and find more clarity, ease, and joy.

As you release what's dimming your light, you start to shine more brightly.

The How-To of "Just Be You!"

One of my biggest frustrations is the advice "Just be you." Not because it's not true, but because no one ever seems to give instructions on *how* to do that. This book is your instruction manual. It was born out of my own need to figure out who I am and why I'm here when I achieved what I thought was my purpose before I turned 30 years old.

You are more than you imagine you are.

Whether you've been lost for decades or feel on track and want to deepen your connection with your soul, this book will help you gain clarity, accept yourself more fully, and have more fun being you. If you're up for the challenge, it will invite you to rethink all of your habits, beliefs, and assumptions about the way life works. As you release what's dimming your light, you start to shine more brightly.

Pushing Through the "Yeah… But" Resistance

This is not the easiest process, because of how we've been conditioned to view purpose, meaning, and success. Some of the ideas may run so counter to how you've learned the world works that you may not even notice yourself resisting. Instead, the ideas will seem unhelpful or make no sense. The mind genuinely can't understand because it has no framework for this new paradigm of purpose.

Alternatively, you may find yourself coming up with reasons why it can't work and won't work for you, specifically, because the "yeah…but" habit is so strong. The ideas in this book aren't meant to be definitive answers. They are signposts to help highlight the intricate webs the mind has woven and start to untangle the unhelpful beliefs keeping us stuck, individually and collectively.

This book points towards freedom, not more dogma.

Some clients have shared that they didn't understand the depth of the transformation they were making until years into the process. They thought living their purpose would be as simple as knowing which career path to choose instead of becoming their true selves. But, you can't just go through these pages and learn or memorize your purpose. Your purpose requires you to engage with your life and allow your lived experience to inform your journey.

Take your time. Let your subconscious slowly guide your conscious mind. If you're here, your awakening has already begun.

Who This Can Help

Thousands of books and courses are geared to those who want to build a better business, discover their creative passion, or find a better job. This isn't one of them. This book is for people who want more.

The "program" we call consensus reality isn't your truth. While there's nothing wrong with wanting to do your best within our tangible consensus reality—we've all got to eat, survive, and thrive—that journey may leave you feeling empty. Trust your inner impulses that something is off for you. If you're wondering what more there is to life, this book is for you.

Whether you call yourself a seeker, a rebel, an outcast, or someone who feels lost and hopeless because you can't get yourself to "get with the program" and just be happy, this is for you.

We're stepping outside of the game of "make money and buy cool stuff" to get curious about bigger questions of meaning, connection, fulfillment, and true joy. Because your greatest joy comes from living your authentic truth.

It's time to know that you've always been right and claim the inner peace and freedom you came to feel and create.

Self-Trust, Not Self-Help

Most self-help advice is self-perfecting in disguise. Leadership, life-hacking, time management, mindset, productivity, relationships, career development, confidence, and personal growth—all attempt to mold you into a better version of yourself.

This book is about setting you free.

Like you, I've tried many popular practices. Get up at 5 am. Exercise and read a book for ten minutes every day. Take cold showers. Follow a budget. Say affirmations in the mirror. They're all about managing and controlling yourself.

Dark Fuel Alchemy® is about liberating yourself.

> *Everything about you is right. Your soul is already guiding you on the perfect path. Your purpose is already unfolding.*

So many self-help books start with, "This is a different kind of self-help book. If you follow these steps, you'll never need another self-help book again." Yet you keep reading them because you're either not taking personal responsibility for your choices, they don't go deep enough to address your real questions, or the tips they're offering feel constricting rather than expanding.

For years, I tried to reconfigure myself into someone more successful, calm, lovable, aligned, wealthy, playful, and the list goes on. I spent $100,000+ on coaches and healers who did their best to help me. After years of frustrating results, I realized everything I was doing to "improve" was a form of controlling myself.

We control when we feel unsafe.

If you've ever done what I've done—fixated on your health, desperately sought clarity for your next step, hyper-minded your diet, tried to find the right expert to help you, organized more or better, analyzed your friends to see who was "toxic" or empowering—then you've tried to radically change your life. For me, the impulse stemmed from being afraid that I wasn't enough as is. I finally realized that if I didn't feel safe in my body, I would always be stuck draining my energy trying to control the circumstances around me or within me.

Here's the truth: Everything about you is right. Your soul is already guiding you on the perfect path. Your purpose is already unfolding.

When you keep fighting what is, instead of accepting and embracing the truth of who you are, you stay stuck in self-perfecting without ever enjoying the freedom of being you. You stay stuck in fear-based consciousness without ever awakening to the love you already are.

Dark Fuel Alchemy® will help you trust yourself, your soul, and life, so that you can stop micro-managing yourself and start basking in your brilliance. If you embrace what is in these pages, I hope that you'll discover the bliss of being you—at peace and on purpose.

Does the Word Soul Make Your Skin Crawl?

Soul isn't a feel-good word for everyone. Many clients have shared with me that using the word soul has been a big hurdle for them in this process. Perhaps you grew up in an environment in which God or religious elders claimed to own your soul. You may have been made to feel guilty, bad, ashamed, or powerless, and your soul was the weapon wielded against you. If so, I'm sorry that happened to you; abuse, including spiritual abuse, is not okay.

Perhaps you align with Buddhist tradition and have heard Buddhism doesn't believe in the soul.

I use soul to mean a force or awareness beyond your everyday consciousness that shapes your perspective. Specifically, I use soul to describe an emanation of universal energy or oneness in your unique form. Like a single blade of grass in an earth teeming with life, you are life too. In this way, your soul is a unique experience to you, yet not of you. It is an animating energy that carries a shared evolutionary directionality. You are part of the whole, yet distinct from the whole in your ability to experience yourself as separate.

The more you play with the process shared in these pages, the more space you may find to open to your wisdom, intuition, and inner knowing.

You are already whole and you already have what it takes to be fully you. Yet you may be holding back from growing into your next iteration out of confusion, doubt, or fear. By grounding you in your soul, this process helps you trust your inner compass as it guides you home to truth. Then, you can surrender who you think you are to the broader life flowing through you.

How to Use This Book

This is less of a book you read once and more of a garden you plant and tend to frequently.

The words lay seeds of new possibilities and approaches. If you read it once, those seeds may be planted but go unwatered, and nothing will change in your life. If you return to it, ponder it, and test out the ideas in your life, then the seeds may start to sprout and bloom.

Living your purpose unfolds over a lifetime. While the freedom this process offers is available immediately, it also grows the more you embrace it. Imagine it like catching a first glimpse of your homeland after years at sea. As you sail closer, the land appears bigger and clearer. Yet, you still have a distance to cover before you can finally touch the shore and be fully home.

Your soul isn't withholding your truth. It's guiding you to become the version of yourself who can fully embody your freedom and magnificence.

How This Book is Organized, AKA What to Expect

There are four parts in this book.

In Part I, you'll see why pretty much everything you've learned about purpose has been leading you down dead-end streets, if not actively making you feel more lost, hopeless, and alone.

In Part II, you'll discover a new roadmap for creating a meaningful, happy life. Some of it may feel obvious, some of it may stretch you out of your mind, both are a good thing. This new framework for purpose will help you navigate your path to your truth.

In Part III, you'll get down to business and gain clarity on your unique purpose. Heads up: the steps and answers won't make any sense if you don't read Parts I & II first, so don't skip ahead.

In Part IV, you'll feel excited about your whole, new, purposeful life and your role in this not-so-subtle revolution to liberate yourself, your purpose, and us all. We'll also talk about next steps for living in authentic presence and what lies beyond this framework.

Little Ways I've Tried to Help You Win with the Book

I have shelves of half-read self-help books, all unfinished for the same reason. If a chapter ends with suggested practices to do, I feel like I have to stop reading until I do them. Unfortunately, the practices are usually super deep (which is probably why they help), or they ask me to clarify something I feel stuck on. Either way, I stop. If I keep reading, I feel both guilty and like I'm not getting the transformation from the book that I wanted. It's a frustrating experience.

To help you succeed, this book has a few (hopefully) helpful features:

- Short-ish sections within each chapter.

  I stay motivated when I'm able to complete a section of a book, even if I only have a small window of time. If a chapter is too long, and I don't have the time, energy, or focus for it, I stop reading. But reading is succeeding.

  That's why you'll find multiple, smaller sections within each chapter in this book. Each section stands alone and relates to the sections around it. You can read one or many.

  The ideas in this book may not be easy, but hopefully, the process of reading it will be.

- Consciousness shifters.

  Nearly every chapter includes a section called a consciousness shifter. These are key ideas that invite you closer to your truth. Together, they lay a new conceptual foundation so you can free your soul and live your purpose.

- Chapter summaries.

  Short, pithy statements reminding you of what you just learned, these summaries show how the ideas fit together and how they build on each other throughout the book.

Plus, they make it easier to revisit ideas. Scan the summaries, locate the concept, and then skip to that section to refresh your memory. This is helpful if you want to tell a friend about something you read (hint, hint) and want to find the section quickly.

- Practices are mostly in Part III.

Here's where the actionable practices live so they don't interrupt your reading flow. The practices won't make much sense if you don't read and understand the new paradigm of purpose first.

The important first step is opening to a whole new way of thinking about purpose. Once you grasp the conceptual foundation, your answers will be more valuable, and you'll see how to integrate them into your life. After helping 100+ people through this process, I've seen who fights the process and who creates a whole new life with it.

The Dark Fuel Alchemy® process is the fastest available path to awakening. The freedom and inner peace you're craving unfold as you embrace the journey. Trust the process.

- Practices are divided into "Do this right after" (the guided exploration) and "Take it further."

The practices are thorough and meant to give you the full experience of clarifying, embracing, and embodying your purpose over time. It takes time to integrate and feel ready for the next step. You can take as long as you'd like to do the practices. You can even do a few and come back and do others months or years later.

To get the most benefit, I highly recommend doing the ones under "Do this right after" immediately following the guided explorations. I'll share this again in each chapter; it's easy to forget what you felt and realized so clearly when you were in the energy of your soul. These initial practices will help you build your capacity to embody your soul's world longer and more often.

Each chapter in Part III also includes practices under a section titled "Take it further." You can do them over the next month, year, or decade. Don't speed through the practices. Give yourself the time to be transformed by them. The goal is to embody a new way of being.

Connecting with your soul and beginning to consciously embody your purpose is about as personal and deep as it gets. If your soul brought you here, you're ready to become who you truly are.

You can find additional journaling prompts and practices in the *Wildly Towards Truth Workbook* available at www.alexispierce.com. The Workbook guides you to integrate the ideas in each section so you can shift more rapidly and fully. It is a good companion if you enjoy journaling and integrating your insights as you go.

What This Book Won't Do

I've spent over a decade helping people live into their purpose, witnessing what works and what keeps you stuck. The majority of purpose-seekers (myself included) secretly wish that a magical Clarity Fairy would wave a wand, and poof!, we would be living our purpose with full hearts and open minds.

But that's not how life works, and deep down, that's not what you really want, either.

Your soul is guiding you to become you—the version of yourself that you both know and are possibly terrified of becoming.

In service to your truth, here are seven habits I promise <u>not</u> to help you continue:

1. Be lazy in your thinking.

    The way we collectively think about purpose doesn't add up. As you'll discover in Part I, it's easy to poke holes in the current approaches to purpose. But these approaches continue to be popular because the alternative requires you to own more power than you may be comfortable wielding and swim against the tide of social conditioning. I invite you to challenge the assumptions you're agreeing to anyway.

2. Fall back asleep.

    Have you ever removed a new pillow or blanket from a vacuum-sealed bag, and it immediately inflates to five times the size of the bag? Your consciousness is like that, too. Once you expand your awareness, it won't shrink back to the comfortable limits you imposed on it before. This is the natural evolution of your identity to expand into the infinite potential of your soul.

3. Search for external answers to internal sensations.

    Almost every program, course, or book is just comforting you as you wander in circles trying to find answers outside of you. They give you steps to follow and systems to navigate, yet they continue to reinforce your baseline assumption that the solution you're looking for is out there somewhere. I help you with the inner journey and invite you back to yourself when you want to default to the seemingly easier but dead-end track of looking outside of yourself.

You can't muscle your way into liberation. You soothe yourself into the truth of who you are.

---

4. Believe your own b.s.

    You are a genius at convincing yourself not to change. Your nervous system is hardwired to avoid the discomfort of the unknown, even if how you feel now is miserable. Your mind and body are on board, too, hijacking your thoughts and emotions.

    I've built in little reminders throughout the book to lovingly call yourself out because it's a matter of when—not if—you run for the comfort of old ways of thinking and feeling. You're not alone.

Navigating your nervous system's innate responses isn't about strength or determination.

You can't muscle your way into liberation. You soothe yourself into the truth of who you are.

5. Wallow in shame or blame.

Shame is the fastest way for your mind-body-emotions to pull the brakes on the train of your awakening. Shame triggers a chain reaction of thoughts and feelings that leave you convinced that you're powerless, worthless, and hopeless. Embracing your purpose is the epitome of claiming your power, worth, and vision. Dark Fuel Alchemy® will help you master turning fear and shame into power.

6. Believe you are broken.

Old paradigms of purpose are failing humanity. Whether you won the lottery of life and still feel scared that you're unfulfilled, or you never got the opportunity to live your dreams and now feel robbed of your chance at purpose, you are not alone. You are not a defective human because the fairytale ending of eternal bliss and contentment didn't materialize (yet). You've just been duped by an inadequate system aimed at justifying power imbalances instead of liberating souls.

7. Try to feel special through your struggles.

When you don't understand the magnitude of your innate brilliance, AKA your purpose, then you may not have a way to rationalize the inner whisper that you are unique and special. Instead, this whisper can get distorted into a badge of honor—if you can't actualize your genius, then you must be special in your misery. Perhaps you are the most lost, most hurt, or most hopeless. This is a good attempt to gain the benefits of purpose without having to claim your power and become the person who lives your purpose. But it's not true.

Your soul is already living in your truth. This process will help you break free from these outdated habits so that you can more intentionally live with truth and purpose, too.

A Beginning Prayer

If you allow it to be, Dark Fuel Alchemy® is the fastest path to awakening. Whether you want to awaken to your potential, experience more freedom, or shift your consciousness towards lasting peace, this process can serve as a roadmap. It is simple—not easy—and it works.

The *Wildly Towards Truth Workbook* is a nice companion to explore the ideas and insights you'll discover here.

Let us end and begin by borrowing from a Buddhist Metta prayer:

May you be happy.
May you know great peace.
May you be free.

May all beings be happy.
May all beings know great peace.
May all beings be free.

PART I

BREAKING FREE

Liberation begins where old paradigms end.

In Part I, you'll discover why purpose has felt so elusive before; confront how current approaches to purpose strand you practically, philosophically and spiritually; and open the door to a new paradigm for purpose focused on true liberation.

*Breaking free is not about
rejecting the past;
it's about boldly embracing
what calls you forward.*

1

A NEW PURPOSE

"I don't feel like my life is a roller-coaster or a spinning top any longer…and it's such an amazing feeling."

Miserable in a Life You Love

Angela had been training for this moment since she was six years old. She could hear her agent's excitement over the phone. "You got the audition for the show!"

"For Broadway?!? For real?" Angela replied in disbelief.

She recalled all the dance moves she'd made up, all the shows she'd put on in the living room throughout her childhood. Now, the ticket to her lifelong dream was only three days away.

"Well, what happened?" I asked Angela a few years later. She had signed up to work with me, searching for answers to her purpose.

"I showed up drunk and bombed." She continued, "I still don't get it. I ruined everything I worked for and hurt so many people when it was supposed to be what I wanted."

I wish this was a unique story—a fluke that only happened to Angela. Yet every day, people wake up miserable in a life they believe they should love.

Actors, sports stars, politicians, entrepreneurs, lawyers, plumbers, teachers, nurses—no one is immune from the void of what feels like a soulless life. Not even money can save you from the pain of that emptiness.

This is the daily legacy of a system designed to promote productivity and profit over soul-level purpose. It leaves you floundering for answers to life's deepest questions, even—and especially—when all your dreams seem to be coming true.

In these pages, you'll discover a new paradigm for purpose that will free you from the endless cycles of striving to achieve goals and then failing to feel better when you achieve them. It will help you understand who you are, the growth path your soul is guiding you on, what to make of your unique struggles, and how to not just forgive the past but understand how it is actively inviting you into your future.

The freedom and authenticity you crave lie on the other side of breaking free from your shell.

---

15 Seconds to Remember Who You Are

Imagine you're holding an egg, white or beige-brown and delicate. It may feel cold or room temperature. It has a gentle heaviness to it and is slightly wider at one end.

Now, imagine cracking that egg into a pan.

The "egg" is now the substance in the pan, part clear, part yellow. What you're holding is the eggshell. What you thought was the egg was just a vessel for the rich, vibrant potential within.

You are the egg.

The freedom and authenticity you crave lie on the other side of breaking free from your shell.

Your soul is guiding you to embrace this transformation—to crack open and reveal your true essence.

Yet, we get so obsessed with *who we have to be* that we forget the true path is *being who we truly are*.

You are not a dancer.
You are not an accountant.
You are not a disability.
You are not an addict.

Those are things you do or experience.

Inner freedom and the bliss it brings lie in centering your purpose back on you and your soul instead of the roles you play and the experiences you have.

Can You Want More Than Everything?

I figured out what I wanted to do with my life when I was 14.

Back then, I was in a youth group with other nice—if not wayward—kids. Our youth group leaders taught us to meditate and led us on Shamanic journeys. I dyed my hair purple and started smoking Marlboro Light 100s at church camp. It was a coming-of-age group.

The minister was a focused woman with a say-it-straight manner and an easy laugh. One day, I asked her how to choose what to do with my life:

"You know Lynn at church?" she asked.

"Yes," I nodded.

"Don't be like Lynn. Every Sunday, she gets up during announcements and asks us to save the dolphins, or trees, or bees, or ocean, or children. She cares a lot, but people view her as a joke. Pick one thing."

So I did.

I picked peace.

Fifteen years later and four years into my dream career, I'd achieved everything I'd imagined:

- ✓ I was part of a dedicated team helping to increase peace around the world.
- ✓ I had a close group of colleagues who were also friends, so work felt like fun.
- ✓ I racked up awards and promotions for my work until I eventually established my own small team of experts ready to deploy to a conflict at a moment's notice.

Because I had worked so hard over two degrees to get there, I had unwittingly convinced myself that it was my purpose. Yet, achieving it didn't feel like what I had expected. Living my purpose—if that's what it was—didn't feel particularly good at all.

Instead, I felt disillusioned and confused. Like I had done it all and also barely scratched the surface of my potential.

It didn't make sense. I had everything I thought would make me feel fulfilled and happy, but I felt like I was playing a part in my own life, and I didn't particularly like the character I was playing.

Why can't I just be happy?
What is it I need to work on? My love life, career, mental health?
What am I meant to do if not this?

I wasn't sure where to turn or who to talk to; I just knew something was deeply off. In retrospect, I was hitting up against my soul's invitation to grow. But I wasn't ready to accept the invitation yet.

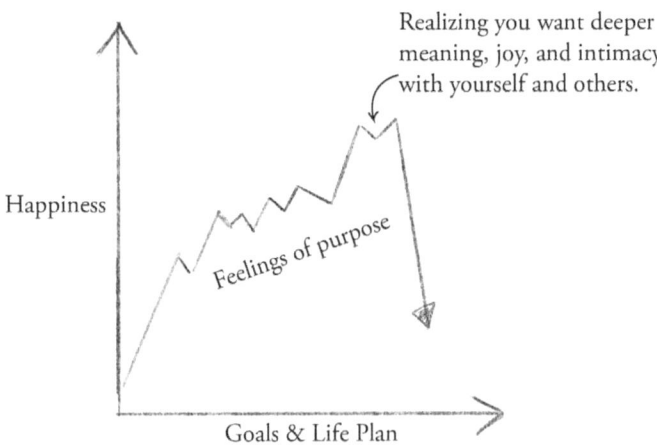

Rock Bottom at the Top

I've noticed clients in a similar position tend to make one of two choices:

1) Move the goalposts.

    For some, achieving the first big goal didn't bring fulfillment. So they set another, bigger goal in the hopes that maybe that one will fill them with contentment and joy.

    This is a common response of serial entrepreneurs, athletes, and artists, as well as students and others. It also captures the social phenomenon of people pining for love, then getting married and pining for a house, then buying one and pining for kids, then having them and pining for a nicer house, and so on.

2) Spiral into despair.

    Others feel a sense of deep betrayal and emptiness after realizing that the life they thought was building to something meaningful is actually an ongoing stream of achievements with no end and no prize. People in this camp often feel confused, believing they have to fake it to continue in their current lives. They may turn to addictions, adrenaline sports, or even a spiritual journey.

After spending a year in this despair, when I left my first career in the government, I wanted to find a new option. I wanted to know who I was beyond the characters I played (and hated) like girlfriend, daughter, and sister. I wanted to find my power independent from the power of my job title. Plus I wanted to discover meaning in my life beyond the socially acceptable meanings of success.

What I found is a core truth within each of us. This truth goes far beyond ability, talents, gender, race, and more. This truth is being called forth by your soul every single day. It will set you free to not only know your purpose but also become who you are.

Consciousness Shifter — Imagine Purpose Like This

Most people assume purpose is like a sunny day. When the skies are clear and the sun is shining, you feel good, know you're on track, and feel energized about life's possibilities. You wish you could feel like this forever. Maybe you just landed the job you want, helped a friend navigate a problem, or had a loving interaction with your child.

The cloudy and rainy days are a different story…

On those days, you feel off-track, lost, and confused about your direction in life. You doubt you'll ever feel clear and fulfilled, let alone live your purpose and be truly happy. These might be times you're going through a breakup, reeling from a bad grade or review at work, struggling with a health challenge, or feeling exhausted and like there's no end in sight to your responsibilities and routine.

Many of us ride this roller coaster every day without even realizing it: feeling unstoppable when life feels like it's going our way, then questioning everything when a crisis or negative event happens.

Here's what I want you to know about both the weather and your purpose: the sun is always shining above the clouds.

You don't have to wait for perfectly clear skies to live your purpose. You just have to change your perspective.

When you understand your purpose from a higher vantage point—your soul's perspective—you can witness the clouds of your life come and go. You can notice how they form and build into emotional storms, how high pressure and hot or cold air blow through and stir up your mind and emotions.

From your soul's view, you can understand the whole picture of your life, like seeing the earth from outer space.

You'll notice where aspects of your life may be off balance, some lush with abundance, others parched for more love, attention, or time. From this level, you are also aware of how the sun and moon revolve like the eternal interplay between the spring and winter seasons of your life. You'll notice how the tides of your life ebb and flow without getting caught in the drama of trying to hold onto the water. You'll understand how cycles of growth and rest, joy and grieving weave together to create an integrated whole.

Your soul's view allows you to navigate life with more clarity and equanimity. You can flow more easily through life because you're not always hunkering down in a storm or holding out for sunny days.

Your purpose is already living in this space of truth and ease. When the mind catches up, you stop limiting your life to just the good days and free yourself to be it all. From that wholeness, you can fully engage with life and experience the authenticity, presence, and connection you desire.

Without Truth, It's Just Guessing

I didn't set out to discover a new approach to purpose. I stumbled into this work helping friends with strategic business planning. I didn't feel comfortable providing random advice, especially since I'd never run a business. Instead, I knew I had to get to the core of their truth with the best tool I had—strategic visioning.

It turns out the highest level vision of an individual is your soul's world. From that world flows the answer to who you are, why you're here, what matters to you, and what may be meaningful to create.

It's not guesswork. It's not my opinion or perspective over yours. It's a repeatable, teachable process to walk you home to yourself.

What Do We Mean by Purpose?

Even though most of us feel like purpose is a deeper, spiritual concept, when it comes to living it, we often default to tangible career paths, job descriptions, and actions. Look up "purpose" in the dictionary, and it's often synonymous with anything from a goal to a task to a frame of mind. No wonder we're so confused!

For some, purpose is an end result: a feeling of having accomplished a purpose. For others, it's the path or journey: knowing that you're leading a purposeful life. Still others use purpose to mean happiness or fulfillment, like an emotional reward you experience if you live well.

Even the most well-known spiritual teachers get a little shaky when it comes to defining purpose. Many describe it as the reason for all human life, which is so vague and big that it's hard to apply to your daily life. Or they narrow it down so much that they focus on the purpose of each moment as an intentional action, skipping over the very real and pressing desire to know why you—specifically you—are here, what makes you different, and how you can meaningfully contribute.

In my work, I've discovered a slightly different definition of purpose. One that encompasses your highest evolution and expression, your deepest pains, and the process of expanding between them. I call the whole process Dark Fuel Alchemy® (more on that in Part II).

Just as the foundation of a skyscraper supports its soaring height, your purpose is an essential element to experience new levels of power, meaning, impact, and beauty. It is the tool by which you access higher states of connection, consciousness, and creation, which then enable you to focus on what really matters (and change priorities as needed in the moment). Your purpose is the portal through which you actualize your gifts, awaken your potential, and create the opportunity to uplift the broader community.

Guiding and Leading at the Same Time

Purpose is both aspirational and instructive. It's something you live into as well as consciously cultivate and embody. Aspirationally, it is how you master being your individual self so that you can also lose yourself in contribution to our collective evolution and expansion.

Instructively, on a day-by-day basis, purpose becomes a lens through which you view the experiences of your life, including your emotions, thoughts, habits, and beliefs.

The benefit of this new approach is that your purpose can then tangibly guide you to:

1) Navigate your current challenges.
2) Understand the unique gifts you share just by being you.
3) Grow in ways that help you feel more whole, content, and fulfilled.

At the end of the day, most of us want our purpose to provide clarity in our lives, as well as spiritual and emotional benefits.

Your purpose is a deeply personal inner game. When you're fully surrendered to it, it's as if no one else exists, and you're in a private conversation between you and your Source. While at the same time, you're acutely aware that everything you do has a communal and global impact.

This is a reflection of a deeper truth that we are all one consciousness. One Life being lived through all of us, like individual fingers on one larger hand. The more you fully embrace your unique role, the more you feel connected and contribute to the whole.

The journey of truly living into your purpose requires all of you. It will change your beliefs, your relationships, and your habits, plus demand you to relinquish all the parts of yourself that aren't authentic and true. In return, you'll be ushered into a new era of deep love, conviction, and peace.

There is no greater peace than living your truth.

100 Words for Purpose

You may resonate with a different word than purpose. Some of the most common are mission, essence, frequency, soul focus, highest truth, or energy. You might also call it God's plan, Kingdom work, or your life's work. Oprah once called it a heart-cry, which I love.

You could use 100 different words, and they would all point towards the same desire—feeling fully alive. Whether you call it meaning, contribution, feeling engaged, playing all the music within you, or knowing you gave it your all, the overarching desire I hear from clients, again and again, is to know that you spent your life present, connected, and expressing and creating from love.

A Note on What's Possible:

You may not believe at this moment that words like bliss or joy or loving yourself or ease or feeling good in your body will ever apply to you. I get it. I didn't used to think it was possible either, and few of my clients believed it when they started. It is. Honestly, feelings of joy and ease and love beyond your wildest imaginings are both possible and closer than you think.

We want to matter, participate, and do justice to the gift of life we've been given.

At our core, we care about each other, and we're willing to give of ourselves to create a better world. This is the beating-heart motivation behind the vast majority of humans I meet. Yet many feel trapped in do-good jobs that actually aren't doing good, see beyond the veil of broken systems, and wonder if anything is worth doing if none of it really matters. The forces of destruction seem overpowering sometimes.

All while the deep, inner pulse to contribute, express, and expand continues.

What Are You Hoping Purpose Will Give You?

It seems silly, yet the deepest questions in life can show up in the smallest decisions:

- Should I go to the gym today?
- Watch TV or go to bed early?
- Change jobs or stick out this one?

Because at the heart of every decision is an underlying foundation of Who You Think You Are.

That foundation is built on the way you've answered much bigger questions like:

- Why am I here?
- Do I matter?
- Is it possible for me to make changes to the seemingly determined course of my life?

It's normal to wonder why you're here.

It's normal to wonder if you matter.

It's normal to wonder if anything you do makes a difference or if it's all just an insignificant, random waste of time on a spinning ball of fire and water in the middle of an endless void.

Before exploring your purpose, it's important to get clear on which questions you're actually trying to answer through clarifying your purpose. A lot of people come to me using the word "purpose" when what they really want to know is how to feel happy and like they're not wasting their lives.

We assign so much weight and importance to finding this answer, but I've found that the answer often doesn't satisfy the desire. That's because most of us are looking for authoritative direction. We want someone to just give us an answer that will solve everything. We want a quick fix, a silver bullet, an easy step-by-step.

Purpose awakens you into a way of being that is much, much deeper than a simple "do this." Of course, it would be nice if some omniscient force could hand us a slip of paper with the answer on it. I'd be first in line! But that would rob of us the point of purpose, which is to choose to become who you are.

Spend a moment right now getting honest with yourself about what you really want to know.

What brings you to this book?
What are you really craving?

Perhaps…

- ✓ More clarity in your career.
- ✓ A better understanding of why life has been so hard.
- ✓ To know what meaning to make of your struggles.
- ✓ A sense of your specialness.
- ✓ A glimpse of who you are beyond the roles you play or perceived value in society.
- ✓ To feel like your life is worthwhile.
- ✓ To understand the point of your life beyond the ups and downs.
- ✓ To tap into more meaning.

Maybe all of the above?

Your purpose can answer all these questions and more. The clearer you are on which questions you'd like to create answers for, the easier it will be to integrate the next few chapters and "work" your purpose once you have language for it. This process will invite you into new levels of truth with yourself, so start by being honest here.

Chapter 1 Summary

- Many people feel empty, confused, and unfulfilled, even if they have seemingly perfect lives. This is the legacy of systems designed to promote productivity and profit over soul-level purpose.
- Like an egg you crack into a pan, you are the vibrant essence within, not the shell. Freedom and authenticity lie in breaking free from external labels.
- Your purpose is playing out in everyday experiences that shift and change like weather. Your soul is above the clouds holding a broader perspective. You don't have to wait for clear skies to live your purpose. You can change your perspective to your soul's view.
- Most definitions of purpose are confusing and incomplete, reducing it to career paths, goals, tasks, or fleeting emotions.
- This new approach to purpose helps you to answer big, spiritual questions, as well as understand your individual gifts, navigate personal challenges with wisdom, and cultivate more inner peace.
- Purpose serves as a tool to access higher levels of connection, creativity, and consciousness—enabling you to focus on what really matters and give fully of yourself to collective evolution and expansion.
- Many people respond to feeling dissatisfied by chasing bigger goals or by spiraling into despair. Both paths can lead to feeling unfulfilled.
- Most people want to feel alive, contribute, and create to their fullest ability.
- Being honest about why you want to understand your purpose makes it easier to integrate the new approach shared in the next few chapters.

Your journey with purpose is a journey of becoming authentically you.

2

WHY YOUR PURPOSE ISN'T YOUR JOB

"Once I understood the expansiveness of my true purpose,…
I no longer had those old doubts and fears dogging my steps… It's
true that when you shift your energy to a higher level by seeing
your true purpose, everything falls into place."

Set Up to Fail

It's not your fault if you feel lost, confused, or disillusioned by purpose. You've been set up to fail by current approaches to purpose, which don't work practically, philosophically, or spiritually.

I'm not a person who buys into conspiracies, but if I were, the current lessons we're taught about purpose seem like an ingenious way to make people feel confused and disconnected from their power, so that they agree to work in a biased system in the hopes of a better future… only to blame themselves when they never achieve a life of ease and happiness.

Over the next few chapters, I'm going to walk you step-by-step through why these current approaches to purpose don't work so that you can finally stop struggling or feeling like something is wrong with you. Then I'll introduce you to a new paradigm for purpose that helps you to be authentically you, contribute your gifts, and also make everyday decisions about your life in alignment with your soul.

The 3 Myths About Purpose That Mess with Your Head

I typically work with people who either feel misaligned or mistaken.

1) The misaligned feel unhappy and unfulfilled and assume it's because their work isn't aligned with their purpose.

2) The mistaken feel like their work is their purpose, but they still feel unhappy and unfulfilled. They assumed an aligned career and material success would also include better feelings, so they must have made a mistake since they don't feel that way.

	Misaligned	Mistaken
Emotions	Unhappy & unfulfilled	Confused & disillusioned
Question	What should I be doing?	Why can't I be happy?
Fear	I'll never figure it out	I must be broken
Inner voice	I have too many interests and no follow through	I'm ungrateful and never satisfied
Current work	My job is not my purpose	My job is my purpose

No matter which group you're in—or if you're a combo of both—these challenges are rooted in the same unhelpful myths most of us marinated in while growing up:

Myth #1 — Your purpose is your job or work in the world.

Myth #2 — If you achieve the social ideal of "success," then you'll be happy.
Myth #3 — Contentment and meaning are your rewards for doing well in the game of life.

Unfortunately, none of these are true or helpful. Let's go through them in more detail, one at a time.

Myth #1 — Your Purpose is Your Job or Work in the World

Most of us have been taught to believe that our purpose is the same as our work or career. Let me burst that bubble for you with 3 questions:

What about babies?
What about people who don't fit into traditional concepts of work?
What about retirees?

Assuming that all people have a purpose, that means these people have a purpose too—even if they don't fit into economic models of what a "productive" member of society looks and acts like.

One of the reasons I feel so much urgency to share this process is because we desperately need to free ourselves from the hold that modern work culture has placed on our souls.

You are an infinite and expansive being with unimaginable creative potential. It's laughable to assume your fullness has to be sandwiched into a definable career path only accessible to you during certain periods of your life and only thanks to the perfectly timed overlap of education, access, and opportunity. This is particularly exacerbated in the United States, where people feel pressured to commit to one specific career path to gain access to health care.

You have the freedom to reinvent yourself.
You have the freedom to break the mold.
You have the freedom to be fully you.

34 | Wildly Towards Truth

This is why—no matter how hard it is or how much the English language fails us—we must reclaim purpose as an essence of our being and not a categorization of our doing.

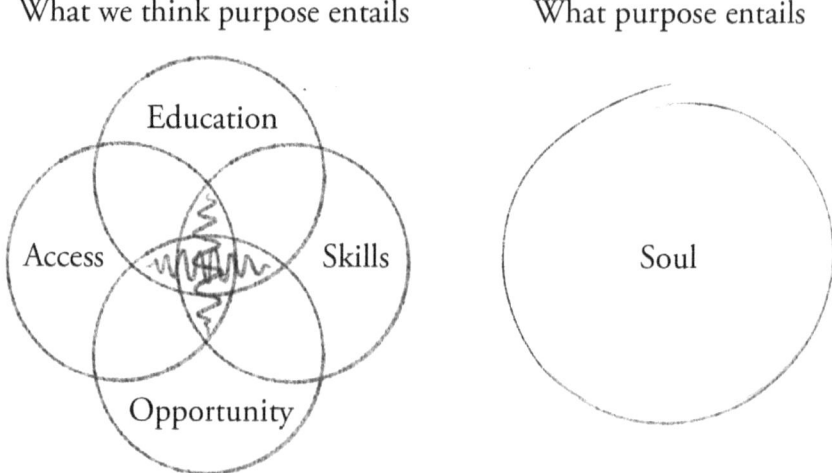

Danger Danger: 3 Ways You Lose When Your Purpose Is Your Career

In the West, it's common to believe that your career or primary social role is your purpose. That belief is reflected in the way we talk about both purpose and the roles we play, paid or unpaid:

"My purpose is to be a teacher."
"My purpose is to help people heal from trauma."
"My purpose is to be a mother."

There are three main reasons conflating your purpose with your career or role is unhelpful at best and dangerous at worst.

1. You lose your identity

Being you is a one-person job. Meaning you're the only one that can do it. But as an employee, you are replaceable.

To be more accurate, YOU are not replaceable, but rather the role you play in a company or institution can always be filled (to some extent) by someone else. The organization can continue without you.

As a friend of mine in the Marine Corps once told me: "You better have an identity beyond the military because The Big Green Machine will spit you out and have your desk filled by the end of the day."

He spoke from experience, having watched his friends and colleagues dedicate their lives, physically and emotionally, to serving an organization that continued to live and breathe without them, often while they floundered to find meaning and purpose outside of it.

I experienced this myself when I left my first career in the U.S. Government. Though they never filled my role directly and I (happily) chose to leave, I discovered once I left that I defined myself by the skills I developed for that job. Without realizing it, I had based my self-esteem, value in society, and sense of self on that role. Which meant that without it, I wasn't sure who I was anymore.

This became clear about a year after I left the government. I was living in northeastern New Zealand and had joined a hiking group to explore the area and meet new people. On one particular hike, a woman I hadn't met before asked me, "What do you do?" I shared that I taught yoga in town, and then quickly followed with, "But I used to be a strategist in the U.S. Government!"

I realized in that moment that part of me worried I would be undervalued and dismissed if I was just a yoga teacher—despite it being the most challenging job I'd ever had. While another part of me didn't want to let go of who I'd been and what I'd done before because it made me feel important and powerful.

For the next few years, I struggled to introduce myself without qualifying my career path. I rationalized it to myself by saying that society only values smart, powerful people and so-called white-collar careers. But in truth, I didn't know how to define or value myself without it.

You might be experiencing this confusion right now. Perhaps you have identified strongly with your role in society—whether it's as a mother, attorney, or dishwasher—and are wondering who you are beyond this role.

Letting go of the belief that your career or role is your purpose is an important first step to embracing your true purpose. When you know who you are on a soul level and feel clear in the gifts that you bring to all aspects of your life, including the roles you play, then you can change jobs 100 times—or never work at all—and still feel confident in your purpose, direction, and value

Your purpose goes with you.

2. You feel unfulfilled

One of the most damaging consequences of conflating your purpose with your career is believing you failed to live your purpose if your career doesn't pan out as you hoped. So often, I see clients holding onto resentments towards their parents, children, illness, traumatic experiences, or money because they feel like they missed out on their chance to live their purpose. Someone or something got in the way or led them astray.

When we had our first call, Lou was in his late 70s and had enjoyed a long and successful career as a chef. The only problem was that he didn't want to be a chef. When he was younger, he had big plans to pursue his dreams as an artist, but his parents discouraged him from it. So he followed their suggested path and now had 50 years of resentment and bitterness to show for it. Even though he liked his job and was good at it, he felt like he'd missed out on the life he was supposed to have—and the purpose that went with who he could have been.

Many people get into a line of work to close a financial gap or because an opportunity comes their way at the right time. They keep going with it because they excel at it, or it's easier to stay than to find something new or risk trying something different. Similarly, I've learned during my fertility struggles that many people feel their purpose is to be a mother, yet some never have biological children. The whims of fate don't exclude you from a life of purpose.

When you feel misled, unfulfilled, or passed over by life, it's easy to feel upset and blame others. These feelings can isolate you even more from the feelings of true connection and contribution you desire. It becomes a self-supporting cycle—you feel left out of true meaning and purpose in life, which causes you to hold back from the life you're currently living, lessening your chances of feeling purposeful and fulfilled now.

Believing your job or role is the only way you can experience a sense of purpose is like finding a romantic partner and then never speaking to any other human again. Tempting though it might be, it puts a lot of pressure on the "One" to fulfill your every need. Your purpose is so big and expansive that it can never be contained by just one expression of it, even if you have the most amazing career or role in the world.

Assuming your job or role is your purpose always leads to feeling unfulfilled.

3. You lose your fullness, AKA your expression becomes myopic

Your purpose is huge. It is you. It runs the whole gamut from your best moments to your worst, and every subtle second in between.

When you expect your role to be your only opportunity to express your purpose, then the persona you adopt in your role becomes the only part of you that is purposeful. The rest of you is relegated to a hobby or fragmented into spiritual you, relationship you, parent you, and so on. Ironically, many people also believe that who they are outside of work or their primary role is the "real" version of them. This confusion can feel like you're switching between roles that you play and juggling competing senses of purpose, instead of feeling like an integrated whole who expresses your purpose across all of your roles.

When you assume your job or role is your purpose, then you also constrain yourself to only what the role allows you to express. That means, on some level, that other people determine how much you can live your purpose. You de facto limit yourself to only the aspects of you that your role allows you to experience. You also have many hours outside of work. You have friends, family, and activities that you enjoy - these are all opportunities to express and live your purpose.

Diane came to me hoping to build out her health coaching business because she felt unfulfilled as a nurse and administrator. She was overflowing with passion to help people but couldn't decide if she wanted to focus on coaching, yoga, art therapy, walking groups, travel, or something else altogether. She felt pressured to choose the exact right focus because it was going to be the thing that finally allowed her to feel fulfilled and purposeful.

Like Diane, you have many facets and nuances. You are an infinitely talented and varied person, and all of your activities are ways your purpose can come to life through you.

When you allow your purpose to be expressed in a variety of ways—some obvious and some more subtle—you gift yourself the opportunity to stretch and grow into your purpose. You allow yourself to be a whole person who is always expressing, exploring, and expanding into new ways of living your purpose. You bring your disparate activities into a coherent whole that is you.

Eight years later, Diane is still in her administrative role and enjoying it. She also has a thriving life outside of her career and allows herself to host art classes and help people with a unique blend of all of her skills when she feels like it. She feels clear in who she is and lives into her purpose every day just by being her.

You are a unique and whole being, fully living your purpose right now, no matter what you're doing or not doing. Your purpose is a gift inherent to your being that can't be separated from you and that you're always discovering more fully, whether your life feels like it's on track or a total mess.

In other words, your purpose is not about what you DO; it's about who you ARE.

Myth #2 — If You Achieve Success, You'll Be Happy

Many of us have been taught to continually achieve as a way of "advancing" through life. We confuse this advancement for purpose or assume purpose will unfold along the way. We rack up awards, degrees, accolades, promotions... all in the hopes that it will get us somewhere.

But where are we hoping it'll get us?

Some people will answer it's getting us more money, more power, more influence. All of which can potentially buy more freedom to choose how to use your time.

But if we pull that thread further, we might discover there's a deeper desire there. A desire to be ourselves, to be undefined, to call the shots in our own lives in our own way. A desire for true freedom, to be able to opt out of the obligation and constraints of the roles we play, so we can just be.

Practicing the art of continually striving and achieving never prepares us to be present and enjoy what we achieve. We get over the next hurdle only to remain unfulfilled. So we fall back on what we know how to do: strive for more.

> *Society is guiding us towards security, not happiness.*

This cycle can continue your entire life. Stuck on the treadmill of trying to get somewhere only to realize you're not getting anywhere—at least not anywhere of meaning and inner value.

Well-intentioned people do their best to follow the "rules" of life and achieve more and more. Deep down, many of us believe we are promised a happy ending if we obey. But society is guiding us towards security, not happiness. To a life that makes sense in our social system, not our souls.

For many of us, the pinnacle of our success is also when our inner world starts to fall apart. This is because we finally peek behind the curtain of striving and realize there's no there, there. No matter how wealthy, famous, or important you are, you still have to do the inner work if you want to be happy, content, and at peace.

This is how I felt when I found myself in my dream job still struggling with low self-esteem, depression, and the echoes of trauma. After 18 years of schooling, I was finally living what I'd worked towards... yet I was an emotional mess. I thought when I had it "all," that I would be the best version of myself and filled with endless bliss.

We're so hyper-focused on creating a sense of accomplishment—and thus happiness—outside of ourselves, we forget that contentment, worth, and peace grow within. Practicing the arts of craving, consumerism, and self-aggrandizing through material possessions will never make us masters of inner contentment. It can't. They are two different ways of being.

Whether you're disillusioned by what you haven't been able to achieve or by a lack of satisfaction with what you have, this is your invitation to start on a new path—one in which living your purpose is an inner game, not an outer expression. This pathway will help you shift your focus to who you're being and becoming so that all of your actions can reflect your essence and your entire life can become an expression of your purpose.

Myth #3 — Contentment and Meaning Are Your Rewards for Doing Well

If you were raised in the U.S. before the 2000s, chances are good that your school bribed you to read books with the promise of a pizza party if you read enough. Or perhaps you waited for the coveted gold star on your homework or class behavior chart. It felt so good to receive approval and acknowledgment!

Most of us were trained from a young age that if we do what's expected (and desired), we'll be rewarded, even if the reward is just to not be punished. This theme continues well into our adult lives and careers when we try to "earn" the freedom to do what we want in retirement through a long career of service. We just assume happiness is a byproduct of our effort because that's the path we're told leads there.

Maybe I was naive, but I truly thought if I did well in the government, had a good friend group, bought a house, and had a clear career path and someday family, my happiness would be guaranteed. So I tried to get those things in place as fast as I could, including pushing to marry the wrong boyfriend and buying a crumbling house just to get it "checked off" the life list. But no matter how sorted my life seemed on paper or how incredibly blessed I was to have so much opportunity, abundance, education, support, and love, none of it took away my internal discomfort. The feeling that I wasn't enough, I needed more, and nothing I did or had would ever be enough. If anything, I felt entitled to even more, because LOOK HOW GOOD I WAS BEING!

I was doing all the "right" things.

Where was my happiness?
Where was my payout of endless love and bliss?
Where was my lasting inner peace?

Unfortunately, no matter how hard you try, you can't earn fulfillment and joy.

As a society, we're so committed to the story that achievements secure our happiness, we feel silly pointing out that it's not working for us. Instead of assuming the system is broken when our successes don't leave us content, we assume that we're broken. Everyone else seems to be progressing nicely, so we must be the exception to the rule. We must be missing the gene that allows us to be satisfied, content, and happy with life. Either that or we're—gasp!—ungrateful, greedy, hard to please, and insatiable.

Ouch.

If this feels familiar, it's not just you.

Most people are in some shade of denial about how empty and disheartening modern life feels.

No matter how good of a spouse you are…
No matter how good you are at your job…
No matter how much you show up for your parents or family or community…
No matter how much you volunteer or go to church or meditate…

There is no happiness prize for good behavior.

There is no point in adulthood when a magical fairy sprinkles you with contentment and bliss, finally validating your efforts all these years.[1] No

---

1 Your religion might promise eternal reward *later*. I'm focused on helping you embrace inner peace and purpose now.

matter how much you achieve externally, you still have to find a way to create happiness, contentment, and a sense of meaning within you.

Growing up is discovering there is no medal at the end of the race. There is no race. There is no time or timer. There is no first or second prize. There is no competition at all. The only running you're doing is in your head because there's nowhere to go and nothing to achieve.

The only transformation is the shift inside yourself from striving to being.

Consciousness Shifter — A New Era of Being

Over-conflating purpose with career achievement is ablest, classist, racist, as well as a host of other -isms. It implies that only those with the access, opportunity, and ability to achieve their career aspirations—exactly as they desire them to be—can fulfill their soul's purpose. That doesn't track with my deeper knowing that if I have a purpose, then everyone must have a purpose, and I suspect it doesn't align with your knowing either.

It's time to untangle purpose from doing and achieving and recenter it in a state of embodied being. It's unsustainable to keep pressuring ourselves into endless perfectionism in the guise of self-improvement, including trying to find the perfect career or role to fulfill our deepest sense of meaning and purpose.

If we play out that assumption, then to successfully live your purpose…

1) You'd have to achieve an extraordinary level of career status + material success in the exact right field for you—which you'd have to discover on your own with no clear guidance.

2) Your success would have no connection to your inner welfare, emotional health, or relationship to community, family, or the larger whole.

This makes the soul sound like a jerk!

It makes much more sense that:

A) Your purpose is about YOU.
B) You have everything you need to live your purpose no matter what your life is like.
C) Your journey with purpose is a journey of becoming authentically you.
D) Peace, fulfillment, and joy are cultivated within and enable you to express your purpose more fully.

Your soul isn't playing by the human rules. It's not judging you, assessing you, punishing you, holding out on you, or shaming you. It doesn't care about your human achievements in a productivity-obsessed system. Your soul is only inviting you into more truth.

It's time to stop setting ourselves up to fail with purpose and fully redefine the game. The truth is, I don't care what job you do. I don't care if you never have a job at all. Because I know in every fiber of my being that YOU are the gift your soul is here to bring, no matter what race, gender, ethnicity, or form your body takes. When you embody your purpose as an inseparable aspect of you, then everything you do becomes an expression of that truth—from brushing your teeth to creating masterful work in the world.

You'll still grow and expand.
You'll still have an individual mission and focus.
You'll even still have an overarching message and desire that inspires change.

But your purpose will no longer be trapped in the limited framework of productivity and economic value. Released from those binds, you can finally be free to define the uniqueness that is you.

Chapter 2 Summary

- Feeling lost or unfulfilled in your purpose is not your fault. Current approaches to purpose set you up to fail and can leave you feeling confused and disconnected from your power.
- There are three main myths about purpose and happiness:
    - Myth #1: Your purpose is your job or career.
    - Myth #2: Achieving success guarantees happiness.
    - Myth #3: Contentment and meaning are rewards or good behavior or achievement.
- Everyone has a purpose, regardless of age, gender, ability, race, education, or access to resources or opportunities.
- Confusing your purpose with the career or role you play has three dangerous consequences:
    - You lose your identity when roles or careers change.
    - You feel unfulfilled because external factors dictate your purpose.
    - You lose your fullness, AKA your self-expression is limited.
- Happiness, peace, and fulfillment are not prizes you can win with good behavior. They are cultivated internally.
- Practicing striving and achieving does not help you develop the skillsets of being present and feeling content.
- Purpose is a state of being, not doing. Your purpose is bigger than your achievements and roles.
- Your purpose is an inseparable aspect of you, which means that everything you do is an expression of your truth.

Your purpose is about your soul's actualization, not your human capabilities.

3

YOU'RE PLANNING FOR PURPOSE BACKWARD

"... I walked away feeling such clarity, as if my mind had been cleared of previous thought patterns and reset to my true mission, with strength and ease."

This Recipe Doesn't Make Fulfillment

All the aptitude and personality quizzes in the world won't add up to you feeling any clearer about yourself or your chances for true fulfillment. They can't because they're looking at your resources—your skills, characteristics, and training—not your truth.

My heart might break if one more person tells me that they know their purpose is to be a nurse or a teacher, but they still wonder why they feel empty and think there must be something more. Typical advice would be to analyze their skills, talents, and proclivities to find a more meaningful career, yet that approach just keeps you trapped in the paradigm of doing at the expense of your being.

This is not a recipe for true fulfillment. It's resource-based planning masquerading as a reasonable way to achieve soul-level satisfaction.

In other words, we plan for purpose backwards and that's keeping you stuck and feeling like you can't live your purpose.

$100 Million in Vaccines Solves Global Peace, Right?

I learned about resource-based planning as part of a government effort to find a new way to respond to complex crises. As a country, the U.S. wanted to provide long-term, holistic support to other countries in need, but the internal budgeting, staffing, and management systems weren't designed for that type of commitment. Basically, we weren't organized for the outcomes we wanted.

Here's a (highly exaggerated) example:

Imagine the government wants to help stabilize a country coming out of war. That's the goal, so then the funding arm looks around for extra money to temporarily divert to this new focus. It finds a bit here and there and allocates a few million in education funds, a few more million for vaccines, and additional millions in military training.

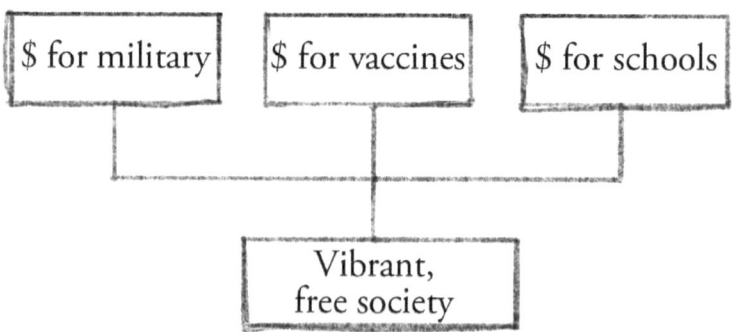

Unfortunately, you can't engender a vibrant, financially viable, free society with only pencils, shots, and soldiers. It takes more than just those elements to create lasting foundations for peace.

Yet, when it comes to defining and living our purpose, most of us make this same mistake every single day.

We're looking at what we have available—our resources—and trying to create massive outcomes that capture our immense depth and breadth and thus hopefully satisfy us on a soul level. It's called resource-based planning, and it doesn't work well to achieve big dreams whether you're a company, country, or consciousness seeker.

A Visionary Alternative

On paper, creating a fulfilling life of purpose is simple:

1) You envision yourself as a happy, contented person at peace with yourself inside and out.
2) Then you identify the necessary and sufficient elements (both are important) to become that person.
3) You embody those elements.

For example, if your best self feels like connection, love, and dancing, then we can guess that to become that person, you'll need community or close relationships with yourself, others, and Source to create a sense of connection, an open heart to create more love, and a flowing relationship with your body and movement to capture the sense of dancing. These categories give you a place to start for how to cultivate the ways you most want to feel and be in the world. The more you are who you want to be, the more you drop the masks of habit and show up for the ways life wants to flow through you.

Each one of these is necessary to achieve the goal (your ideal way of being), and together they are hopefully sufficient to guide you there.

This is an example of planning based on the outcome you desire. This way, you get to bring all of your network, resources, skills, gifts, talents, community, plus miracles to bear on creating what you really want.

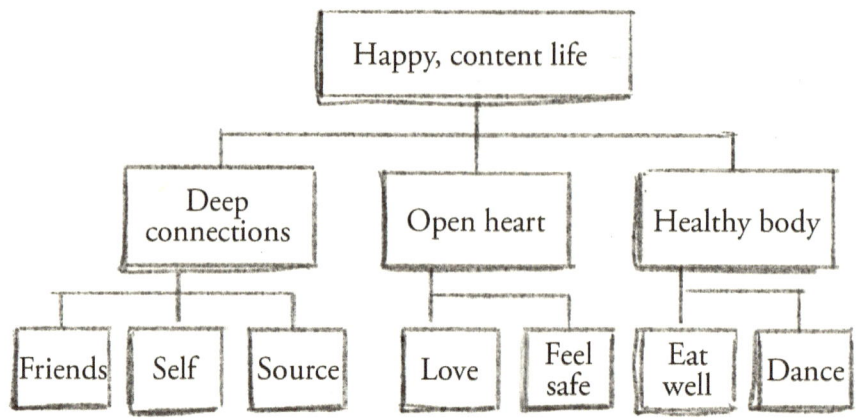

Unfortunately, most of us learned to plan backward and do it without thinking.

We learned to focus on the tools and resources we have and try to cobble together an outcome that will suffice, even though it's usually not the whole picture.

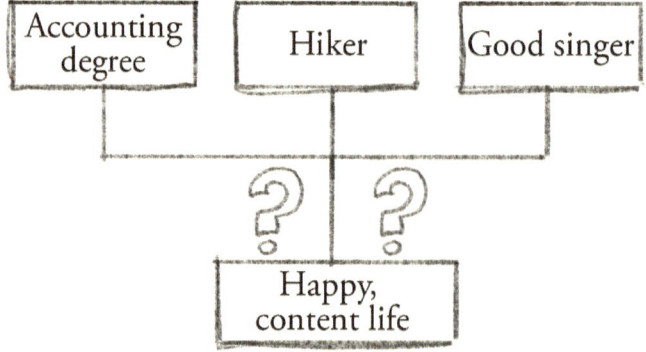

This backward planning is a recipe for lackluster results in any industry. Applied to your purpose, it's a guaranteed way to feel unfulfilled.

Shana & The Permaculture Massage Accounting Movement Center

When Shana came to me, she was in her mid-50s and desperate to create a business and quit her 9-to-5. The problem was that she couldn't figure out what type of business would feel truly fulfilling, and she didn't want to settle at this point in her life.

She was debating going to massage school, even though she was already a certified accountant. She was also fascinated by somatic movement and helping seniors feel safer in their bodies. Beyond that, she dreamed of owning a permaculture farm and growing her own food.

Imagine if we tossed all of these skills and interests into a bowl like ingredients for a salad. You could shake, chop, and dress those ingredients all you want, and they're still unlikely to create a coherent or appetizing meal.

It's possible to cobble together a business from those ingredients. She could run or work at a retreat center that doubles as a permaculture farm while offering massage and movement training for guests and also being the accountant for the center. Humans are creative and you can make almost any combination work if you really go for it.

But the overall approach—assuming that feelings of joy and purpose will flow in abundance if you get the exact right combo of all of your interests and passions—is limiting.

Your purpose is a state of being that informs your doing; not something you're doing in the hopes of changing your way of being and feeling.

Consciousness Shifter — You Can't Cobble Your Way into Purpose

Trying to create a sense of purpose from your resources doesn't work for two main reasons:

1) You can't account for everything you might ever be interested in, skillful at, or inspired by for the rest of your life.
2) Your purpose is about your soul's actualization, not your human capabilities. (More on that in Chapter 7.)

Your purpose demands flexibility and, more importantly, all of you. It is a total devotion to your becoming.

Your purpose is a state of being that informs your doing; not something you're doing in the hopes of changing your way of being and feeling.

When I left the government and started helping small business owners with strategic planning, I quickly realized how often we default to resource-based planning, and how totally inappropriate it is when your goal is freedom, happiness, or a sense of true purpose in life.

Instead, we need to start with vision.

What do you actually want to achieve? Not as a list of accomplishments, but from the perspective of what your soul is cultivating and creating through your very being.

From there, we can identify all of the elements that support the unfolding of that vision—whether you already have them in hand or not. This leaves room for miracles and for life to support and guide you. In other words, it leaves room for growth and evolution. It also allows you to continually deepen your understanding of what you think you want and how you want to feel without getting trapped by your previous choices.

Planning backward isn't the only habit or belief making it hard for you to truly know and live your purpose. Let's dive into some of the others next.

Chapter 3 Summary

- Most of us plan for purpose backward. We try to create big dreams from the skills and resources we already have.
- No combination of skills or talents will feel like your purpose, because purpose is a reflection of your being, not what you do.
- Resource-based planning limits what is possible and keeps you stuck taking action without ever feeling fulfilled.
- Vision-based planning starts with who and how you want to be and then allows your actions to flow naturally from your state of being.
- Your purpose is a total devotion to your becoming.
- When you focus on your soul's vision, you can work with all your resources and leave room for growth, evolution, and life's miracles.

Your purpose is a one-person mission to live into the truth of your soul.

4

OTHER LIES ON PURPOSE

"...decades and decades and BOOM... melted one of the largest limiting beliefs I had with 'purpose'"

Dying of Good Ideas

Your purpose is a one-person mission to live into the truth of your soul. To become the fullest possible version of yourself and expand continually along the emotional trajectory that captures your soul's truth. While that last sentence will make more sense in Part II, the point is that your purpose is not your job, passion, strengths, skills, talents, service, or role in the world.

So far, we've explored why conflating your purpose with your career leads to frustration. We've also considered why common methods for discovering your purpose don't create greater fulfillment. Now let's burst a few other belief bubbles about purpose that may be holding you back from fully embracing yours.

Punishing Kids with Passion

If you are—or have—a child in school between the ages of 14 and 18, then you're probably well-versed in the "find your passion" messaging. Children are asked repeatedly from toddler age to adulthood what they want to do when they grow up. Many respond with fantastical answers, like "astronaut-fireman-football player" (which, by the way, is totally possible). As kids get older, they may respond with more expected or "reasonable" answers, like doctor, lawyer, mechanic, or engineer.

For kids who say, "I don't know," the next question is often, "Well, what are you passionate about?"

There are two main reasons why passion is not a reliable pathway to purpose:

1) Not everyone is driven by passion.

   Not everyone needs or even feels the spike of excitement or emotion that comes from diving deeply into a topic. Some people feel interested, perhaps in the form of not being as bored as they are by other topics. Some people feel good being engaged with a team or friends, and they don't care what the topic is. Others enjoy their hobbies but don't want to make a career out of them.

My chiropractor's son is smart and gets good grades, but he doesn't know what he wants to study in college or do later in life. Well-meaning advisors have tried to help him by asking what he's passionate about, but other than playing video games with his friends, he doesn't feel excitement in that way. Their questions make him worry there's something wrong with him instead of helping him feel confident in his decision-making about the future.

2) Not everyone can "afford" passion.

Passion is often a privilege for kids of a certain socioeconomic class who have the support and opportunities to explore what excites them. Some kids learn that they "can't afford passion" because it implies pursuing an interest that would take energy away from making money to survive.

For example, Lou from Chapter 2, was actively discouraged by his parents from pursuing his passion for art when he was younger. His parents came from a lower-income background and worried he would never create the financial stability they wished for him if he followed his love of art.

If we exaggerate the passion-based approach to purpose over time, we end up with a few radically different, archetypal outcomes:

A. Kids who get to pursue their passion and are fully committed to their chosen identity and role.
B. Kids who pursued a passion and now feel burnt out and wonder what else life is about.
C. Kids who took whatever job they could find and now feel left out and behind because they still don't know what their passion is or how they can find and live it.

D. Kids who took the best job they could find and are angry that they never got to pursue their potential and feel held down by the system.

Exaggerated Archetypal Outcomes of Conflating Passion and Purpose	
A ◦ Pursued their passion. ◦ Still fully committed to the identity of that role.	**B** ◦ Pursued their passion. ◦ Now burnt out. ◦ Wonder what else life is about.
C ◦ Took any job they could find. ◦ Feel left out and behind. ◦ Still don't know their passion or how to find and live it.	**D** ◦ Took best job they could find. ◦ Angry never got to pursue their potential. ◦ Feel held down by system.

Does one or more of these feel familiar? I was in the top right box, which led to my quest to better understand my purpose and eventually write this book. Our future generations deserve more options than these boxes.

The more we focus on passion, skills, and talents as foundations for understanding your purpose, the more we continue to alienate people from actually living their purpose. We also continue to perpetuate social inequities in the name of potential.

Here's what I want you to know:

- ✓ You don't have to feel passionate to have a purpose.
- ✓ You don't have to feel passionate to be happy.
- ✓ You don't have to be single-mindedly focused on one career path to be fully you.

Your purpose is available to you no matter if you feel inspired, get to go to college, have a supportive family, or if none of those are true. Your soul's purpose is not tied to your gender, race, class, mobility, or ability.

It IS you.

The goal is to be authentic; passion is a tool best used by those who want and like to feel it.

Passion and the Anti-Force

"But, Alexis," I feel you exclaim, "I *want* to feel passion! That's why I'm reading this—I want to lose myself in something. That's how I'll know I giving it my all and living my purpose."

I get it. We love feeling in love. We love being carried away by a book or a movie. We love going all-in during a game or project.

There is a difference between losing yourself in the hopes that it will help you feel better and answer the underlying questions you have about your value in the world and how to make your life meaningful, and giving yourself fully to the inspiration flowing through you. The latter requires you to claim your meaning and value first. Similar outcomes, but they feel very, very different in practice.

It's like the difference between hoping the "One" will make you feel complete and happy, versus loving who you are and enjoying your life, and then feeling like it gets better when you find someone you like.

I'm not trying to suck the fun out of your life and say passion has no place. My goal is to introduce you to a level of truth within you that exists regardless of whether or not you feel passionate, because passion is not a pre-requisite for living into your purpose. Nor is all passion the same.

In my government career, I was led by a passionate vision. I felt possessed by it in some ways. I knew what could be and believed that creating it was right for the country and the world. It was a vision of possibility I was compelled to actualize.

When I left the government, and even today, I'm not filled with the same level of clarity and drive as I was then. I believed that my unshakable conviction was a sign of my purpose, so it's disorienting not to feel it. Passion was my main motivating force.

Since then, I've tried lots of ways to find passion, including focusing on what I didn't like…

- I can get passionate about people sitting on the couch waiting to die instead of fully living.
- I can get passionate about how the foster care system in the U.S. fails parents and kids.
- I can get passionate about how standard medical care just patches problems instead of getting to the root cause of issues... how doctors don't even understand basic biomechanics or breathing techniques, let alone the complexities of how trauma impacts the nervous system and the nervous system impacts your physical, mental, and emotional health.

Eventually, I lose steam on all of these topics because they stem from what I don't like, not from what I know is possible.

The most enduring passion comes from your vision.

When something just is to you, then you don't have to amp yourself up or convince yourself into it. It's not a job that you turn on and off or leave at home. It's not something you retire from or eventually tire of. It's the truth as you know it should be—that's that.

This is why people like Nelson Mandela, Susan B. Anthony, Mother Teresa, and Sojourner Truth are so inspiring decades or centuries later—their vision still calls us into their truth.

Commitment waivers. Passion waivers. Vision remains.

The process you'll experience in Part III will help you gain clarity on your truth so that you'll have a level of vision that inspires you. Sometimes that inspiration will feel like passion; other times it may feel like quiet conviction. Still other times, it may feel like an idealistic burden. As long as it's calling you forward and inviting you to live more fully and authentically, it's helping you live into your purpose.

Purpose Is Not Your "Why" or Motivation

Your soul's purpose is a driving urge that influences everything you do, think, and feel. It's continually calling you forward. Your soul is ruthless in its efforts to shape you into a clear channel for your truth. Yet, none of this may register in your conscious mind. Your purpose is built into the fabric of your life, and you may not recognize it as a unique experience of soul or purpose.

> *Your soul is ruthless in its efforts to shape you into a clear channel for your truth.*

Your "why" and motivation are pointing towards a more conscious choice. These might be the reasons you find to continually renew your energy for a project or focus, especially when questions arise like, *What am I doing?* or *Why do I bother?* Your why might be to provide a better life for your children, to end world hunger, or to feel like you gave every bit of yourself in service to life (the latter is often the motivation behind why people crave deeper purpose).

Your why and motivation spark energy. They generate momentum and drive. They move you from where you are now towards a future you believe is possible.

By contrast, your soul's purpose feels more like a pull energy. It's drawing you forward, whether you are aware of it or not. It's like the urge that makes salmon swim upriver in the spring or the invisible force that causes the flowers to bloom. I like to imagine it's like a thread pulling you through the eye of a needle so small that you have to shed layers of false identities to make it through and become your true self. This pull is beyond your consciousness and ingrained into the fabric of your being.

Both energies invite forth your talents.

Both require your full dedication.

Your why helps you consciously develop your potential; your purpose helps you become the person who lives your truth, regardless of whether it matches your idea of your potential.

Ideally, they work together to support you in developing your skills, surrendering in service to a cause that's bigger than you alone, and remembering that you are capable of more than you believe is possible.

In the worst-case scenario, your purpose and why conflict and interrupt the flow of your vital energy. Sometimes, you may be so convinced of your goal and attached to a specific outcome that you may close off pathways of growth and expansion. I did this repeatedly in the government. For example, I turned down my first job offer and almost turned down the second one, because I couldn't see how small arms control or immigration policy could lead to my dream of working in international conflict resolution. Luckily, a lack of other options forced me to surrender, and it turned out immigration policy was a direct path to my bigger vision and desires. That path has continued to unfold into the work I do today.

Continuing to move through open doors with awareness guides you into greater purpose.

Holding a Clear Channel — i.e. Opening Versus Controlling

Your soul is focused less on life working out well for you (money, success, health, happiness, etc.), and more on sculpting you into the best transmitter and receiver of your truth. Your soul is tuning your inner radio dial to find the clear channel, while also helping you figure out how to stay on the station once you've found it. You may notice that even now you have moments of clarity, similar to how a TV station comes in better while you're holding the antenna. Your body grounds it, like a good conversation, yoga retreat, or favorite podcast may help ground and clear your mind now.

The path of purpose is about learning to hold that clear channel in yourself.

Over my adult life, my motivations and conscious why have changed significantly, even though the thread of my purpose weaves through it all. At first, I wanted to be a global changemaker and work in the United Nations or at the U.S. Department of State and have dinner parties with my imagined husband and feel like a power couple. I wanted to feel important—to feel like someone who mattered.

My why had to do with ending war and suffering. I believed in doing the right thing for the country and in creating a better world for all. In that way, a thread of my why has continued—I still want to end suffering and war, create peace, and change the world. It just looks different in its expression. Now it has more to do with opening my heart, having amazing experiences with my (now real) husband, ending generational lines of trauma, and creating safe spaces for others to embrace their truth. Of course, I also want to make money, surrender to my creative potential, and see how far I can push the limits of what I think is possible for me.

My soul is pulling me forward through these different iterations of my career and identity as I deepen my understanding and more fully embody my truth. It doesn't really matter what I think I should do or should be, because they're all a pathway to becoming more me if I allow them to be. My soul is guiding me through an inner process using everything it can, including my conscious motivations and why.

When Your "Why" Leaves You Empty

Even if you have a strong why, purpose is still important because you can fulfill your motivation or why and still feel empty afterward. I got to have my dream job, feel important, and do meaningful work in the government. Yet, once I reached a certain level of success, I felt like there had to be more to my calling than what I was doing. Like any goal, achieving your why may not bring you the lasting joy, inner transformation, or contentment you desire. You may even feel like you gave your all and lost yourself in the process.

Purpose requests your all, but gives you back yourself along the journey. Purpose is always guiding you to feel more full, fulfilled, at peace, and joyful.

Lastly, you don't need motivation or a why to live your purpose. Purpose is the journey of your life, period. It's happening whether you choose it or not, and it's playing out in your life every day already. As you bring conscious awareness to your purpose, you can better understand the ways your soul is guiding you in every area of your life. Then you can start to work with your soul to create a life of radiance, joy, and meaning, even if it ends up wildly different from your conscious goals.

You're on the right path if you're becoming more fully you.

Consciousness Shifter — Purpose Is Not Your Mission Or Life's "Work"

I'm going to split a few hairs here in the hopes of creating a bit of breathing room for you around your purpose. I decided to include this section, because I recently received a marketing email from a business owner sharing how they went through a painful life experience, found their way to the other side, and now they believe it's their life's mission to help other people through similar painful experiences.

It's a story many of us are familiar with and perhaps even use ourselves. At its best, it has deep, spiritual roots; helping others achieve enlightenment or salvation once you've attained it yourself appears in many traditions. Used superficially and only about your career, it can limit you living into your purpose.

The process you'll discover in Parts II and III will lay out a new way to conceive of your purpose that informs your work without unwittingly limiting you in it. In the meantime, let me share three points on why viewing your purpose as your life's work or business mission sets you up for disappointment. I also invite you to revisit Chapter 2 for a refresher on the three main reasons why tying your purpose to your career or a specific role is unhelpful at best and dangerous at worst.

> A) Life gifts you with lots of challenging and painful experiences. Focusing on just one may limit you from expanding through others.

We'll dive deep into this in Part II. For now, the important part is that you don't have to define yourself by one big struggle. In my experience, most of us misinterpret the invitation that challenges present from the soul's perspective. That means we also miss the opportunity for growth into purpose that they provide.

There's nothing wrong with sharing what you've learned and experienced. This entire book is a version of that—I was struggling with purpose, discovered a new approach that makes way more sense, and now I'm sharing it with you in the hopes that it helps you achieve inner peace and freedom faster.

Yet I don't have to define my entire life by that insight, conflate this process with my soul's mission, or view that struggle as the defining issue of my life. That would be skipping over the interwoven gifts that lie in healing from sexual assault, improving my relationships, restoring harmony in my nervous system, repairing my gut, and trying to have a baby.

Life is always gifting you opportunities to become the person who lives your purpose more fully. While it's admirable to be inspired to help others, your purpose is far bigger than any one specific life lesson.

B) Your purpose is more about who you're being than what you're doing.

True purpose invites you to surrender who you think you are and enter into a state of authentic presence and receptivity to life and your soul. In that state of being, the actions you're inspired to take may not always fit within the confines of a chosen persona, role, brand, or career. Yet they're still on purpose in the sense that your soul is calling you forward into new awareness and awakenings.

For years, when I would tune in and ask for guidance in my business, all I felt in response was "meditate." That wasn't very helpful, since I was broke and needed money, so I largely ignored it. A decade of hacking it out in business later, I realized meditation is exactly what would have ushered me into becoming the person I needed to be to create my dreams and succeed more easily.

Your soul is guiding your being and becoming, not your doing. In that sense, no "work" can ever be your life's work, because you are already your main mission.

C) Your responsibility is to birth the baby, not choose which baby to birth.

At every moment you are pregnant with exactly what you need now to evolve more fully into your purpose. You don't get to choose the baby you are pregnant with. Your responsibility is to do your best to cultivate, birth, and shepherd the creation on your heart.

That responsibility may require you to drastically renovate your inner and outer worlds. It may invite you to take big turns in your life and career to let go of beliefs and habits that hold you back from becoming more fully you. If you cling to a business or career or idea of your life's work because you think it is your purpose, you may interrupt the flow of your actual purpose trying to move through you.

So yes, your career is a life's work. It is also part of your life's work. But your actual mission is to live into the truth of your soul. It's to become the fullest possible version of yourself and expand continually along the emotional trajectory that captures your soul's truth. Everything else is how you choose to express your truth in a human social and economic system.

The key is to not limit yourself by confusing the ways you express your purpose—career, business, hobbies—with your purpose itself. Then you'll be able to move in faith with your soul, while continually evolving yourself and the ways you contribute.

Strengths Tests Won't Help You Get Clear

As we uncovered in Chapter 3, trying to use your strengths to understand your purpose is resource-based planning, and it doesn't work. Some of the most talented people are also the ones who share feeling the most desperate for purpose. That's because doing something well does not inherently imbue that activity, its creations, or your life with meaning or fulfillment.

Your strengths, skills, talents, and personality have a big role to play in the ways you choose to express your purpose. They are like the teammates and your purpose is like the team. As the players hone their mastery and work together, the team is more unified, focused, and artful in its mission. This is why trying to search for purpose without first going through the steps to fully embody your unique truth spins you in circles. Purpose requires you to become you so that you can then more fully develop into your purpose.

Purpose Isn't About Meaning, Either

Your purpose isn't about finding meaning in your life. It's about how you create and use meaning to become more authentically you and follow the trail of your soul.

You can assign meaning to anything. That's the fun of being human. You get to choose. That choice is power. When you feel disconnected from your purpose, it's often because you're also disconnected from your power of choice.

I'll share a lot about the power of meaning-making in Part II. For now, know that your purpose isn't the meaning you make of your life. Meaning can change, and we're in search of truth. It's who you become in service to your soul, which involves wielding the power of meaning.

If your life was a beaded necklace, the events of your life, welcome or unwelcome, are like beads. Your purpose is the thread that connects them. You can create a distinct meaning for each bead that either empowers or disempowers you. This process will help you choose a more purposeful meaning by showing how everything you experience relates to the larger thread of your purpose.

Service Is a Consequence, Not Your Purpose Itself

You've probably seen a similar quote before:

> Your purpose is not the thing you do. It is the thing that happens in others when you do what you do.

While I don't disagree in the full expression of purpose, it's not a helpful pathway to understand and embody your purpose. The majority of us are struggling with purpose, not because we don't know how to give and serve, but because we're not rooted in a strong enough sense of self to be able to withstand the level of surrender needed to truly show up.

There are steps into embracing purpose that are required before we attempt to lose ourselves in service to others. When you're living the truth of your soul, you cannot stop yourself from being of service. It is an inherent part of who you are. Yet, when you attempt to serve as a way to shortcut owning your worth or escape from having to embody your truth, you stay stuck in unfulfilling cycles of transactional giving based in coping skills and trauma responses.

Dev was a brilliant hypnotist and tour guide for the subconscious mind, yet he couldn't seem to make the money he needed. He gave and gave, offering his unique mind-rewiring journeys for $10 when others were charging $100+. He believed that if enough people benefited from his work, he would not only feel validated but eventually succeed.

It's advice many of us have heard before: show your value and give generously and then you'll be rewarded. But this approach skips over a key ingredient—you must embrace your value first. Dev had all the skills. He was an undisputed master of his craft. Yet, he was over-giving and under-receiving, because he wasn't convinced of his value in the world. He knew intellectually that he mattered and his work mattered, yet the old patterns were strong and he defaulted to people-pleasing when sharing his work. He longed for results to help him feel more confident when more confidence is what would help him see better results.

For most of us, moving into our purpose isn't about serving more. It's about claiming and embodying our brilliance so that we feel safe in ourselves and can show up fully in service.

God's Work Doesn't Work as a Paradigm for Purpose

Depending on your faith, your purpose is inherently about surrendering to God's plan and allowing yourself to do God's work in the world. You are stretching into your purpose when you are truly living that energy of devotion. Let's be honest though: very few people are showing up with that level of devotion.

The rest of us tend to look to God for answers without fully embracing our gifts or taking responsibility for how we're working with life. In that way, viewing your purpose as God's work can end up much the same as wistfully hoping for an answer that magically changes everything without having to change yourself. You may wait for a clear sign or until you're directed when, in truth, you're receiving signs and nudges every moment of every day.

The process I guide you through in Parts II and III will help you connect the dots from your faith to your daily action so that you understand how to actualize God's plan for you and start living it with courage and conviction.

Every path can guide you towards purpose if you allow it to awaken your heart to deeper truths while dropping the identities, beliefs, and habits obscuring your truth.

Chapter 4 Summary

- Many of the ways we think about purpose can hinder us from embodying and living with true purpose.
- Passion is not required to live into your purpose.
- Your purpose is always with you, even when passion or motivation wanes.
- The ways you express your purpose are not your purpose itself.
- Your purpose is a way of being that flows into your actions, not something you do to hopefully change how you feel.
- Your soul is ruthless in its efforts to shape you into a clear channel for your truth.
- Your purpose is a driving urge that influences everything you do, think, and feel.
- Purpose and your "why" can work together but are different. Your why helps you consciously develop your potential, while your purpose helps you become the person who lives your truth, regardless of whether it matches your idea of your potential.
- Your purpose isn't about finding meaning in your life. It's about how you create and use meaning to become more authentically you and follow the trail of your soul.
- You cannot serve your way into self-worth and purpose. Service flows from your purpose.
- True purpose invites you to surrender who you think you are and enter into a state of authentic presence and receptivity with life and your soul.
- Every path can guide you towards purpose if you allow it to awaken your heart to deeper truths while dropping the identities, beliefs, and habits obscuring your truth.

Living your purpose is about receiving the aliveness coming through you and responding to the impulses you're gifted.

5

WORKING WITH LIFE FOR TRUE PURPOSE

"This is such an intense, deeply life changing process. You should put up a warning, 'Caution: May cause earth shattering discoveries.'"

The Thorn in the Side of Your Otherwise Tolerable Life

Many of us feel lost and confused about who we truly are, and also frustrated that we can't find a way to express ourselves fully. We look at others and compare how we feel to how we imagine they feel. This can happen whether you're the creme of society's crop or feel like the last rung on the social ladder.

If I had that kind of money, I'd be so happy…
Sometimes I just wish I was a hairstylist and life was simpler…

It doesn't matter who you are or what kind of life you have; comparing yourself and feeling like you're missing out is normal when we're taught to look outside of ourselves for happiness, fulfillment, and purpose. At best, it can inspire curiosity about other possibilities for your life. At worst, it can precipitate what I call *existential depression*, which is when you don't want to die, but living feels pointless if you can't access and fulfill the potential inside you.

Let's explore the extremes:

At one extreme, there's Bryson. Bryon is a well-known actor. He's at the top of his game, yet feels more confused and alone than ever. Everyone thinks they know him, while he feels like he's playing the character of "Bryson." It's not that he's being fake; it's that he is terrified by how empty he feels, even though he has the career, house, money, car, and influence he always wanted. For a while, he thought if he just bought more stuff or got better roles, then he'd feel better, but the feelings only got worse. He's tried drugs, alcohol, and sex to numb the pain and even went to rehab. He feels dumb and ungrateful trying to explain to friends that he feels like he's missing something because everyone says they wish they had his life. He wonders if there's a truer version of himself beyond the roles he has to play that could help him feel happier, even if discovering it risks everything he's worked so hard to create.

At the other extreme, you have Tonya. Tonya is stuck in what feels like an endless loop of working to survive and is barely scraping by no matter what she does. She has a close friend group, kind kids, and good relationships. She volunteers, goes to church, and has regular time with her friends and for herself. She's doing all the "right" things but still feels like something is missing. *Is this all there is? Just working and trying to make the best of what you have?* she wonders. She has so many creative dreams that she wants to pursue, but she doesn't have the money, time, or support to do them. She wonders if she'll ever get to become who she knows she can be or if she's just stuck in this routine forever.

In both these examples, we end up with the same core questions:

What is the point?
Who am I meant to be?
Is this all there is to life?

Whether you've come to these questions through existential depression or spiritual curiosity, these are often the deeper thorns in the side of our otherwise manageable lives. Sometimes, they're barely noticeable, but sometimes, late at night or in moments alone, their sharpness catches us off guard. Then no matter how busy we get or how much we toss and turn to avoid the pain, the ache of them remains.

These questions point to our craving for a deeper understanding of the meaning of life itself, as well as our role within it. While many spiritual traditions provide a broader context that can feel satisfying in the moment, many of us want tangible answers that connect the dots between the big picture and our daily actions. We want answers that span from the creation of the universe to what we're meant to do in the next five years. We want both big and specific meaning.

This new approach to purpose helps you close the gap between your life and Life itself. It will help you navigate the very personal, practical questions about who you are and why you're here, as well as your broader spiritual aspirations related to your soul's evolution and the evolution of the universe. All of it will help you explore how you want to answer the big questions of life for yourself so that you can feel good and move forward with more clarity and confidence.

Consciousness Shifter — Life Is You and You Are Life

Life will never skip over you. It can't, because you are life itself being lived through your unique perspective—God incarnate in your personal experience.

Language doesn't allow for this level of unity and creates a false separation between the "I" and the "other" for the sake of convenience. It might be spiritually accurate, but it wouldn't make much sense to describe the awe you felt in looking at the stars with the statement, "I was gazing at myself and felt such reverence in my presence. I felt so small in relation to my vastness."

We default to referring to life as something outside and wholly different from us to make sense of our lived experience. To rank and sort animal from object, you from me, cause from effect. These are the realities of human life.

On the spiritual plane, it is all one in a giant continuum of consciousness and experience. Our lives are like popcorn, suddenly transforming from hard kernel to fluffy morsel when the time is ripe for our individual consciousness to burst forth and be part of the show. Yet, the pot we're cooking in and the fire that ignites us are both life itself expressing through us.

Living your purpose is not so much telling life what you want to do, but receiving the aliveness coming through you and responding to the impulses you're gifted. You aren't responsible for the way life is flowing. Your responsibility is to show up 100% in all your gifts, talent, and skills, and be in service to the needs of life in the moment.

I share the popcorn analogy because, to understand this new approach to purpose, you may have to fundamentally shift your underlying beliefs about who you are, what life is, and how it all works. There is no right or wrong. I am not claiming to be the authority on what's true in life for you. Rather, I'm presenting an approach that I've found creates some space and softening in myself and others. It seems to connect the dots in more helpful and empowering ways than other methods of approaching purpose. Yet it requires that we divest from those ways of thinking that haven't led us toward the inner peace and freedom we desire.

So for convenience's sake, while I'll use language that implies life and you are different entities, please note that all of this is rooted in an understanding that there is one Life and you are one of its infinite expressions.

Life Is Always for You

The most beautiful truth of life is that it is always for you. Now that can feel hard to believe—if not infuriatingly wrong—when we feel hurt, abandoned, abused, or cast aside by life. But it's true.

Life is ALWAYS unfolding for you.

A Note on Blame Versus Responsibility:

Allowing all of life to be for you is not that same as you causing every experience. It is not trying to excuse anyone's behavior or blame you for the violence and abuse that other people have chosen or perpetrated against you.

You can take responsibility for making lemonade from the lemons life gives you without having been the one who grew the lemon tree and dropped all the fruit on your doorstep.

Working with life is believing that the lemons are not on your doorstep to sour your life, prove that's all you're worthy of receiving, or make you squirm in pain when they rub into your open wounds. Instead, it's knowing that you can feel more and more powerful with every lemon you squeeze, as you create a soul-awakening nectar that restores you to your wholeness.

The key is that while life is always *for* you, it's never going to *do it for you*.

You have the free will to decide if you're going to step up and work with life or not.

Every experience you have is an invitation to become more fully you.

For example, imagine you love running but twist your ankle. After months of rest and physical therapy, you finally get back to running only to hurt your knee. Then you finally work that out, only to have balance problems. (By the way, this is basically my husband's experience as soon as he crossed the threshold into his mid-30s.)

From one perspective, you might believe that life just isn't going your way. You finally found something you love, running, that makes you feel good and is healthy. Yet no matter what you do, you keep getting smacked down. In this way of thinking, you're doing the "right" thing, but an invisible force is preventing you from advancing. You're the victim of these unfair whims of fate.

As you'll explore in Part II, there's a different way of navigating at it all together. An approach that invites you to dig deep within yourself, transcend the victim-perpetrator paradigm, and embrace life entirely as an opportunity to expand.

Your purpose lives in this perspective.

Your purpose is an expression of your highest truth including the deep pains and fears that currently keep you from living that highest truth. It's the kick you get from running and the frustration of your injury.

They go together.

You expand into your purpose when you accept the invitation life is giving you and grow, even and especially when that invitation is wrapped in struggle, hurt, and pain. The answer is inherent in the question, and your purpose is inherent in the challenge.

Square One and a Green Door

Abrahamic religions give us a linear sense of time and spiritual growth. We start at point A and journey until point Z. For some, that means we are born in sin and do our best to achieve salvation.

If we overlay this new approach to purpose onto our inherited beliefs about time and growth, it might look like this:

You're minding your own business, moving along your spiritual journey, focused on perfecting yourself to be worthy of salvation. Then you see a green door. You touch the doorknob and it hurts. It's like every fear you've ever had zaps through you in an instant.

I'm not worthy.
Nobody will ever love me.
I'm truly alone and destined to die alone.
[Insert your favorite fear here.]

Even though it hurts, you muster the strength to brave your fears and open the green door anyway. On the other side, you feel better. You did it! You lived through the pain and learned that you're stronger than you think. You survived and now feel more centered and capable.

Except, oh wait. *Is that another green door?? Are you kidding me? I just went through that!*

Your mind is racing—*did I not get the lesson? What is life trying to teach me? What did I do to deserve this? I swear I'm a good person!*

It can feel like you are back at Square One, doomed to repeat the same challenges over and over without ever "getting anywhere."

I use quotation marks because our religious heritage has convinced us there is somewhere to get to—a point in time, space, and personal growth where life will suddenly be peaceful, calm, quiet, and happy.

But life is change.

Life is always and only eternal change and movement.

There is no "there" to get to, other than your experience of this moment right here. Unfortunately, we're poorly practiced at being present and content, and exceptionally well practiced at continually striving for the next and the next thing. Our deepest beliefs and assumptions about what's true in life reflect this pattern of striving but not achieving, including feeling punished when seemingly bad things happen.

But there is an alternative way to approach life.

Endlessly Spiraling Green Doors

Imagine that time isn't linear, but more like a spiral. On that spiral, we're in a moment in time, while also continually growing and expanding. The spiral moves both upwards and outwards—refining and expanding at the same time.

As you move along the spiral, you encounter 1000+ green doors. Each one is painted in the same color of pain or fear that cuts you to your core. Each door is different, but they're all the same green because your deepest fear is always the same. This is the disempowered side of your purpose.

When you are allergic to peanuts, you notice peanuts everywhere. The same goes for the disempowering feelings of your purpose.

When a certain pain feels so true that it convinces you over and over of your deepest fear, you start to notice that pain everywhere. You make the same meaning out of every experience because you're convinced that fear is true.

> *In many ways, pain is the most holy aspect of your purpose.*

Not all growth experiences have to be painful, but the ones you're ignoring as invitations into your purpose most certainly are.

In my work, I've discovered that, in many ways, pain is the most holy aspect of your purpose. It is what often ushers you through the next doorway of personal growth and into a whole new understanding and embodiment of who you are.

But only if you accept the invitation.

Life will never force you to make a new meaning or feel differently about an experience. It will just keep giving you the invitation over and over again to choose to feel differently in yourself.

It's Groundhog Day all over again for your soul:

Your boss micromanages you.

Your partner belittles you.

Your parents disrespect you.

These experiences don't mean that you are inherently small and unworthy of respect. They're invitations for you to claim a deeper sense of self-respect within.

Every time you notice a green door in your life, imagine what would be different if—instead of sighing with frustration *here you are again!*—you dug deep, found the inner growth in the experience, and walked through the doorway into an all-new way of being. Imagine if each challenge ushered you into a new and deeper understanding and sense of self.

This is what it's like to live your purpose.

The Soul Doesn't Stop

Your soul is ruthless.

You will be continually invited to claim your truth in deeper and more nuanced ways throughout your life. In other words, you're going to keep coming across green doors.

For me, my green door makes me feel like I'm not enough. I was facing one when I didn't get the final promotion I wanted in the government. Another time was when my boyfriend of five years dropped me off at work and never spoke to me again. When I couldn't figure out how to get my business going no matter how hard I tried. When I finally did get my business going and then overstretched myself and burnt out emotionally and physically. Going through fertility struggles… Every one of these is a green door that stirs up my deepest fear that I am not enough and never will be. They exist not because I'm doomed to be less than, but because I'm destined to claim my inherent worth and enoughness.

If, right now, you keep feeling the same type of fear or pain over and over, excellent. You're on the cusp of truly understanding your real purpose. I invite you to consider what life is inviting you to claim deep within through this experience (I'll help you with this in Chapter 15).

No matter how much we want someone else to fix it, make it easier, or give us the answers, life will never give you a pass on your purpose, because YOU are meant to grow into it.

Your purpose is yours to claim.

Yours to embody.

Yours to choose and express.

Life will not force you. You have the free will to be miserable and interpret everything that happens to you as a cruel twist of fate that proves you're a victim. I tried that for years, and it's a perfectly valid way to move through life. But your soul doesn't believe that, plus it won't help you live a life of purpose and joy.

Your soul knows that in your truth, you are capable, whole, and ready in every moment to claim the brilliance that is already alive within you.

The sooner you surrender to life's invitations, the sooner you'll feel content with who you are, inspired in your purpose, and at peace with life.

Misreading the Soul's Signals

My mind has a few favorite hits that it plays anytime I have a down day. The soundtrack goes from *Your life is meaningless, Nothing you do matters,* and *You'll never amount to anything,* to the epic ballad *You're doomed to be trapped in an endless cycle of unfulfilling work because you don't have the skills, network, courage, creativity, or money to be who you really are.*

Ugh.

Even when I was engaged in objectively meaningful work in the government and impacting the country as well as the international community, every few months, the soundtrack would start playing, and I'd question everything. One of my go-to ways to feel badly about myself back then was comparing myself to a friend or colleague stationed abroad in a crisis:

They're making a real difference. They're helping real people. They're out there pulling refugees off boats and drafting peace treaties, while I'm just writing policy in some office out of harm's way….

On those bad days, the only reason I could find in my mind for the difference between us was that I was a selfish coward scared of testing myself in the real world. On good days, I honored my innate talent for big-vision thinking and coordinating unified responses to unimaginably complex situations. But the secret worry that I was a coward carried through.

So I did what most humans do when faced with big fears about whether or not they are a good person. I got even busier, masked my sadness with caffeine, numbed out my fear with alcohol and food, tuned out my thoughts with TV, boyfriend drama, and happy hours, disappeared into my job to make me feel important and powerful, and stayed up late so I'd fall into bed exhausted with no time for deep thoughts.

It worked... for a while.

But eventually, if you're lucky, you can't play the avoidance game anymore. Your inner truth kicks in, and your old coping strategies no longer make sense.

For me, I realized I was punishing myself. Not because I was bad or mean, but because I was afraid that I wasn't good enough for my own dreams and the feeling of potential inside me. I was in my perfect career—shining at the top of my game with job offers and promotions being handed to me every year—and I still felt like a fraud.

I felt like I was playing at my work. Like it wasn't real; I wasn't real.

I remember sitting in my cubicle watching the "real adults" walk between meetings.

They look happy. They seem okay working every day and then retiring. They seem content with 'real life.'

I interpreted all my yearnings for more—all my impulses to break free from the work-to-pay-bills system and unleash my creativity—not as my purpose coming forward more clearly. Not as my soul speaking through my discomfort. But as a sign of immaturity.

To me, it was proof that I didn't fit in. I didn't truly belong. I was a phony and not adult enough.

In truth, it was my purpose adeptly at work, propelling me into greater aligned action.

Two Ways the Soul Screams

Perhaps you felt that way before too. Like you're playing the *role* of you. Like you're wearing a mask at work and with your friends and family, while the real you is secretly watching from behind the scenes.

These can be scary feelings because they make you feel alone. You may feel like the only one who can't seem to be happy. As if there is something flawed or broken about you.

These feelings aren't "off purpose." They are signs that you're hanging out in the disempowered energy of your purpose and craving a new experience within yourself. Before we dive into that, let me lay out how I see these tough feelings play out in clients because understanding the patterns is the first key to being free from them.

In my experience, this fear that you're flawed or broken manifests in two main ways:

1. You check out

It's unnerving to feel like you'll never be happy. You may wonder what's wrong with you and if life is even worth living. For some, this becomes a dangerous flirtation with suicidal thoughts. For others, it's the more general feeling I call existential depression. That's when you don't want to die, but you're not sure living matters if you can't be happy and fulfill the potential you feel inside you.

To ease the pain and fear, you may turn to drugs, alcohol, sex, or other addictions. Anything to both distract from the emptiness and also feel a rush to prove to yourself that you're not a numb, heartless robot of a human.

For the world's social elite, the disconnect between outward success and inward emptiness can lead to wild swings between feeling filled by creative genius and then empty and small as an individual. Imagine closing a huge deal, recording a new hit song, or unveiling your new design and feeling so on top of the world. Then you go home at night after the excitement wears off and you're just you again. All the same problems and struggles. All the same frustrations and fears. Your spouse is annoyed with you, your kids think you're the worst, and you start remembering all the aspects of yourself you don't like, too. How can you be so seemingly big and important in some areas of your life and feel so small in others?

Even if you're not on a Who's Who list, you may have experienced symptoms of existential depression.

Here are a few of the ways it might show up:

- You feel enraged by world affairs while also feeling like nothing you do matters, and it's pointless.
- Your personal goals feel meaningless against the vast expanse of life's dark—if not evil—emptiness.
- You feel tired, bored, and disinterested in conversation, and everyone annoys you.
- Your normal tricks to soothe yourself into feeling better don't work. Eating doesn't satiate you, venting doesn't stop the frustrated feelings, and sleeping doesn't take away the heaviness.
- You don't actually want to die, but you find yourself thinking or saying there's no point in living if you can't fulfill your potential.

In my 20s, I turned to adrenaline. I'd trigger my fight-or-flight nervous system because it was the only way I could identify feelings that I understood and knew how to handle. Sky-diving, picking fights with my boyfriend, pushing myself to run harder and faster... these let me feel an energy surge of power, even though deep down I felt out of control and lost in my purpose. I was scared my life was a waste or a fluke, but when I got that rush, at least I knew I was alive.

This is also why so many of us stay busy all the time. For me, government work was quite literally one global or homeland security crisis after another, and while I hated the buzz of my BlackBerry, I loved the constant distraction and stimulation. Stress is a socially acceptable excuse for an unregulated nervous system, and I was unwittingly all-in on being dysregulated.

Fortunately, this road runs out eventually. You need more and more of your chosen distraction to drown out the voice of fear inside you—and many people have a wake-up call during that time. You might also call this period a "dark night of the soul," or what I now know as the disempowered energy of your soul not-so-gently nudging you towards greater purpose.

2. You get angry

Feeling hopeless, despondent, disappointed, trapped, and/or anxious can also make you feel powerless. Like a wild animal trapped in a cage, you know you don't belong there. Your soul won't allow it. So you subconsciously move up the food chain of emotions from hopelessness to anger.[2]

Anger is powerful. Anger has a sense of self implied in it. YOU exist in anger, and you come to your own defense and rescue.

Anger is self-protecting and self-awakening at the same time.

When I was in the government and worrying I'd never live up to the potential inside me, anger sheltered me from my fear. It let me keep going and feel strong against the one thought that could cut me off at the knees: *I don't matter.*

Sometimes, it's easier to blame someone else for how powerless and hopeless you feel instead of facing the deeper question of if you truly are capable. It's easier to be angry than to feel vulnerable or scared.

So we point the finger everywhere but inwards:

It's not my fault I'm unhappy and unfulfilled; it's life's fault for leaving me behind!
It's HIS fault for attacking me.
It's THEIR fault for hurting me.
It's my parents' fault. They are why I'm like this.

Blame can help us in the short term. It is a safe haven when we feel out of control and helpless to find our path. But in the long run, blame—and the anger that fuels it—is unsustainable. It wrecks your relationships, makes you feel tense inside, stresses your body, and convinces your mind that the world is unkind and unsafe.

Eventually, it turns the fear that you're alone into a reality.

---

2   David R. Hawkins, Power vs. Force: The Hidden Determinants of Human Behavior (Carlsbad, California: Hay House, Ince., 1995, 1998, 2004, 2012), 90-91, Map of Consciousness®.

Luckily, anger is another disempowering energy of your soul's purpose. When you learn how to use your emotions to find yourself on the landscape of your purpose, then you have a roadmap of how to make your way to feeling more empowered, fulfilled, and whole. You can appreciate the coping skills and trauma responses you once relied on to survive and allow them to start to fade into the background as you develop new, more authentic ways of being in the world.

The Easier Hard Road

Since you're reading this book, I'm willing to bet you've tried getting angry or losing yourself or both, and now you are looking for another way to know your life matters. A better way. A way that connects you with the truth of who you are on a soul level, helps you know in your bones who you're meant to become, and then live it with confidence and clarity.

You're in the right place.

In my journey, blaming others, raging against life, and disconnecting from my real feelings eventually stopped being helpful tools. I didn't like how they made me behave and feel, which just added to the shame and isolation of already feeling broken beyond repair. If that was the easy way out, I was willing to take the hard road instead. I was willing to confront the fear that I wasn't enough for my own potential.

One of the first challenges I gave myself was to question my own beliefs and assumptions about life:

- *If it is easy for me to toddler-style tantrum flop into believing life and I are both meaningless, isn't it just as possible that life is meaningful?*
- *Are some days good because I feel like my life is meaningful, and that puts me in a better mood? Or does my good mood make me think that life is meaningful?*
- *Is the only roadblock between me and feeling happier my doubt that I matter? Or that it is possible to feel happy? Or that I have a bigger purpose?*

Over time, I discovered the simple answer is yes. There is no proof, and we'll never know for sure. But you get to choose: live with the hope that you matter or succumb to the fear that you don't.

After spending years tapping into the deepest truths available to us through meditation, reflection, and dedicated study, here's what I now know to be true. I invite you to feel into the words below and realize this truth already exists in you too:

You have a purpose. You were born with a purpose, and you'll die with a purpose. It is as inherent to who you are as the very concept that you exist.

Even if you've been feeling lost, hopeless, or confused for decades, you still have a unique purpose. You can feel fulfilled, you're meant to feel fulfilled, and you can create a meaningful life. This becomes clearer as you shift your allegiance from the fears of your mind to the truths of your soul.

In return, you just might have to give up everything you know about yourself and purpose to become that person.

When you allow yourself to be fully you, you stop fighting with life and yourself in an attempt to be different than you are and finally soften into a deep, sustaining inner harmony that creates ripples of peace through your life and the world.

The Metaphor that Saved Me

Imagine yourself as a blade of grass. There are millions of blades of grass in the world, yet each individual blade of grass is unique and different. Why?

Why not have one overarching meta Grass instead of so many individual ones? Because they each serve a purpose. Each blade of grass has a role to play in the collective experience of grass.

Similarly, you have a unique role to play in the collective human experience. Call it a puzzle piece or strand of the intricate web—you matter. Your energy contributes to the experience of the whole.

The more you understand, own, and express your unique purpose, the more you contribute to a loving, expanding, peaceful world.

That's why this book and my life's work (notice I didn't say purpose) are dedicated to helping you understand and embody the truth of who you are. When you allow yourself to be fully you, you stop fighting with life and yourself in an attempt to be different than you are and finally soften into a deep, sustaining inner harmony that creates ripples of peace through your life and the world.

When you embrace your unique gifts and the perfection of your being—just as you are—you become an emissary for ease, confidence, and contented wholeness. Then your sheer presence can uplift and inspire others, as it was always meant to do.

You are the gift.

Not what you can do or how much you've accomplished. Just you. Just by being you, appreciating you, and most importantly, loving you.

When you embrace your unique purpose, you have the roadmap to understanding and loving yourself for your being—for who you inherently are. Then the struggle to prove yourself and seek validation falls away, and you become a living embodiment of love.

The goal isn't to achieve some external purpose. It's to become the person capable of fulfilling the infinite potential already within you.

Excavating the Human Purpose

If we're all unique blades of grass in a vast field of the world, then what's the point of human life in general? Grass prevents erosion and knits together dirt. But what about us? What do we add?

You might believe our collective purpose is to serve God or be ourselves, and any number of other beliefs. To me, they all point toward the same truth.

Before digging into your specific, individual purpose, it's valuable to spend a few moments considering the beliefs that underpin your view of life in general. These beliefs can either bolster you during dark days of doubt and insecurity or affirm your worst fears and leave you feeling even emptier and more alone.

I started exploring my beliefs about life about eight months before I resigned from my government career. I was taking a month off on doctor's orders because I was experiencing symptoms of post-traumatic stress disorder after being raped by a colleague the year prior. Though I'd been in therapy for months and already changed jobs to avoid seeing him while the investigation was underway, I found myself blanking out and "waking up" at my desk not knowing how long I'd been sitting there, staring at nothing. I was also responding with excessive anger and indignation to even the smallest hiccups or challenges at work. At a particularly low point, I wore a sleeping bag over my dress in a meeting with the CIA to express my resentment over the air conditioning temperature, which had been set to accommodate men in suits, not women appropriately dressed for the heat of summer. With both my professional reputation and emotional welfare on the line, I traded in my time off for a few weeks at home.

While that might sound nice to you, my home wasn't any less stressful. My house at the time was what I not-so-jokingly called a "tearer-downer" instead of a "fixer-upper." Unfortunately, I didn't have the money to tear it down. Instead, I tried to piece together a renovation hoping to sell it, so I could quit my job later in the year.

During those winter days at home, I saw only the contractor involved in the renovation and one neighbor who was determined to keep me fed. She claims I ate nachos 24 days in a row before she intervened, and I don't doubt it.

Most days, I spent all my energy trying not to cry. My emotions were a revolving door: enraged, hopeless, helpless, enraged, hopeless, helpless, in a continual cycle. Yet this time at home was also a turning point.

As the rawness of my stress started softening, I poured myself into releasing the past so I could move into my future. I started questioning my own beliefs.

Was the world friendly and safe for me to relax? Or was life inherently harsh, uncaring, and every woman for herself? I wondered.

My pain had brought me to the threshold of my power, and for the first time, I was flirting with who I was and wanted to become. I was tired of feeling tight, tense, and defensive, but I wasn't convinced it was safe for me to relax and trust life, either. I needed to know more about why we are all here and what it all means.

Living for the Fun of It

Questions like *Why am I here?* and *What does it all mean?* are as old as human thought. Answers to these questions are at the root of our religions, spiritual traditions, and scientific study.

For some, the answer is nothing—a vast emptiness with no meaning or reason. For others, human life is a reflection of God. A judgment, game, or opportunity for the One to experience itself in millions of ways through each individual.

Humans are unique in that we possess conscious thought and the analytical prowess to wonder *why* in the first place. While the rest of life is caught up in the daily demands of surviving, humans are gifted with reflection, contemplation, and self-awareness—with the ability to make meaning.

I joke that practicing Yoga and gaining awareness will ruin your life because once you are aware, you can't stop being aware. You notice everything! All your foibles, fears, coping mechanisms, bad habits, and, most painfully, the gap between how you feel now and how you desire to feel instead.

Without the clear direction and framework of your purpose, a little bit of self-awareness can lead to over-analyzing, self-doubt, and feeling imperfect or inadequate. Your purpose helps you channel your awareness into tangible action so that you can make powerful and intentional choices in your life.

But even if you lived your unique purpose every day of your life and felt like your life had meaning, you might still ask the bigger question of why exist at all.

My favorite explanation comes from the Hindu creation story.

In Hindu mythology, life as we know it was created out of a sense of *lila [pronounced lee-la]*, or divine play. God is whole and complete, so there could be no need or want for anything more; God already is ALL.

From that state of wholeness, God created humans, Earth, and the entire Universe just for the fun of it—for the sheer bliss of creating. Just because. In short, we are an expression of pleasure, joy, and fun.

This creation story helps me connect with a sense of my wholeness while also explaining the creative wonder that drives me to explore and desire more. I can be both, and. Whole and creatively expanding.

Being Whole and Always More

Perhaps you have also felt a simultaneous knowing that you are enough combined with an urge to be more.

This is your soul's legacy and gift to you: In every moment, you are the fullest expression of life itself, and yet life is continually growing, changing, and evolving.

In other words, you are already whole. You are already living your purpose. And there is an infinite well of creativity and potential within you that is revealed as you own yourself more fully. If this sounds a lot like the purpose of life is to love who you are to discover more of who you might be and contribute fully to a greater whole with your unique gifts—that's because it is.

As one blade in the broader grass of life, you grow and evolve too. Each new height you reach or new depth of emotion or understanding is a new experience for Life as it lives through you. All the while, at your core, you are intimately connected to all of life, which is whole and complete. You are always your blade of grass.

It is not the nature of life to stagnate. It is not in your nature to stagnate. Even if you feel like you've been stuck, confused, or spinning your wheels, internally, you have been changing. You have been meeting new edges of frustration, new depths of impatience, and new levels of determination. Even your pain has been guiding you toward expressing your purpose more clearly and fully. Because you are part of a bigger happening—life is happening through you.

However you choose to view the origins and reason for human life, in this book, I assume that the overarching human purpose is to love and be loved. Just as the overall purpose of the collective grass is to be grass, humans are here to be and to be loved. Why? Because if God is whole and One, then that Oneness can only be love.

As my former New York license plate once said in a nod to Bob Marley: "1 life 1 love."

You are your own blade of grass, but we're all sprouting from the same earth, which is humming to the tune of Life itself: the tune of love.

So then what about you?

What's your unique flavor of love and be loved and how do you discover it?

You'll explore answers to these questions in Part III so that you can find a way into your body, make peace with your own experiences, and experience a new way of being. When you are embodied in your wholeness, everything you do has a purposeful resonance and impact.

This is not about you finding the answer and then becoming, but rather becoming so that you can finally live your own answers.

Chapter 5 Summary

- Life is always for you, yet it's not going to do it for you. You have free will to work with life or not.
- Your purpose is an expression of your highest truth, including the deep fears that keep you from living that truth.
- The soul is always inviting you to embody your purpose more fully, even when it feels scary, hard, sad, or painful.
- Challenges and seeming setbacks ("green doors") are invitations to embrace your truth more fully, not punishments or signs of failure.
- There are two main ways feeling flawed or broken manifests:

  1) You check out.
  2) You get angry.

- A "dark night of the soul" is the disempowered energy of your purpose not-so-gently nudging you towards greater truth.
- Your emotions help you to find yourself on the landscape of your purpose and make your way toward feeling more empowered, fulfilled, and whole.
- You matter. Like a single blade of grass, you uniquely contribute to our shared whole.
- The goal isn't to achieve an external purpose; rather, it is to become the person capable of fulfilling the infinite potential within you.
- Self-awareness can lead to over-analyzing, self-doubt, and feeling imperfect or inadequate. Your purpose helps you channel your awareness into tangible action and intentional choices.
- The path of purpose is not about you finding the answer and then becoming. It's about becoming your fullest, most authentic self so that you can finally live your own answers.

PART II

CHARTING A NEW PATH

The journey to your truth is not a straight line but a spiral—each turn invites you to see familiar terrain with new clarity and deeper wisdom.

In Part II, you'll discover a new roadmap for purpose, stretch beyond your mind's current understanding of purpose, and learn how to navigate the path towards your inner truth.

You may notice some topics from Part I are explored again in Part II. This is because learning isn't linear. There is a cyclical nature to the mind and life. We revisit ideas over and over again from new perspectives as we slowly embrace new ways of being. As you embody new levels of consciousness, you have new insights and make new connections, even with the same material. It's like listening to your favorite song and hearing a new chord you hadn't noticed before. This book is designed to help you deepen into yourself and spiral home to your truth.

*Purpose is not a single point;
it is a path that widens as you walk it.*

6

YOUR SOUL'S WORLD

"Getting clear on my soul's world has reframed everything."

Your Inner Truth

Your incredible uniqueness comes down to one specific factor: your soul has its own understanding of the world.

Think of it like your personal movie playing in your head. You have a distinct and special version of reality that you're living in your mind. Everything you do is an effort to bring that reality to fruition on earth, not because you have to, but because *it's already true for you.*

Your soul's world[3] is your truth.
It's what you know is right and possible.

Real-World Roots

I discovered the soul's ideal world while helping friends with strategic business planning. In my government days, I helped implement a vision-based planning model to create tangible outcomes in complex crises. It may seem obvious to plan based on your vision of the outcome you want, but as I shared in Chapter 3, most of us learned to plan backward. We look at our resources and try to cobble together a solution that will feel good instead of deciding what we desire and allowing miracles to unfold to achieve it.

After I quit my job, I moved to a small town in northeastern New Zealand. I joke that I wanted to go somewhere far away, green, and warm, and I got two out of the three (it wasn't particularly warm). At the time, I had this feeling that if I could just be alone and isolated enough, I would be able to discover a deeper sense of self. Like, I would be able to get to the bottom of who I am if I didn't need to be who people expected me to be.

Maybe you've felt this way before too. If you had a fresh start or could shed your daily habitual relationships of "sister," "daughter," and "girlfriend," you might catch a hint of who you really are.

I desperately wanted that. I felt as if my entire personality was defined by how other people perceived me. Some people thought I was an entitled brat. Others thought I was deeply kind and generous. I wanted to believe and receive the loving feedback and yet lived in fear that I was actually a deeply flawed and bad person. Living alone on a mountaintop in New Zealand was my attempt at trying to clear out the noise of other people's opinions and find a deeper truth.

---

3   I use the phrase *soul's ideal world* to capture the entirety of truth your soul will unveil for you. You may experience it as a vision with images, or you may experience it through smells, sounds, body sensations, or a deeper knowing. This is less about your physical senses, and more about your inner senses (more on that in Chapter 10).

(By the way, this is a perfect example of a game the mind plays to keep you waiting for the perfect time or circumstances to be able to find clarity, calm, or contentment. You feel convinced you need quiet time or space to reflect—or to leave your spouse or job like I did—to be able to figure out your next course of action. Luckily, it's usually not the case. It's a distraction technique to keep focusing on external changes instead of turning within, and I fell for it hook, line, and sinker.)

After eight months in a secluded mountain town, I ventured back into the world and took a job at a Yoga studio on the South Island. While that only lasted a few weeks, during my time there, I helped the owner create a new strategic vision for his company.

He was a brilliant and kind-hearted guy, both dedicated to helping people and completely overwhelmed. His studio was in a huge space in an old school with lots of potential for community events and workshops. That meant he was also juggling big bills to keep the place running and continually looking for and being approached by potential partners. With money on the line and his family's future at stake, he wasn't always able to see clearly which opportunities were the best fit and which might be taking his business in a direction he ultimately didn't want to go.

The benefit of strategic visioning is that you gain clarity on your deepest truth and reason for being. As I helped him through a simplified version of the planning process we used in the government, I got my first peek into a soul's world. As we drilled down to his highest vision for himself and his life, we accidentally tapped into his soul and why he was here.

A few months later, I was back on the North Island helping another friend with strategic business planning.

He was also a business owner and well-known in his field. He'd been successful for years and was now looking for the best way to expand in the future, especially in an ever-evolving industry. As I walked him through the strategic visioning process, I again got to witness a soul's world coming forward. At the time, I wasn't sure what I was witnessing, but I felt something bigger was unfolding.

A year later, when I returned to the U.S., I started helping growing and emerging business owners clarify their big visions. Time and again, we tapped into something new—a space beyond their desires and goals that felt more like heaven on earth than a tangible business mission.

The more people I worked with, the clearer it became that each one of us has a unique understanding of the world that we're living every single day, whether we know it or not.

Impact of Your Vision

Your soul's ideal world impacts every aspect of your life—from what seems unfair or unjust to what feels right, honorable, and "normal" to you. It influences everything from the careers you choose to the TV shows you like, from what social issues inspire or enrage you to how you respond to events and experiences in your life. Your vision filters through your entire life.

Your ideal world is quite literally the movie of reality running in your head. I say this with all seriousness. The reason you are different than other people is because you have a different version of what's "true" running in your mind.

Your soul's world defines that difference.

Discovering the soul's ideal world has been pivotal in my life because now I understand myself and others on a whole new level. All the aspects of your personality that you think are your preferences, quirks, or politics are actually deeply rooted in what your soul knows to be true. It also helps me guide clients, not based on my own opinions, but to live in alignment with their truth.

First Contact

I remember the first time I felt my soul's ideal world:

I was probably eight or nine years old. A story had just come on the evening news about something awful, maybe a child being forced to commit atrocities in a war. Every part of me reacted to the unjustness of it.

THIS CANNOT BE. THIS IS NOT RIGHT, my insides screamed.

This level of knowing—when you feel something is deeply off and not the way it *should* be—is a hallmark of your soul's ideal world. You're not just being a softie or empath or bleeding heart or whatever dismissive term you've used to justify feeling so moved by the world. It is your soul expressing loudly, using the only tools that it has to communicate with you: emotions, sensations, imagery, and symbolism.

Your Soul's World Makes You Unique

Your soul's world defines what's true for you. It is the core of who you are. It is also inseparable from your experience here on earth.

There is no aspect of your life untouched by your soul's ideal world because it is the deepest element of your uniqueness. It is the fingerprint of your individuality right before your consciousness merges back into Oneness with all of Life.

As we explored in the previous chapter, if the general human purpose is to love and be loved, then your soul's vision sets the tone for what flavor of love you embody and how that love is actualized through you.

It is what makes you a unique blade of grass in the broader species of grass. It is also the source of your purpose.

Over the years, I've had the honor of guiding 100+ people to discover their souls' worlds and corresponding purposes. While there are frequently common elements (we're all One after all), each person has a distinct focus and priorities that end up creating vastly different outcomes. It's similar to how different kinds of cake are made with the same base ingredients but can create endless variations based on the flavors you add.

Your Soul's World is Just One Question Away

On some level, you already know the truth of your soul. You are always in conversation with your soul, even if you don't realize you are having a conversation. The process in this book helps you learn how to make that communication conscious, trust what you discover, believe yourself, and/or be a willing partner in living your soul's truth.

When I meet with new clients, I often get the impression that they're expecting me to hypnotize them or go to some special psychic place and then tell them what their soul says. Each time, I laugh because, while I'm an expert at building a bridge between your conscious mind and your soul and facilitating the conversation, you're the only one who knows your truth!

I'm frequently surprised by the details and direction people share about their soul's ideal world. Nothing can replace the power of you understanding and claiming your own truth.

Unfortunately, most of us are accustomed to outsourcing our inner wisdom. We look to psychics, tarot cards, and tea leaves for answers. We take personality assessments and online quizzes, desperate to learn the deeper truths of ourselves in the hopes that it will reveal a new clarity and direction.

I've tried all of it, and often from a place of wishing someone else would just give me the answer. This usually leaves me feeling unsatisfied and even more desperate for clarity. These tools and their purveyors aren't meant to be milked for answers. They work much better when we come to them feeling empowered and use them to integrate and consider new perspectives instead of hoping they'll solve life's mysteries for us.

Let It be Simple

True transformation and inner peace come from tuning into your truth and learning how to honor and live it authentically for you. No matter how much you wish someone else could just give you the answers, that defeats the point of your soul's journey. The point is to become YOU, and that happens within you.

This process is simple and, in many ways, obvious. It should be. Because the answers are already there within you, just waiting to be understood and implemented intentionally. It isn't that you don't know or that life is holding out on you. Instead, you've forgotten how to connect with your truth.

One of the main reasons I wrote this book is to help make your truth available to you. Knowing your soul should not be reserved only for those with the privilege and access to pay for programs or private support. I'm committed to creating a revolution in how we define purpose and think of our journey in life. I hope that someday this process will be taught in schools. As new generations grow up clear in who they are, we can begin to cut ties with the distorted belief that we're only valuable to society when we perform and produce, and instead start truly embracing our inherent worth.

Let this process be simple. Let yourself honor the truth that's already within you. Let yourself become who you were always meant to be and live your gift in the world.

Creating Heaven on Earth

Your soul's ideal world could also be called heaven on earth. In this context, heaven means an experience of pure bliss and completion or wholeness, not a specific religiously affiliated location. Your soul's world is how you know life could be for the planet and everything and everyone on it.

The soul begins to express clearly when the mind has deemed the conversation irrational and impossible. At that point, the soul is free from the imagined constraints and restraints of the mind. That means that your soul's world does not have to play by the rules of our shared, consensus reality. The more leeway you give it to be different than the world we live in, the more clearly you'll see what's true for your soul.

Connecting with your soul's ideal world is like remembering what you knew before you were convinced out of believing yourself. It reflects what's most real for you. Because it is a space of pure truth, it also allows you to experience your pure essence.

As you trust your truth and embody the essence of your unique world, you become evidence of the heaven that is possible within us all.

Going Beyond the Mind

The soul only knows potential and truth. It knows what is universal because it lives beyond individual fears and worries. It holds the torch of what's possible for humanity—even when the mind believes it's impossible.

By contrast, the mind only knows limitations and practicalities. It's concerned with patterns, safety, and making ideas a reality. The mind is like a hands-on, fix-it person who's been shoved into a management role. Their skill set is valuable but ill-suited for the task at hand when you want to touch into purpose and peace.

When the mind and soul work together to actualize the soul's ideal world, magic unfolds in your life. People call it synchronicity, manifesting, and even luck. It is the natural result of understanding that your soul's world and purpose are much, much bigger than your dreams of personal abundance or success, and then aligning your actions to your truth instead of desires.

The Soul's Goal

You're not here just to be wealthy or travel or have nice things. That's not the goal of life from a soul perspective. That's the goal from a fear-based perspective where there are a limited number of "winners" who dominate others, and being one of those winners is the ultimate way to ensure your safety and survival.

You don't have to search very long in the online archives to find examples of seemingly successful and wealthy people who still feel unfulfilled and crave more. Often, they don't realize that it is the soul craving more, so they continue to build, invest, and expand in the tangible world, even though it doesn't fill the inner void.

Most of us have been taught this is the aim of life: do your best to create safety, power, and freedom externally through things like money, influence, and possessions.

Unfortunately, the soul doesn't particularly care about all that. Yes, we are creative beings and love to create. Yet, creating tangible experiences is a means into purpose, not the goal of your purpose. Creating is the tangible how to experience an intangible becoming. The becoming is your purpose.

Your soul's ideal world reflects your true desires, beyond those that arise from need, fear, or social and cultural messages. It is a representation of what you want to experience for yourself in your life and what you know is possible for all of us.

Your soul is willing to risk everything you believe you are to become who you truly are.

Consciousness Shifter — Becoming a Portal for Truth

On a soul level, you are here to create a possibility for all of humanity to expand and deepen into a fundamental experience of love in all of its forms.

In this way, your soul is inviting you—and all of us—closer to becoming the perfection of God-energy manifest into form. Each one of us holds the essence of an aspect of truth and wholeness. When you allow yourself to embody that truth within your being, you become a portal for others to touch into that truth themselves.

This is how we help each other come home to ourselves.

This is how we experience heaven on earth.

The soul is willing to take risks to do that. It's willing to risk everything you believe you are to become who you truly are and create its vision on earth. It doesn't need you to be perfect. Instead, it invites you to fall forward into a deeper understanding of the real you beyond your idea of you and continually crack open your heart to the relentless, communal, and expanding nature of Life itself.

So, yes, your soul's ideal world is unrealistic. It's massive and beautiful and impractical in many ways. But it's also the truth as you know it and the driving force of your life. When you surrender to its beauty without judging its difficulty, you begin to accept yourself on a whole new level.

You begin to love the love that you are.

Is Hate Truth Too?

If the soul's world is the source of your personality, values, and even politics, then you might wonder about people who preach hate, division, and discrimination. Are these part of their souls' worlds? If so, what does that mean about the future of our world if, for some people, their inherent truth is hate?

You're safe to take a deep breath because hate isn't part of the soul.

In my experience, people who focus on the limitations, flaws, or differences between people are expressing those opinions from a place of fear. They are feeling into the opposite of their soul's world, and instead of using that tension to discover their deeper truth, they are reaching outside of themselves to blame others for their discomfort.

Reaching outside of yourself is the root cause of all violence.

Living your purpose and fully experiencing the magic of your soul is an inside job. It requires you to take everything personally in the sense that all of life is for you. The fear, pain, struggles, and traumas are invitations for you to claim your truth more fully. (More on that in Chapter 9.)

People who blame, shame, discriminate, harm, or try to subjugate others are trying to create an inner sense of power at the expense of others. Fortunately, that never works in the long run. True power is a deep knowing of your rightness within, and that can't be gained through righteousness vis-a-vis others.

This new approach to purpose gives you the tools to both empower yourself to live your purpose fully and rewire your mind to realize that living your purpose is an inner game, not an outer expression. Once you shift your focus to who you're being and becoming—and work with life to use all of your experiences to expand into your truth—then your actions will reflect your essence, and your entire life will become an expression of your purpose.

People who are sharing messages of hate and violence are not living in truth, but rather reactive fear. The soul only knows love, connection, and unity. The soul understands hardship as a pathway for self-understanding, power, and growth, but it doesn't trade in hate, inequality, or discrimination.

What Your Soul Knows for Sure

After helping people put words to their souls' worlds for over ten years, I've noticed a few commonalities. While each ideal world focuses on unique elements, they often have similar core feelings. Many of these feelings overlap because they all point towards the same ineffable truth at the heart of the soul—a knowing of a union beyond our human understanding.

At its simplest, this union is the feeling of love in its purest form. In each vision, the focus and way it's emphasized and expressed is unique, but it always comes down to love.

Some of the emotions at the core of many worlds include:

1) Respect – a sense of mutual honor and consideration, as well as a freedom to be who and how you are without judgment or fear. Some share a sense of being celebrated for your individuality and valued for your unique contributions.

2) Knowing you're held – a feeling that you are supported in what you do and who you are. It's a sense of being safe to take risks because the net is always there without shame or judgment.

3) Faith – a belief that everything is okay and always turning in your favor and for the greater good of all.

4) Connected – a sense of Oneness throughout humanity as well as with Nature. It's the feeling that you are inherently part of Source and thus a valuable part of the whole.

5) Contribution – a belief that everyone contributes in the way they can and are best suited for, and there is space for everyone to be valued and cherished for their role. Some note a sense of expansion and growth in this contribution, while others share a more laid-back sense of contentment or even creative expression.

Safety shows up frequently too, but in the soul's world, safety functions as a given or a consequence of a deeper knowing. It's a reflection of being safe to be yourself or safe to trust in God / Life / Source. Unlike in this shared reality, every soul's world is inherently safe for the nervous system, and people naturally flourish and thrive. You could view safety as a prerequisite to entering the realm of the soul since, on a soul level, there is no danger or existential threat. The soul is and always will be.

But Aren't You Just Being Idealistic?

Idealism is believing your soul's world verbatim and insisting that life is like that now or no one is or ever will be okay. Living into your purpose is trusting your truth and choosing to embody it in yourself regardless of how scary or different our shared reality feels.

That is an act of courage in a world that relies on you being a spiritual coward.

Your soul speaks in symbolism and imagery meant to spark sensations in your body. Your soul's world was never meant to be a literal translation of what's possible. Instead, it reflects important values and themes that you stand for and care about.

That means your ideal world isn't some naive, pie-in-the-sky wish. It's not the creation of a fanciful, immature mind. It is your soul sharing with you exactly what is true for you.

When you stand for that truth, you set out on a path most will never even realize is there, let alone travel down. It's a path of self-liberation that requires you to focus on yourself, stretch beyond yourself, and knowingly relinquish your ideas of yourself all at the same time. It invites you to take radical responsibility for who you are being and the meaning you make out of life, which includes challenging every thought and response you've been taught and have habitualized.

Your soul's world is not a delusion that you'll never live up to; it's the very real truth you already embody and are expanding into.

As you become conscious of your ideal world, you're invited to embody the essence of that world (your purpose) and live it fully. This is how you deliberately live into your purpose and impact our shared reality just by being you.

Not only is it the bravest commitment you could ever make, but in my estimation, it's the most important as well. Imagine if we're all puzzle pieces in the larger whole. Expanding into the fullness of your piece serves and supports us all. This is how your spiritual journey contributes to all of our awakening.

Liberate yourself for all.

The focus is on you, because that's where you have the power to make real change and impact, yet the result is for everyone. We're in this life together, experiencing it individually.

Does "Ideal" Mean Perfect?

"Ideal" can be a loaded word. The ideal body, ideal partner, ideal career. In my lifetime, it's made me feel like I'm competing against everyone else for a perfect outcome to prove that I'm winning at life.

In our consensus reality—which is rife with competitive and transactional relationships—we often use ideal as a lateral description. It points to one thing or person being better than another.

His face is more ideal for the ad campaign than hers.
She has ideal birthing hips.
This house is in a more ideal location.

One option becomes more desirable, with all the jealousy, comparison, and belittling that comes along with that.

The idea of "ideal" creates pressure to be better, perform, and strive for perfection. It gives you the marker against which you can measure both what's externally desired and how much you're failing in comparison.

That's not how I'm using the word here.

In the context of soul and purpose, ideal is a vertical description. It describes the difference between this shared reality and your truth. Your soul's world is no better than my soul's world. There is no lateral comparison between them.

Everyone's soul's world is their own ideal, not to strive for, but to recognize as the background truth, like an operating system. It is the inner map against which all of the experiences of your life are compared.

That doesn't make your ideal world perfect or something that should be imposed upon others. It also doesn't mean that your experiences in our consensus reality are bad in comparison. Ideal is highlighting that a deeper truth exists, that it is pure in its essence, and that it is unshakable.

Can Your Purpose and Vision Change?

In over ten years of guiding people to discover their soul's truth, I've never seen a purpose change, but I have seen the ideal world change. I recommend people repeat the soul's world process at least once a year because it frequently reveals new layers of nuance that can help you better understand aspects of yourself, your values, and your current life.

Change is the fundamental nature of life. In your soul's world, change is a sign of personal growth and evolution. Like any relationship, as you build trust connecting with your soul, you'll understand its imagery and offerings better.

One of the most powerful aspects of the soul's world is that it helps you identify your current priorities, both in your life and in your personal healing. Perhaps you feel your immense potential but also feel overwhelmed because you don't know how to close the gap between who you are now and who you want to be. The soul always shows you the next step you need to take for inner and outer growth if you know how to identify the signs.

Your soul's ideal world is always changing because it's inviting you to be present. When we are present, we are attuned to what is sacred and allow ourselves to shift into a state of reverence, openness, and awe. If your world was always the same, your experience of it could become routine, and your behavior could become so habitual that you act without paying attention, like driving to work along the same route or brushing your teeth.

The body lives in this moment. Your power is available in this moment. Your purpose is actualized through your embodied being in this moment.

Chapter 6 Summary

- The reason you are different than other people is because you have a different version of what's "true" running in your mind.
- Your soul's ideal world is how you know life could be for the planet and everything and everyone on it.
- Your soul's world impacts every aspect of your life—from your dreams and personality to your sense of what is right or wrong.
- Living your purpose is about understanding your soul's world, trusting its truth, and embodying its essence.
- Your soul's ideal world isn't literal. Your soul communicates through emotions, sensations, imagery, and symbolism.
- Safety is a prerequisite to entering your soul's world because, on a soul level, you are whole and can't be harmed.
- Understanding your soul's world helps you align your actions with your truth so you feel more purposeful in your life.
- Creating is the tangible how to experience an intangible becoming. The becoming is your purpose.
- Many souls' worlds have similar feelings because they all point toward the same core truths.
- Your soul's ideal world is always changing because it's inviting you to be present.
- Your purpose doesn't change.
- Focusing on your soul's world and purpose is in service to everyone because your life is where you have the power to make real change and impact. We're in this life together, experiencing it individually.

Your purpose is like a pathway guiding you to a broader awakening.

7

YOUR SOUL'S PURPOSE

"This is a BIG THOUGHT... but... I am beginning to BELIEVE I AM ME. It is so huge... so expansive and so empowering. I have a feeling that I am so much closer than I ever thought to a launch pad of my true life's purpose. WOW!!!!"

Your Pathway to Liberation

Your purpose is your pathway to liberation. Like footprints appearing on the ground, it shows you where to step next as you learn to dance with all of life and surrender to the experience of being human. Purpose brings you home to the magic and the majesty that is you and enables you to more fully embrace life as you are and as it is.

In the simplest terms, your purpose is how you bring your soul's ideal world to life. It is the key or linchpin to making the world of your soul possible. Without your purpose, your soul's reality would be identical to our shared reality. Because of your purpose, your soul's world unfolds instead.

This is a radical shift from believing your purpose is your career path or a way of using your talents to help others and hopefully make a bit of money. For too long, we've focused on purpose as a doing-ness. This is a holdover of a society that has both prized the individual above the collective and reinforced productivity as the main meaning of contribution.

You are so much more than what you do.

Fortunately, there's a revolution unfolding to reclaim your wholeness beyond the skills you can provide in society. There's a renewed focus on your whole being and a reclaiming of your value as a human, without additional action required. This new approach to purpose invites you to unhook from old narratives smothering the flame of your spiritual being, while simultaneously inviting you to embrace our interconnectedness and a shared responsibility towards each other for our collective liberation.

Defining Purpose

Your purpose is how you bring your soul's world to life. It's an essence you embody that, when you live it fully, ushers in the full potential of your ideal world. For you, it functions as your guiding light. A deep, inner beacon calling you forward and encouraging you to stretch beyond your fears, assumptions, and personal suffering to fulfill a bigger destiny—the bliss of being you.

I like to imagine it as a curtain between our shared, consensus reality and the ideal world of your soul.

On this side of the curtain, people are suffering from the pain of a specific belief, misconception, or feeling. Life hurts. We struggle.

Once you pass through the curtain into your soul's ideal world, you are imbued with a fundamental truth—a knowing, belief, or feeling—that allows you to become and feel like the people in your soul's world.

The basic idea is that some doubt, fear, worry, or belief has to shift to bring your soul's ideal world to life. Your purpose is the fundamental truth or knowing that replaces that doubt, fear, or worry and thus allows for your soul's world to unfold.

Your focus in this lifetime is to embody your fundamental truth so fully that you:

1) Radiate it from within.
2) Gift others the experience of it.
3) Awaken to the nature of human experience and truth by continually expanding into it.

In this way, purpose transforms from the old model of service or career into a pathway for awakening. It becomes a lifetime journey that invites you to:

- ✓ Claim your essence and potential.
- ✓ Own the power in your suffering, and—as a famous parable of the Buddha suggests—turn the arrows of life into inner flowers.
- ✓ Drop your resistance to life and instead work with its ever-changing mystery to empower yourself more and more.
- ✓ Go inward to see the patterns and responses holding you separate from bliss.
- ✓ Know our shared Oneness and connection in your being, not just intellectually.
- ✓ Go beyond a limited sense of self to contribute with your whole self.
- ✓ Experience presence.
- ✓ Spontaneously respond to life's experiences instead of manipulating your responses based on your preferences.
- ✓ Rest in the innate joy and bliss of being.

In the larger puzzle of life, your purpose defines your unique puzzle piece. When you live it fully, your piece can slot in and complete the collective picture. It's your special flavor of love that helps heal the world. It's how you create heaven on earth, right here, right now, for yourself and everyone else.

Consciousness Shifter — On the Trail of Purpose

You might assume that your purpose is only the big, shining vision and truth you're here to embody. But the art of living your purpose functions more like a pathway guiding you toward a broader awakening. Along that pathway, you get to make choices about which direction you go and how long you visit certain ways of being.

I'm an aspiring hiker, so I'll use a hiking metaphor.

Sometimes, the pathway of your purpose will meander through open fields where the sun shines and wildflowers bow gently in the breeze. You'll feel amazing, unstoppable, and free. The path before you will be clear, and you'll see your destination in the distance like the promise of a warm bath and a hot meal after a long day on the trail.

Other days, the path will seem to disappear into a wood so dark and chilly, you'll shiver with each tentative step. The air will be so heavy and hazy, you'll have to squint your eyes to see as you trip over rocks and stumps in the path. Every crackle of leaves or snap of a twig will pause your breath and your heart as you wait, wondering what gruesome horror may surprise you next. You'll feel terrified, alone, and hopeless. The path will feel grueling, with no end in sight, and you may feel doomed to a journey of misery and struggle.

Both of these trails are part of the pathway of living your purpose. While we might shy from one and embrace the other, they are both necessary parts of the whole experience of becoming you. So are the tedious stretches of the trail — the ones with no big views or noteworthy features—as well as the lonely days when you don't come across another person, and the more social moments commiserating with others over a snack by a cool stream.

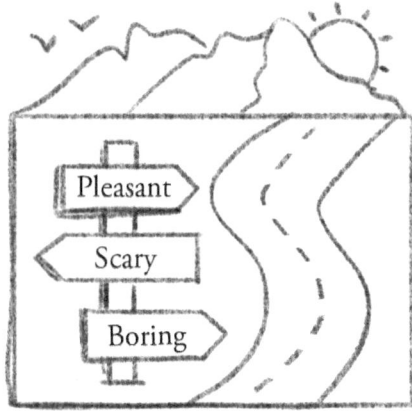

Similar to hiking, the "goal" of your purpose isn't to get anywhere per se. Some pinnacle moments may make you feel like you're on top of the world. Yet the true gifts of the journey are what you discover about yourself, who you become, and what you experience along the way.

I share this metaphor because it's easy to think of purpose as something you're either doing or not doing. On days when you feel lost and frustrated with your life, you might feel like you haven't "found" your purpose. On days when you feel meaningfully engaged with life and connected to others, you may feel like you're finally living your purpose.

Your soul knows you're on purpose either way.

If you're on the trail, AKA you are alive, you are living your purpose.

Regardless of the weather (your emotions) or the trail conditions (your situation), you're making your way through life one breath at a time.

This is the path of purpose.

Your soul is always guiding you through exactly the right section of the path for your broader expansion and awakening. Your job—and the part that makes it feel like you're living your purpose—is to grow wildly into the truth life is leading you towards.

Disempowering Yourself out of Purpose

Because you are always living your purpose, the best question to ask isn't "How do I find my purpose?" but "How am I avoiding the power of my purpose in this moment?"

If you're always living on purpose and it's inherently part of you, then you can't lose your purpose or be separated from it. Instead, the key to intentionally living with purpose is to claim the power that your soul is inviting forward within you now.

The challenge many of us have is that it's easier to feel small, insignificant, and victimized than it is to face the fears that come with anointing ourselves as powerful. Plus, we confuse true power with social power, which celebrates wealth and dominance over inner mastery.

Outer possibilities lead to disillusionment; inner possibilities lead to liberation.

As you move toward understanding your innate purpose in Part III, I invite you to keep questions of power top on your mind. You are never without purpose, though you may be more comfortable feeling disempowered in relation to it.

One of the main ways we collectively disempower ourselves around purpose in society is by linking purpose and career, so the next few sections will help you continue to unravel that connection.

Beyond the Work Persona

When I was in my first career, even my most applauded skills felt fake. Work felt like a game I was playing, as well as a burden on my soul. It was strange to have something as important as planning for global peace or homeland security feel like a role that I was playing—a character that I was good at performing. Even now, I can slip back into that analytical, strategic, politically-savvy character. It's fun, and she's good at the role of strategic scheming and negotiating. And she's not me. Or at least, not all of me.

- *Do you feel both excited and trapped by your work personas?*
- *Do you enjoy the feelings of confidence and aptitude you get from your job while also resenting that you have to work and the demand it places on your time and lifestyle?*

Many of us feel that the modern definition of "work" is not quite right. That there is something soul-destroying about giving your life to a job in the hopes of being able to buy your freedom later. While this book isn't directly about dismantling capitalism or modern economic structures, it's important to honor the parts of yourself that are telling you something is off or wrong.

You're allowed to trust yourself, even when it goes against how the whole world seemingly functions. This inner voice is the same one that is continually guiding you toward greater fulfillment and peace. Allow yourself to hear it.

Should You Quit Your Job?

Many people sell "purpose" as a shorthand for discovering your aptitudes and turning them into profit. I'm not that person. I don't believe everyone should leave their jobs, start their own business, or travel the world in a caravan. That approach still holds purpose hostage to the confines of a capitalist, careerist culture.

I'm not interested in helping you feel better within this system or milking aspects of your life for money. I care about helping you liberate yourself and creating an entirely new system that centers your soul, your wholeness, and your role in our collective evolution as a community.

Over the past ten years of supporting clients to embody their purpose more fully, the vast majority have stayed in their current careers. That's because your soul is already guiding you to the perfect circumstances to become the next evolution of yourself and embody your purpose more fully.

Greater purpose isn't always about quitting your job, but rather fully embracing what is so you can accept the invitations your current life is offering you.

When you think about purpose only in terms of what you do, you miss the opportunities that are right in front of you to expand into who you are.

Turning Obligations into Soul-Level Gifts

During my last year in the government, I felt miserable. I knew I was quitting, so on bad days, I wanted to march into my boss's office and resign right there on the spot. The stress didn't seem worth it, especially as I navigated the aftermath of trauma. All I wanted to do was be at home, sleep, or be outside.

Since I was experiencing the impact of PTSD, the duties I had enjoyed and congratulated myself for performing well in my work persona now seemed ridiculous. I was infuriated by spending days negotiating the perfect phrasing for Departmental memoranda. It seemed so pointless and misguided when real-world crises were happening every minute to real-world people. *How could grown adults take themselves seriously arguing about commas?* I raged inwardly.

Perhaps you resonate with feeling disengaged or disenchanted with your work.

Yet I knew I had to stay. I had to complete one final year to be vested in the government retirement system and keep the employer contribution to my account. Also, my house wasn't ready to sell, and I needed the income to cover my bills. Even though I was having a breakdown—or on good days a breakthrough—I wanted to see it through. That was the loving choice for me.

To make staying longer tolerable, I decided to think about my job differently. Instead of an obligation, I started to wonder how it could be a gift to myself.

I asked myself questions like:

How is this job and this situation supporting and nourishing for me?
How is this the loving choice?
Why is this exactly the right place for me at the right time?

Surprisingly, answers came:

- The slower pace of my last role allowed me time to have the "blackout" periods and still perform my work duties.
- A new project allowed me to engage with new people, which felt uplifting and exciting compared to continuing with the same conversations and colleagues I'd had for years—which now felt grating and personally upsetting.
- The salary increase allowed me to more quickly fix up my house and prepare to sell it so that I could eventually quit.
- The health insurance allowed me to pursue therapy and other forms of personal support.
- Fewer meetings around town meant I could slow down my nervous system and get into a routine every day.
- I was part of a team, so I could work collaboratively, which was particularly helpful since my analytical mind wasn't working as well as it had been before thanks (again) to trauma.
- Plus, I was no longer the boss or lead on the big projects, so I could let go of the responsibility to keep track of everything.

When we stretch ourselves, there are usually benefits to our current situation. Often, those benefits point us towards ways we are ready to step into our purpose more fully.

Like the metaphor of getting caught up in the "weather" of our daily lives, when you zoom out to the perspective of your soul, you can see a bigger picture. From that vantage point, you are most likely on the path of your purpose, even if you can't currently see the forest for the trees.

It is easy to resent our jobs and the feeling that we have to do something. For me, challenging myself to view my career as nourishing helped me start to claim more power in my everyday life. Everything starts to transform when you believe that every aspect of your life is inviting you to expand into your truth.

I didn't know what I was doing at the time, but I was using the disempowered feelings of my purpose to propel me into embodied truth.

That's the beauty of your purpose. You're already living it, which means you can expand into it more fully right now.

But Aren't You Meant to Serve?

Many people come to me with a belief and desire to contribute. They often tell me that their purpose is to serve others. That's what they learned from their parents, and that's what they teach their children about purpose, too. When I was first wondering about my purpose, the question I asked myself was, "If my future daughter asks me what I did to help the world, what will I say?" The drive to contribute is natural and a reflection of an instinctual understanding of our shared Oneness.

The belief that purpose is service is compounded by guidance from venerated heroes such as Mahatma Gandhi and the Reverend Dr. Martin Luther King, Jr.

Mahatma Gandhi is often cited as saying, "The best way to find yourself is to lose yourself in the service of others."

Reverend Dr. Martin Luther King, Jr. repeatedly urged people in his sermons and speeches to consider what they are doing for others.

While their remarks are inspiring—and accurate—they skip over two key pieces that most modern purpose-seekers miss:

1) It's not about just serving, but serving with your whole, embodied self.
2) There's a difference between fighting for freedom and showing up for your accounting clients or marketing job.

Most of us approach serving from a place of codependency, confusion, and a half-filled inner cup. That type of service is transactional. You're using yourself as a tool to gain self-esteem, brownie points from parents or neighbors, eternal salvation from God, or some other outcome you desire to feel better about yourself.

Serving this way is unsustainable, draining, and damaging to yourself and others. It keeps us stuck in old paradigms of taking from each other to try to patch our inner feelings of deficiency and lack. It also tries to find purpose through service instead of allowing service to flow from purpose. This will always leave you feeling unfulfilled and like, no matter how much you give, you are still not enough.

True service is a natural outpouring of feeling whole and accepting in yourself.

When you are fully embodied in your essence, your very presence is transformational for those around you. When you are no longer consumed with wondering who you are and how to feel better in your own skin and you accept yourself as you are—the perceived good and bad—then you discover more energy to show up compassionately for others. You become a force in your being. It's no longer about you, so you can allow your efforts to be about others.

Finding yourself through service works, but only if your understanding of finding yourself is showing up fully in your passionate gifts and allowing yourself to stretch beyond what and who you thought was possible. That type of service illuminates truth. It stretches you into yourself—into your fullness—which is the foundation from which you can offer support to others.

Most of us don't find this level of service in our jobs as cashiers, drivers, consultants, artists, or CEOs. Yet we keep asking these roles to provide us with purpose while simultaneously pressuring ourselves to serve more deeply and genuinely. We assume there is something wrong with our hearts or intentions when we feel jaded and burnt out, instead of realizing that there is a fundamental difference between transactional service and whole-being commitment in service to your soul's world.

You have the potential for the freedom-level visions these men shared. Your soul's world outlines your true mission—the mission pumping through your veins and pulling you forward every day. Allow your conviction to be to that vision. Then your service will guide you into your fullness as well as contribute to the world.

Your soul evolution is an inner expansion, not an outer expression.

The Inner Game

Your soul evolution is an inner expansion, not an outer expression.

Purpose is about *becoming* the fullness of you, not necessarily how you then express that fullness in your life.

Most of us are focused on the problems in the world that we'd like to solve: hunger, childhood poverty, homelessness, corruption, and so on. Sages and wisdom teachers across cultures and generations continually remind us that the first step to changing the world is changing ourselves. That's because we hold the roots of craving, greed, violence, objectification, and more within us. We see the fruit from those trees outside of ourselves without realizing that we're tending the soil inside each of our own minds and habits.

I like to say I can live my purpose just as much by washing the dishes as I can working as a high-level strategist or a Yoga teacher. That's because living my purpose is about who I am and how I feel in myself. From that place, I can express it through everything I do. This frees me up to respond spontaneously to the needs of the moment and the people I'm with, which is like purpose in motion because you can bring your full self to the moment.

The awakening you're seeking is a way of being related to how you're feeling. You can feel both empowered and disempowered in your purpose. When you are attuned to where you are in your inner experience, you have the power to choose differently and move towards living your truth more fully. It's understanding the whole experience for the perfection that it is—the totality of life, encompassed in every aspect of your experience.

While that sounds freeing, it's also painful. We don't want the responsibility. We certainly don't want to confront the doubt, fear, and pain within us or admit how it's revealing itself through our thoughts, beliefs, and actions. It's easier to feel we are innocent and the world is the problem.

Purpose is an inner game. *your* inner game.

Living your purpose is about fully embracing the game within yourself and working every aspect of your life to propel you into the embodied empowerment of your truth. (Then eventually, beyond to pure presence in the bliss of being you.)

These aspects include your beliefs, fears, thoughts, worries, emotions, stressors, common phrases, assumptions, nervous system responses, reactions, personality quirks, ways of talking with people, coping skills and trauma responses (CSTR), and more. Even your traditions, inherited bias, and humor are treasures for you to mine. These are the stepping stones in your path to greater awareness, fulfillment, embodied power, and purpose.

It's all *for* you.

The Fight Between Truth and Thought

The English language fails us a bit because purpose is defined in terms of doing.

We don't have language around being our purpose.

Doing is an expression of purpose. Who you are is the being of purpose.

While a deeper part of you might agree, it often doesn't translate to the logical part of your mind that's like, "Yeah, but a purpose is something I do..."

You may experience a continual back-and-forth between your heart and your head:

> Heart: "I get it. I'm here to embody my soul's deepest truth and bring it into the world through who I am so people can experience it through me and everything I create. As I cultivate peace within myself and with life, I naturally embody more truth and bliss, so I'm in service to uplifting humanity."
>
> Mind: "Wait, what's my purpose?"

I feel this struggle. I've gone in circles with it myself. No matter how deeply I understand the evolutionary and revolutionary power of this new approach to purpose, my human mind only wants to ask, *What am I supposed to be doing again??*

Like all major shifts in consciousness, the paradigms don't go together. The one that we're gifted through language in our current society and the one that we're unveiling now from the soul.

If you keep coming back to feeling confused about purpose and craving direction, it's likely because you've been trained to think about life in a "do this, get that" paradigm.

That paradigm is transactional and rooted in a desire to belong, be safe, and feel loved:

If I'm a good girl, then they won't hurt me.
If I study hard, then I'll get a good job.
If I make a lot of money, then they'll finally respect me.

These are all valid ways we try to care for ourselves in an imperfect and unjust world. They are also attempts to manipulate life to give you the outcomes you desire so that you feel more safe and in control.

But life is wild and unpredictable. Society is unfair and inequitable. Beyond all that, you don't have to *do* to earn your purpose. You already *are* your purpose.

Truly embracing this new understanding of purpose means upgrading your relationship with life and how you define success. It means stretching beyond your quest for security into true service, which requires you to claim your whole, holy power.

Luckily, the payoff to this upgrade is more ease, confidence, love for yourself and others, and even bliss.

Abdicating Your Power and Claiming It Back

Life is trying to empower you, not disempower you. When you continually look for guidance as to what you "should" be doing to live your purpose, you abdicate your power to the idea of a "right path." But when you *are* your purpose, you have the power to either choose your right path or make your path right.

You may not be used to feeling or thinking of yourself as so powerful. This new way of understanding purpose may be uncomfortable. It invites you into an entirely new way of being in relation to life. It may feel easier to stay disempowered and wait for the answer to your life path to fall from above.

I've continually dipped my toes back into the pond of powerlessness over the years. I ignore my inner voice and seek out input from others, believing that my truth can't be trusted. I ask my husband and friends for advice, look to doctors to fix or heal my fertility, and hire people in the hopes that they'll somehow grow my business better than I can.

The impulse to find answers outside ourselves is adorably human. When you catch yourself doing it, you can laugh and have compassion for yourself. Of course you want someone to help you in the areas you feel most confused and powerless! Yet, these are life's invitations into the power of your purpose too.

On a soul level, the choice is to stretch yourself to live fully, which means showing up fully. It may be uncomfortable, but you commit to following the call of your soul and becoming, even when that means claiming power you feel safer wishing others would wield instead.

I invite you to shine the light of awareness on areas of your life where you may be hoping for magical answers rather than becoming the person who lives your purpose. It's like wishing to be at the top of the mountain without hiking the trail. The path is for you, and becoming is the way you move in truth.

Chapter 7 Summary

- Purpose is how you bring your soul's ideal world to life. It is the key or linchpin that makes the world of your soul possible.
- You help others experience the magic of your soul's truth when you embody and live the essence of your purpose.
- Every aspect of life invites you into greater truth and purpose, even your struggles.
- You're "on purpose," whether you feel amazing or horrible. The journey of your purpose is like a hiking trail with highs, lows, and every possibility in between.
- Because you are always living your purpose, the best question to ask isn't "How do I find my purpose?" but "How am I avoiding the power of my purpose in this moment?"
- Purpose invites you to stretch beyond disempowering fears, beliefs, and habits to fulfill a bigger destiny—embodying the bliss of being you.
- There is a difference between transactional service and whole-being commitment in service to your soul's world.
- True service arises naturally when you embody your purpose.
- Life is trying to empower you. When you look for guidance as to what you "should" be doing, you abdicate your power to the idea of a "right path." When you *are* your purpose, you embrace your power to either choose your right path or make your path right.
- Doing is an expression of purpose. Who you are is the being of purpose.
- You don't have to prove your value or worth or achieve "success" to live your purpose.

Every thought, sensation, and emotion can propel you into greater truth and purpose.

8

YOUR DARK FUEL

*"This is a process like no other that I have come across…
and it worked for me like nothing else has."*

The Duality of Wholeness

Humans experience life in duality.
Hot / cold.
Like / dislike.
Love / fear.

While we might understand on a deeper level that all is One, it's easier to get along in society using dualistic thinking.

For example, if you rejoiced when someone shared a fatal diagnosis with you, people might be hurt or offended. Collectively, we have defined illness as bad, and we have expectations for how we engage with each other when things are bad. We are expected to act sad, express concern, and use calming and soothing voice tones. Many of us rely on these same social mechanisms around death, which is also culturally assumed to be bad, at least in much of the United States. On the other end of the spectrum, births or weddings are generally considered to be good and we often wish the parent(s) or couple congratulations.

Illness and death = sad and bad.

Birth and marriage = joyful and good.

Purpose has gotten tangled up in the same human habit of labeling and categorizing life into good and bad.

Purpose is typically considered good. We want and desire clarity and presumably will feel good once we have it. But feeling lost, confused, and unable to gain traction in life is assumed to be bad. We tell ourselves it's a waste of our time and talent. It may even feel childish, immature, or irresponsible.

While these are natural and valid feelings, they are also the outcome of a culture that values productivity over exploration and doing over being. It reduces purpose to an is-or-is-not for the haves-or-have-nots.

When you embrace your wholeness, you liberate your purpose from these limiting frameworks. You don't have to change how all of society functions to live into your purpose. Instead, you can bring a new consciousness to the ways your soul and purpose have been trapped in these paradigms and use this new awareness to propel you into greater purpose.

The hiking path metaphor gets closer to describing the experience of living your purpose. Even then, you might assume a path has a beginning and an end, and the beginning is where you are now, and the end is where you want to go. This spirals you right back into duality because where you want to go = good. Where you are = bad. It implies that we are growing beyond something unsavory that needs to be transcended, healed, or matured to live our purpose. While I'm all about continually learning and maturing, they are not prerequisites for living your purpose. You're living it fully already right now.

The gold in this new approach to purpose is that it calls you back into wholeness anytime you realize you're viewing purpose through the lens of duality. It continually points you away from shaming yourself when you feel lost or unsure of yourself and invites you to claim your ability to make empowered meaning out of all of your experiences.

The Light and Shadow

For years, I described the wholeness of purpose using the duality of light and shadow. On the outside, you shine your light, and everyone tuned in can see and feel it. On the inside, you're often living in the shadow, doubting the very thing you naturally gift others. That means your purpose isn't something to "find," but rather something you allow yourself to claim and embody within.

I'm now moving away from the light / shadow language for two main reasons:

1) I'm uncomfortable with the continued implication that light = good and shadow = bad, and that shadow is a secondary effect of light and not inherent in its own right. This has tentacles that wind their way through our psyche and prop up structures of white supremacy, anti-blackness, and racism.

2) Many people subconsciously assume the light side is their actual purpose and want to "transcend" their shadow as quickly as possible, even though that misses the entire point of this new approach to purpose.

Over the years, I've realized that any language about a spectrum, poles, or spiral of expansion triggers a deeply ingrained assumption of good and bad. We are so desperate to be saved from our fears and doubts that we default to idolizing the good and avoiding, if not demonizing, the hard, painful, and difficult. I share this because no words adequately explain an embodied knowing of your completeness, rightness, or wholeness. It takes skillful awareness, especially in the beginning, to catch the habits of the mind that prefer the presumed good over bad.

In the next section, I do my best to offer a model for purpose despite the limitations in language. As you read, I invite you to:

A) Notice when and if your mind starts creeping into dualistic thinking or desiring an endpoint at which your purpose will be "solved," and you'll finally feel clear and better.

B) Feel beyond the words to the freedom that's possible if you embody your wholeness now.

To help, let me share a few different images and metaphors that point toward the truth that language cannot quite capture.

Whole—and Polarized—Like the Globe

Imagine your purpose is like the globe. It has two hemispheres with two opposite poles. One hemisphere and pole are characterized by the empowering aspects of purpose like meaning, bliss, connection, and contribution. The other, the disempowering aspects like doubt, insecurity, and fear.

Notice if you already want to pack up your bags and move permanently into the empowered hemisphere. Yet, it's all your purpose. Your globe is whole.

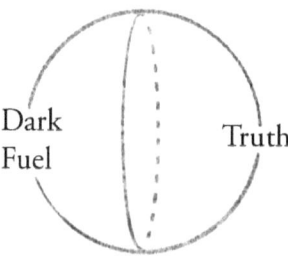

Your purpose functions like a globe of a certain emotion or truth. It's a whole and complete experience, which includes the opposite experience too. These emotional experiences are most intense at the poles, with varying shades of the emotion or embodied knowing throughout the whole hemisphere.

I call these hemispheres Truth and Dark Fuel.

The way you live your purpose is by continually locating yourself on the map of your purpose globe and using every thought, sensation, or emotion to propel you into deeper truth. I call this process Dark Fuel Alchemy®. (I'll share more details about Dark Fuel Alchemy® in the next chapter.)

The Yin and Yang of Your Purpose

Like the yin and yang symbols, Truth holds within it the seed of Dark Fuel, and Dark Fuel holds within it the seed of Truth. Just like joy holds within it the seed of sadness, and sadness holds within it the knowing of joy. Each emotion implies the totality of the experience of that emotion, including its opposite.

The two poles of your purpose define both the ultimate pinnacle of your soul's lived experience on earth and the pain of its absence that continually propels you to embrace and embody your Truth more fully.

Neither pole is better than the other or "good" or "bad." You need both of them to fully express and expand into your purpose. In a practical sense, your purpose is to express and expand into them fully.

Consciousness Shifter — Finding Yourself on the Inner Map

You're here to be the totality of your purpose globe and embody every aspect of that emotional sphere. To make it easier to navigate, the poles help you know where you are on your inner map—either feeling more or less empowered in your purpose. In our hiking metaphor, they help you figure out if you're in the sunny meadow or slogging through the scary woods. They help you navigate and work with life to grow into your truth.

You feel good and radiate your purpose when you fully embody the experience of your Truth.

Living your purpose is about consciously using every point on this globe to bring you back to that core, key Truth. That's why I call the other hemisphere Dark Fuel. It propels you into an empowered claiming of your true nature.

For example, my Truth is knowing I'm enough.

My Dark Fuel is feeling not enough.

To live into my purpose and work with the duality life is offering, I can notice every time I'm feeling not enough—for example, comparing myself to others, shrinking, people-pleasing, second-guessing my choices—and view it as an invitation to dig deep within and claim my Truth that I am enough just as I am.

As I feel more enough in myself, the more I gift the experience of enoughness in the world just by being me. I may also contribute in more meaningful ways because I feel enough to share my talents and skills in overflowing service, rather than getting hung up on whether I or the experience is good enough.

This is how every experience brings you more fully into your truth and purpose. Everything is an invitation to expand into *you*. You naturally gift your purpose to the world.

Putting Purpose into Words

Many words can describe the two hemispheres that create the wholeness of your purpose "globe." Some of these words can be helpful; some can spin us back into judging our struggles and wanting to transcend them for the magical promise of a perfect, purposeful life.

Purpose / Core Wounding

One of the most common dualities used to describe these hemispheres is Purpose and Core Wounding. I've used core wounding myself as a shorthand to help people understand what I mean by Dark Fuel because the feelings are similar. The drawback to using core wounding is that it sounds like something we need to fix before we can permanently move into the promised land of our purpose. It sounds like something is wrong with us or fundamentally broken, like an insurmountable obstacle or flaw in your being. Dark Fuel helps remind us that painful thoughts and emotions are also part of our purpose and are meant to help us claim our truth more fully, not suffer eternally.

Empowered / Disempowered

These are clarifying words to describe the two main ways you feel in your purpose. In the Truth hemisphere, you move towards feeling more and more empowered, clear, joyful, connected, and content being you. In the Dark Fuel hemisphere, you experience feeling disempowered and the related feelings of hopelessness, fear, doubt, and disconnection. What I like about these terms is that, like Dark Fuel, the answer is right in the language: claim your power, and you alchemize what is painful into what strengthens you. The pathway of actualizing your purpose becomes clear—find truth and power in the moments you feel most lost and powerless. These are the terms I use throughout this book.

Joy / Growth

You might resonate with this wording. Joy captures the essence of the Truth hemisphere. It feels like being on purpose and continually expanding into your authentic self. Growth is a reminder that all the tough beliefs and feelings aren't the life sentence they may seem, but rather a gentle prodding from life to grow into your truth. The only hiccup with this language is that it implies growth doesn't happen within joy.

Growth happens within the whole experience of living your purpose, including joy. Purpose is an inner evolution focused on growing within and into yourself, as well as within and into community. Sometimes that growth feels like a letting go of tension you didn't realize you were holding. Sometimes, it feels like hitting your head against the same wall after decades of similar painful experiences.

Regardless of how subtle your aha moment is or how tiny your step towards authentic bliss is, joy and growth intertwine at every phase of your entire journey.

Beauty / Repulsion

These terms capture the felt experience or even outlook you may have when you're in the Truth and Dark Fuel hemispheres of your purpose. Truth opens us to the beauty of life. We appreciate and accept our gifts, allow for others to shine, and find meaning in the interconnectedness of all life—from the flower blooming to the baby being born to the intricate dance of cars moving on the highway. By contrast, we're often repulsed by the feelings and challenges we face in the Dark Fuel hemisphere. The struggle to live our purpose can be captured by how we avoid this part of our purpose and the power it holds.

I share these additional examples to help deepen your understanding of why I use the terms Truth and Dark Fuel and to help you catch when your mind defaults to unhelpful frameworks that limit your potential.

Truth just is. It is the enduring, ineffable foundation from which our concept of ourselves, our souls, and all of life grows. Like a single, clear radio station in a remote area, everything we feel is in reference to Truth—the further we get from it, the more "static" we experience in our thoughts, emotions, and sensations. The closer we are, the clearer our inner channel.

In the words of 13th-century mystic poet Jalāl al-Dīn Muḥammad Rūmī, "When you feel a peaceful joy, that's when you are near truth."

Dark Fuel is our standing invitation from life to embody our Truth more fully. It might look or feel like something bad, unwanted, or "low-vibe", but it is the action arm of Truth. Like the intense pull of an oppositely charged magnet, Dark Fuel is always drawing you into your Truth. The further you are from being ready to embody your Truth, the less intense that pull will feel. The closer you are to a breakthrough and evolving into a whole new level of Truth within yourself, the more powerful the pull will feel.

What Truth Feels Like

You may expect truth to feel like angels singing with giant flashing signs that say "yes!" Instead, truth feels neutral. Joy comes once you learn to stay in truth and open your heart to expressing your true nature of peace, happiness, and purpose.

Anytime you're feeling "static," it's a sign that you're not in Truth. Just like a radio signal, the further you go from your clear inner channel, the more you'll feel static in the form of confusion, insecurity, fear, and doubt. Decisions, relationships, and even the basics of making it through your day may feel fuzzy, unclear, and hard to understand. By contrast, when you're connected with yourself and your truth, you'll have clearer access to your intuition. You'll hear your soul's guidance (even if you don't follow it). You'll feel more at peace with yourself and life.

It's that simple.

Static isn't a bad thing, though. We want to make it bad and stay in clarity forever, but again, everything is happening for you. Static only exists in reference to truth, which means that if you can notice and recognize the static for what it is, you already have one foot back in your truth.

The more intensely you feel static like confusion, doubt, or fear, the more the pressure builds like water pooling behind a dam. There is nothing wrong with pressure building. When you aren't continually tuning into your clear station, then you may need the frustration of static to propel you to take action, including inner growth.

This is Dark Fuel. This is the threshold of the doorway into your next expansion. The reason it's the same "green" door is that you often default to the same static. It's like your favorite non-radio station: insecurity, doubt, fear, confusion.

Truth Feelings	Dark Fuel "Static"
Clear	Unclear
Calm	Stressed / frazzled
Open	Defensive
Unflustered	Confused
At peace	Worried
Generally positive thoughts	Indecisive
	Second-guessing

Bracing for Emotional Whiplash

Many of my clients experience what I call *emotional whiplash* after connecting with their soul's truth. This happens because you feel really good in the expansive nature of your soul's world and then crash afterward. This is normal and happens to almost everyone to some degree. It can be especially intense after the first time you visit your soul's ideal world.

Emotional whiplash describes how it feels when your old habits of feeling and thinking come flooding back after feeling so open and free in your soul's world. While you may not have noticed—before connecting with your soul—that you felt tense, hopeless, or angry, it becomes obvious after the bliss of your soul's world. Now that you have truth to compare to, your "normal" way of being feels terrible.

For some people, it can feel as if every aspect of your life just got worse. The mind can chime in to convince you that you're doomed to be miserable and that there's no point in trying to feel better. You may even decide it's better not to connect with your soul because you can't possibly ever feel good enough to live that way.

Emotional whiplash is strong enough to make some people quit the process altogether. The mind and body are masterfully attuned to exactly which strings they need to pull within your thoughts and emotions to keep you safe (i.e., the same). The more you can remind yourself that the first step to living your truth is realizing where you are on your inner map, the less scary these feelings will be. They're giving you information to better understand the journey ahead of you. Using the radio station metaphor, emotional whiplash means your inner "radio dial" had previously been tuned into a lot of static, so finding the clear channel now is a big release and change. The more you practice tuning into your soul's world, the easier it will be to toggle between it and the static of your daily life.

Do You Have to Suffer to Expand?

You don't have to go through pain to get to your purpose. This is not a journey of earning your purpose. You don't have to prove yourself on the emotional obstacle course of life to earn clarity, meaning, or fulfillment.

Many people have stories of incredible hardship that awakens them to their power and potential.

We love these stories, and we covet them. Homeless to multi-millionaire. Cancer scare to radiant health and self-love. Abuse victim to empowered survivor at home in their body. The actor who drives to Hollywood with $10 in their pocket and lives in their car before getting discovered and booking a multi-million-dollar role.

If you're not one of these people, you may have felt jealous of them previously. They have such a clear story of perseverance and triumph.

You may even wonder, *What big hurdles have I overcome? How am I supposed to know my purpose if I haven't done anything big like that?* Business trainings literally teach you to identify a problem that you have overcome and offer the steps you followed as a business product—and then call it your purpose.

This may leave you feeling even more hopeless and lost in the quest to discover your purpose. *I haven't gotten to the other side of anything, at least not to the point of feeling healed and successful. Isn't that why I'm looking for purpose in the first place—to help me feel whole and finally be successful?* (Note how the old paradigm of purpose as career and a means to money and power creeps into these thoughts.)

On the flip side, you may feel trapped by the confines of your narrative if you are one of these people with a transformational story. You may want to grow beyond defining yourself by past experiences. They may no longer feel like identities, but, as a client beautifully described it, "a distant echo."

You may feel firsthand that you no longer need to believe that pain created your transformation or was your only path there. You may not need to invest in your story as a trauma or problem to overcome, but rather as the perfect step in the inevitable evolution of your expansion. If so, you may be craving a deeper understanding of purpose because you've traveled to the end of believing your transformational story was your purpose.

There is no proscribed path and no required service in pain to earn and achieve your purpose.

Unraveling Cause and Effect

Dark Fuel Alchemy® is not cause and effect, and Dark Fuel is not the cause that creates the effect of feeling purposeful. There is no proscribed path and no required service in pain to earn and achieve your purpose.

The relationship between your Truth and your fear is not sequential, meaning you don't have to feel fear to access Truth. You don't have to go through pain to get to purpose. Even the imagery of the spiral and the green doors is a description of a perspective and potential pathway, not a requirement for living into your purpose. It's a way to invite your mind beyond how you may currently conceive of dead-ends, roadblocks, and "life lessons" and open to a more expansive possibility of deepening into your Truth and power. It's like using a map to discover where you are and how to navigate onwards, not requiring yourself to travel somewhere unpleasant before you're allowed to visit where you want to go.

Like the two *yin* and *yang* hemispheres of a globe, pain and purpose are like paradoxes held at the same time. There is a magnetic force between them because one side is not complete without its opposite. A concept can't exist without the depth of its corresponding not-concept. Embodying your purpose is holding both, all of it, and swimming in the tides of the pull between them.

Dark Fuel shows you how to use fear, struggle, and hardship to find more power and thus catapult yourself into the power of your purpose. This is not meant to imply that suffering is the only way to access your power or that embracing power is the only use for pain and fear. Instead, this framework helps you remember you have power and you are powerful so that you can stop struggling against life and start more fully living your gifts and contributing.

The Doing of Purpose

You're already living your purpose. You're doing it every day, all the time. Your soul doesn't clock in and out. It doesn't take a vacation while you're going through yet another unfulfilling relationship or the motions at your job. The soul doesn't need you to find or realize anything to do what it's already doing—continually and constantly inviting you into greater truth and bliss.

That said, humans are doing animals. We love to take action and do things. So here's a way to think about your impulse towards action:

The *doing* of your purpose is all the ways you choose to express and play out the emotional experience that is your purpose. That means the whole "globe." This includes the pinnacle Truth that lies at the heart of your soul's ideal world, as well as all your personal struggles now and in the past, and everything in between.

Your purpose is playing out in every experience of your life. When you identify where you are on your emotional globe, then you can use every thought, sensation, and emotion to move you closer to your highest truth.

You are *always* living your purpose.

Until now, you may have been only conscious of the Dark Fuel, the experiences that touch into your biggest fears and pain. In my mentorship, I've noticed that people can almost always name their deepest fear right away. It lives on the surface, ready to pounce at the slightest hint of a bad day, unusual look, or careless word as evidence that you really are worthless, useless, broken, or an unlovable waste of space. While the mind may not register these thoughts, they show up as feeling deflated or back to "normal" when you have finally been feeling good.

As hard as it may be to wrap your head around it, these are the doings of your purpose, too. It just might not feel like it because you haven't yet used this pain to fuel you into more authentic Truth.

The path of your purpose is to alchemize what feels disempowering into unshakeable power.

When Purpose Feels Good

Living your purpose starts to feel good when you consciously recognize the Dark Fuel feelings of your purpose and use them to become even more confident in your heart-expanding Truth.

For me, feeling not enough is like the background music of my life. Even when I'm doing well, the fear is playing quietly behind the scenes, distorting my actions and reactions. Many of the painful experiences of my life have reiterated this fear, and even felt like they were proving it... like when I didn't make that final promotion in the government. Or in my business, when I undercharged and over-delivered for years because I was terrified people would be mad at me. Or more recently, when I've struggled to get pregnant and felt unworthy of this common rite of womanhood.

These experiences are all invitations for me to realize my worth and value. To decide that I am enough no matter what. To embody my Truth in the face of my biggest fears. But they feel terrible.

This is the path of your purpose: to alchemize what feels disempowering into unshakeable power.

When I started taking my own advice and working with my struggles as Dark Fuel, I started coming alive with a new confidence and clarity that had been previously cloaked by insecurities. I showed up for the invitations in these experiences and used them to become even more myself. I stripped away years of unhelpful beliefs, stored emotions and trauma in my nervous system, as well as default assumptions that weren't supporting me. On the other side, I found more ease, openness, understanding, compassion, connection, love, and joy. It didn't change the past, but it brought me closer to my authentic self so I could live in better integrity with my soul.

Life is happening for you. All the good, all the bad, all the everything. Dark Fuel is how you work with life to expand into your fullness.

The Seduction of Shadow

Let's be real though... our hard thoughts and feelings are compelling.

It's tempting to feel that life is unfair, holding out on you, excluding you, or whatever you may believe about why you don't feel at peace and on purpose yet.

From a spiritual perspective, this is a lazy approach. It's easy to blame the world. It's easy to think that you're broken, uniquely left out, or incapable.

There's a payoff to those beliefs, and the payoff is not having to change. Instead, we expect and demand life to change.

I'll share my gifts when I finally get the right opportunity.
I'll feel confident when I have the money and influence.
I'll speak my mind when I'm in charge and no one can touch me.

Perhaps you've had thoughts like these; I know I have.

For years, I held back in my business because I wanted to see results and guarantees first. I didn't realize it at the time, but I was looking for validation that I was smart and my views were acceptable and helpful before I was willing to own my perspective.

I would deliver incredible trainings and personal support and then second-guess myself behind the scenes. I would obsess over having the right language or the right offer. I told myself I was too deep, no one understood me, and my work was too long-term for our instant gratification culture.

While all of these beliefs may seem reasonable and true to the mind, they also trapped me as a victim of life. By victim, I mean in comparison to a creator. Someone who is impacted by other people's creations but doesn't feel empowered to create themselves.

Even though I came up with programs and projects all the time, I didn't trust or stand behind my creations. I didn't believe they were good enough, and a part of me was waiting for a gold star (or money) from the Universe to show I could believe in my own thoughts. This is one of the reasons I started this book ten full years before I finished it.

In short, I was scared and used that fear to stay stuck in the Dark Fuel hemisphere of my purpose. It was like I grasped the "dark night of the soul" part but forgot the fuel part, so I just stayed there believing my insecurities. It was easier for me to look for reasons *out there* for why my dreams weren't coming true and blame those reasons instead of facing the fears in me that were causing my lackluster outcomes.

Let me be clear that I'm not saying everything is your fault. I don't believe that; life happens. And you have the opportunity to take responsibility for the meaning you make of events in your life and how you respond to them.

This is your true power. Creating meaning that uplifts and supports you so that you can move towards losing who you think you are in service to becoming who you truly are.

This is Dark Fuel Alchemy® at its finest. Turning your inner mess into purpose-filled gold.

Chapter 8 Summary

- Dualities like love/fear, good/bad, and right/wrong help you navigate life, but they aren't helpful for understanding purpose.
- Your soul is not judging or assessing life as "good" or "bad"—all of it is for you to live into your purpose.
- Purpose functions like a globe with two hemispheres:
  - The Truth hemisphere is who you are beyond roles and expectations. It often feels like joy, contentment, clarity, ease, or other empowering emotions.
  - The Dark Fuel hemisphere is why living your Truth seems impossible. It often feels like fear, worry, hurt, shame, or other disempowering emotions.
- Living into your purpose is about consciously using every point on your "purpose globe" to align you with your soul's truth.
- Dark Fuel Alchemy® is the process of using what feels disempowering to propel yourself into greater Truth and purpose.
- Truth feels neutral, like a clear radio signal. Staticky feelings like confusion or doubt mean you're not in Truth.
- Static only exists in reference to the clarity of Truth. If you notice the static, you're on your way closer to Truth.
- *Emotional whiplash* is when you feel down after feeling so open and free in your soul's world. It's normal and gets better the more you practice embodying the feelings of your Truth.
- You don't have to go through pain to get to purpose or endure fear to access Truth. You can also expand in joy and ease.
- You claim your power when you make empowering meaning from your experiences instead of feeling victimized.

*All experiences are equal in their potential
for enlightenment.*

9

LIVING YOUR PURPOSE WITH DARK FUEL ALCHEMY®

"Warning: Side effects may include moments of breath-taking clarity and readjustment of your perceptions."

A loving reminder that even though you may remember some of these topics from before, you're spiraling deeper now. You're allowing the mind to explore more nuance as you embody a new consciousness. You're spiraling home to your truth.

Consciousness Shifter — Sources of Power

Your Dark Fuel stands alone as a source of power in and of itself. At a certain point in your journey of embodied purpose, you may no longer view aspects of yourself as needing to be fixed or healed and other aspects of yourself as feeling better or more evolved. It all becomes power.

From that consciousness, you get to pick and choose where you source your power from, because all experiences are equal in their potential for enlightenment. That power also becomes in service to the circumstance; your presence calls forth the thoughts, actions, and feelings that spark expansion in the moment.

You might already have experience with this type of responsive presence. Perhaps you encourage your children, team members, or friends differently based on the type of motivation and affirmation that best connects for them. In one of my recent meditation groups, I marveled at how one member inspired me to respond with soothing gentleness, while another brought out more blunt language and sarcasm. As you surrender to the moment, you release your ideas of who you have to be and stretch into using all your tools in service to the person in front of you. Everything in life becomes in service to you so that everything in you can become in service to life.

> *There is no prerequisite for being you, and you can realize your truth in an instant.*

Dark Fuel Alchemy® is a roadmap towards a new understanding of life. It gives you a model for how to navigate where you are now to who you are meant to become and how you want to feel. The biggest hurdle I witness in this journey is not that people don't know their truth, but that they don't believe they can get there. They feel powerless and confused about their role vis-a-vis life.

Renegotiating your relationship with pain and suffering is integral to claiming your power because much of human life is spent feeling powerless in relation to immense suffering. From self-doubt to addiction, anxiety to hunger, poverty to war, craving to trauma—you confront the many faces of suffering every day.

This is a pathway for liberation.

To truly move towards liberation, bliss, and living in harmony with your soul, you need to reckon with your understanding of suffering.

Why is it there?
What is it for?
How much do you take personally?
How much do you let impact your beliefs about yourself and your potential?
What is your responsibility to feel the suffering versus awaken bliss?

Let this be a training manual of sorts to help you jog down a path I've been slowly meandering. Dark Fuel Alchemy® is a shortcut—the fastest route I know into the power of being fully you and thus embodying your purpose. It's meant to give you directions from where you stand now, not define one route as the only option. There is no prerequisite for being you, and you can realize your truth in an instant.

The Unshakeable Truth of Finding Answers Within

In my soul's ideal world, the world is at peace, and everyone feels deeply at peace. This is the outcome of people knowing they are whole and enough, which allows them to show up fully for others and to fully play their part in the larger whole.

For my soul's ideal world to work, individuals have to ditch feeling deficient at the doorway of this reality and step into knowing they are whole. This takes courage and responsibility because the alternative is waiting for something or someone else to make you whole and enough to fully live your life.

When you see it in writing like that, it's absurd to wait on anyone or anything outside of you to anoint yourself with permission to be you. But many of us are living this way without realizing it.

We're holding back, waiting for the silver bullet of clarity, opportunity, permission, or approval to grant us entry into our purpose. Perhaps you're waiting for the Clarity Fairy to wave their wand over you and give you the confidence you need to trust your inner voice (clarity is courage turned into trust through action).

It's easy to believe the messages of your fear. It's tempting to agree that your deepest worries of being worthless, unlovable, disconnected, broken, or isolated are true. That would excuse you from having to fully live. After all, if you're broken, you don't have to play. It's your "get out of life's hard stuff free" card. You're too worried to connect, too insecure to take a risk, too afraid to be vulnerable. Ironically, staying stuck like this *is* the hard part.

Believing you are anything less than capable and a miracle in progress feels bad because it's not your ultimate truth.

You *know* your soul's world is true and possible.

Your soul knows what people could truly achieve if they had your soul's truth knowing too. It knows you're meant to feel good.

Otherwise, feeling so bad wouldn't, well, feel so bad.

This is why it's called Dark Fuel. Tough thoughts, experiences, and feelings are not some broken, irreparable part of you to be shunned and transcended. They are your continual invitation to claim your truth more fully. Because in a world where everything exists, the meaning you make determines your experience.

The Hard Part of Change

The hardest and most enduring task of living your purpose is breaking the habit of looking outside yourself for answers and uprooting the seeds of disempowerment it causes.

Humans consistently default to looking outside ourselves. We almost automatically look around and blame other people, circumstances, companies, governments, and so on. Not because it's true, but because it's easier.

It's easier to feel left out than to face how powerful and uncomfortably extraordinary you truly are.

We've even created whole philosophies dedicated to convincing us that God is outside of us—and that we are arrogant or bad if we dare claim our gifts and think highly of the talents we've been given.

Mistaken Humility

True humility is owning your gifts so wholeheartedly that you can stop thinking about yourself and what you're lacking and start being in skillful service to others. What could be more godly than using your all in service to others?

I know I'd rather have a surgeon who nonchalantly mentioned they've performed a procedure a thousand times and has the best outcomes than one who downplays their achievements.

We borrow from the confidence of others to feel steady in ourselves, especially as we navigate challenging experiences. We find security in their self-belief because it moves us closer to feeling neutral and thereby Truth. How we typically think of humility is distorted and messy. It is a form of manipulation trying to gain validation. When someone doesn't need validation, the motivation behind their actions is cleaner. They have the emotional space to think about you instead of being cluttered inside by their own coping skills and trauma responses.

The more at peace you are with your gifts, the more you can be of service to others just in your embodiment, aka how you are in your own skin.

Wrestling with Arrogance

True humility is owning your brilliance. It took me almost a decade to begin embodying this, even though I understood it intellectually for years. In the intervening time, I had to create a stronger foundation of safety in my nervous system so I could open my heart to being connected in community and feel safe sharing myself.

Writing this book was both the outcome and part of that process. I started the first draft ten years before I wrote the version you're reading today. I needed time to grow so I could share these ideas from loving overflow and not desperately needing you to agree, approve, or cheer me on.

My work is not for everyone. Very few people will probably ever "get it." But I know it changes lives and has the potential to change how we approach purpose for generations.

Before, I felt like I needed to convince everyone to see its potential—to see me. Now, I'm more centered in myself and my enoughness (my soul's Truth), so I can share the inspiration that comes through me using all of my skills like writing and speaking without taking it personally.

It's not about how you express but that you trust yourself to express when, where, and how you are inspired.

Humility is claiming your gifts. If you continually hone your skills and talents, you can be an even better steward of the healing that flows through you for others. Your job isn't to judge the message, ideas, or healing, but rather prepare yourself to be the best channel for it.

Your job is to become the best doctor, teacher, parent—the best YOU in all your chosen roles—so that you can be guided by your soul to express your Truth in the moments it's needed most. This is how you become your whole puzzle piece.

It's not about how you express but that you trust yourself to express when, where, and how you are inspired. This is a realization of the prayer "God, use me," or Mother Teresa's famous metaphor of being a little pencil in the hand of a writing God. She could not have served in this way without being devoted to her path, following her inner guidance, and using all her skills in service to her divinely inspired mission.

So take a mental note. Perhaps dog-ear this page. Your ongoing area of awakening will be remembering that this journey is about becoming more *you*. Along the way, you'll discover new ways in which you've subtly abdicated your power in the hopes that someone else would answer life's questions and fix you. This, too, is Dark Fuel to propel you further into your authentic truth.

This is the human paradox. Every emotion and belief is an option. The truth lies in being able to rise above the clouds of everyday life to understand the higher calling and show up fully even when you aren't sure of the path ahead.

Trusting Your Deep Wisdom Within

Looking outside of yourself for answers is heart-achingly human. You're not the only one who does it; it's fairly universal. That said, you are the only one who can walk yourself to the other side of it—and start referencing your deep wisdom within one realization at a time.

Almost everyone who hires me knows exactly what they want and need. Yet they pay experts like me to help them through a process to feel confident in claiming their desires.

It seems silly, but we do it all the time.

We defer to others, ask around, get second opinions, or read reviews. By checking outside of ourselves, we feel like we're lowering the risk involved in our decision-making. We trust the crowd consensus and the first-hand experience of others. This works when evaluating a hotel or buying a new gadget online, but it's a miserable way to run your life.

Because no one has ever chartered the path that you're on.

No one can tell you which so-called "mistakes" will lead you to gold and which ones you could've skipped. No one can feel their way through your future or know all the intricacies of your past. No one else can feel the confidence and courage that come from accepting and validating yourself.

No one else can dream your dreams.

Because of that, no one has the answers for you. Not even me. I can help you become the person who finds and trusts your answers within, but I cannot choose your path for you. No one can.

Emptying Yourself and Choosing More

Deep down, you probably don't want others to determine your path because it robs you of your fundamental right: the right to change. You get to grow, change plans, and reinvent yourself. You can change your mind, your career, your attitude—all of it.

That's why limiting yourself to one career path or one way of expressing yourself also limits who you think you are and can be. If a choice feels liberating and aligned with your truth, go for it. Go all in on your chosen style and identity. But don't forget you *can* change the minute that identity feels constricting for you.

As I write this chapter, there is a back-to-school commercial on TV that demonstrates this freedom perfectly. In the ad, a young boy is asking if his parents remember how much he loved dinosaurs in the past. He reminds them that last year, he wanted a dinosaur lunch box, book bag, toys, pens, and more. Now he says he's changed. He only wants shark-themed items.

You can make a radical change just because you want to, too.

You can break free from the imposed limitations of the characters you play and the beliefs you hold about who you are, who you're not, and what's possible for you. This is how you liberate yourself to be you in every chapter and moment of your life while also making space to change to meet the needs of the moment. You become spontaneous and responsive presence.

You become clay that can be molded to suit what's needed. Not because you have to change to be liked, approved of, safe, loved, or accepted. But because you are so grounded in your Truth, you can surrender into being an open and receptive vessel for who Truth is inviting you to be in the moment. A cup for someone to pour their fears into. A pitcher to fill up an empty heart. A wall to shield a child from harm. You show up fully for each moment and respond without judgment. This is liberation. This is the power of continually coming home to your truth and allowing your soul to guide you moment by moment.

Taking the Wheel

The power and challenge of this new way of living and new concept of purpose is that you are in the driver's seat.

You get to save yourself.

You get to heal yourself.

You get to determine if your life is worthwhile or not.

If I could let you in on one secret to radically changing your life that is also foundational to Dark Fuel Alchemy®, it would be this:

You make the meaning.

Life happens. You start new jobs, people die, you win a prize, a friend moves away, you meet the love of your life, someone you love gets sick, and on and on it goes. The changing events of life are its only guarantee besides death.

Perhaps you read that list of events and reacted to each one.

Perhaps you labeled some of them "good" or "bad" or "fortunate" or "unfortunate." (Our old friend duality popping in again.)

Perhaps you believe that some mean you're blessed and others mean you're being punished. (The victim and earning paradigm revisiting.)

Those assessments are in your mind. Life doesn't judge the event. Life just lives and keeps on living. It is neutral. Like a new coloring book, life is just a sketched outline. You add the depth and color that make it miserable or marvelous.

Turning Miserable into Marvelous

If you want to change your experience in life, the first place to look is in the meaning you're making of life.

You will experience pain.

You will experience hardship.

You may even experience things no human should ever have to experience.

And you have the free will and power to make those things mean whatever you'd like.

Some people will decide that their suffering means they are bad. They'll believe they are being punished by God or are an inherently flawed human who deserves to suffer and is destined for misery.

Beth was worried she was not a good person. A regular student in my meditation class, she was a caring, considerate woman who believed she was too judgmental of others, and this trait made her bad. Ironically, she continually judged herself about judging others as a way of trying to keep her judgment in check and assure herself she was a good person. The fear of being deeply flawed influenced her thoughts and actions behind the scenes. She frequently tried to prove to herself and others that she was a good person, which often made her tense and tired.

Others may not settle on a concrete meaning but always hold a seed of doubt—wondering if the pain they've experienced means they are unworthy, unlovable, or incapable. That doubt will spread roots throughout the rest of their life, infesting their relationships, dreams, hopes, and self-esteem with insecurity and deference to others to reassure them that they're okay and acceptable.

Maria was an incredibly successful saleswoman. She flew in for a weekend retreat, and we met up the night before for dinner. Over our meal, she shared with me that she'd been excommunicated from her religious community a decade before. While this group has all the markings of a cult and many people would feel grateful for a chance at life outside of it, she still felt hurt and confused about why she'd been removed. She had been ripped away from everything she knew and everyone she loved, and she worried it was because she wasn't good enough. While this hadn't held her back in her new career, it created a big wall between her making friends and dating. She carried the guilt for a decision she didn't make and worried something was wrong with her.

There's another option:

You can choose a meaning that supports you.

No event in life comes with a built-in meaning.

Life's not a new pair of pants that comes with a tag and clear instructions to wash inside out and hang to dry. As much as you might want to categorize events as blessings and sins, it's truly about perspective, context, and how you want to feel about the experience.

If you want to create an all-new, empowered relationship with life, change the meaning you're making.

Instead of believing your ex dumped you because you're unlovable, choose to believe they freed you to become who you truly are.

Instead of thinking you missed out on a job because life is unfair, choose to believe that you needed to feel rejected and hopeless so that you would finally make real changes in your life and stop settling for scraps.

This is Dark Fuel Alchemy® in action.

Beth chose to see the humor in the endless circle her mind was running in—judging herself to stop judging others. She realized her judgment habit was a way to try to feel safe. Now that she had better tools to take care of herself, she could feel her hurt and fear and tend to herself gently. Maria started practicing being more vulnerable and sharing parts of her past with people. This opened a pathway for others to show how much they loved and valued her, and for her to slowly build trust that she wouldn't be punished or abandoned again.

Alchemy in Action

When I first drafted this chapter, my husband had just been laid off from his job. A few people we told reacted with compassion and expressed sorrow. It makes sense... in the U.S., we socially agree that losing your job is bad.

But I was elated.

I chose to believe it was a gift and the moment we'd been waiting for to scale my business to the next level with his help. To me, it felt like the opportunity of a lifetime.

This applies to trauma too. Even horrible trauma—that no one should have to experience—can become a source of empowerment if you find a supportive meaning for you. I've helped many people, myself included, find deep healing in the worst pain they've endured. In my darkest moments in the government, when I didn't understand why I had endured multiple sexual assaults over my life, I decided it was a wake-up call to end patterns of victimhood in every area of my life.

This is the magic of reconceptualizing your suffering into your Dark Fuel. Even experiences that you never wanted can become an empowering opportunity for your expansion.

It's not about making things okay or learning lessons to earn more ease. It's about choosing to claim power where you feel disempowered.

Running Away on the Fear Train

For many years, I carried a story that something was wrong with me. I saw evidence for that belief everywhere. Many friends "ghosted" me—three of whom disappeared right after telling me that we'd be friends forever and I could trust them with anything.

I spent decades making these painful experiences mean that I couldn't trust others and that I must be fundamentally flawed. Why else would they drop me? There must be something wrong with me—if only someone would tell me what it was!

When I started exploring self-development, I went into it looking for answers to what was wrong with me. I thought that if I could figure out what perfect and whole looked like, then I'd be able to see what I was missing and why I was so unlovable and fix it. Years into my relationship with my husband, I still act out this story and catch myself waiting for the moment when he'll get fed up and leave me.

Embodied beliefs run deep.

Luckily, my husband has helped me live more fully into my own work and realize I don't have to make these experiences mean anything about me.

From that new perspective, we can open to all new insights.

The Soul's Perspective on Timing

In many of the relationships mentioned above, my coping skills and trauma responses were front and center. I was fortunate to be around people who loved me for who I truly am, but the closer they got, the more I panicked and responded in ways fueled by trauma and fear.

When I met my husband, he was able to roll with my reactions. The increased safety helped me start to regulate my nervous system and feel more steady in myself. That meant I was able to notice and soothe myself through my fears more easily. This combination helped our relationship work when others couldn't.

I share all that because it took me years to realize that maybe my ex and other friends didn't leave me because I was broken, but rather because none of us had the skills to navigate my trauma.

That doesn't mean I am bad or wrong or unlovable or flawed or destined to be abandoned by everyone in my life.

It means I wasn't ready to move through that trauma and feel more empowered at the time I was in relationship with them.

It's all for me.
It's all for you.
Life is unfolding at the pace of your nervous system.
You get to choose what it all means.

A Peek into the Next Phase of Awakening:

When you come into a relationship of acceptance with yourself and life, events don't need meaning at all because you're not taking life personally either way. You're able to be present and respond to the needs of the moment without judging yourself or others. You're moving into full service.

Invitations into Truth

Most people talk about challenges in life as "lessons." I don't believe in that. Here's why:

1. I don't believe that anyone is keeping score or grading you.
2. I don't believe there is an ultimate "right" in every single moment beyond what's right and aligned for you.
3. I don't believe you can "fail" at living, which lessons imply.

Instead, I use the word invitations.

If you believe humans have free will, then the concept of a lesson probably doesn't jibe with you either. How can there be a "right" answer if you can choose whatever you want? How can you get it "wrong" if everything is available and all experiences are potentially valuable?

The more I tune into myself and the truth of my soul, the more I'm aware of the paradoxes of life.

- ✓ I feel held and trust it's all okay… even though the future is unknown and unpredictable.
- ✓ I feel a sense of familiarity as if it's all been done before… even though I'm also scared about what I can't guarantee.
- ✓ I'm in a continual state of becoming… even though I am already whole and complete.
- ✓ The vast unfolding of life feels inevitable… even though I have free will. *(With this one, I've landed on the understanding that free will is the freedom to create the meaning I choose about events already unfolding and, when meaning no longer matters, the choice to follow the impulse of the soul or not.)*

Life is guiding you in a continual process of becoming more fully yourself, which means the events of your life can't be about whether or not you pass or fail. That would imply that some people will have wasted their lives or gotten it "wrong." It would also imply that there's a gatekeeper who decides if you get to be fully you and that you aren't whole already right now. Personally, those ideas don't line up with the ways I feel and understand life when I embody my Truth.

Everything in Relation to Truth

Your Truth is like your soul's gravity continually pulling you deeper into yourself. As static on the radio increases the further you are from a clear channel, the "static" in your life is only frustrating in reference to your Truth. No matter how messed up, discouraged, or lost you feel, these feelings are intense because they are in contrast to the ease of your Truth.

Truth is a blank screen, and tough thoughts and emotions are neon lights; they only stand out because the Truth is always and already there. Just like a neon arrow flashing "this way," Dark Fuel is pointing you straight to your Truth if you can stop focusing on the specific thought, event, or feeling and see the bigger picture.

Life is continually inviting you to expand into yourself. You can take the invitation or not. The grand paradox is that you are already whole. You are already, at every moment, your fullest expression of yourself. So you don't *need* to take the invitation. You don't *need* to change in any way. You just might not feel as good and reach the levels of inner peace and bliss you desire.

Invitations are life's way of showing you the path from Dark Fuel to Truth.

Drama Tornadoes

Drama tornadoes are seemingly urgent and fixable problems we use to distract ourselves from the deeper, scarier questions at our core. They're ways you avoid the work of becoming you and embracing your purpose.

When I'm live on a video call, I demonstrate this by wiggling my fingers at the bottom of the screen. As my hands dance around, people inevitably start watching my fingers.

"Why are you watching my hands?" I ask. "The real show is back here."

We've all fallen prey to the allure of drama tornadoes at some point.

Once my daughter gets through this tough patch…
Once I find a new job…
Once I help my mom find the right doctor…
Once I declutter the house…

The specific options are endless, and I've heard hundreds. They're the reasons we use to stay stuck in the spinning daily tasks of life, thinking that *if we could just get that off our plate…*, then we'd have time for the big stuff like inner work.

It's a trap. You'll never get through the seemingly urgent and fixable stuff. There will never be a set moment when you are "there," and everything is settled and ready for you to do Big Work. Drama tornadoes are endless because we need them to be endless.

They subside as soon as you decide you're ready and willing, and you have the support you need to stay the course. Or, more accurately, your willingness to get caught up in them subsides.

- You partner with your daughter instead of taking over for her.
- You stop using your energy hating on your job and decide to look for another one, or not.
- You ask for help or experience the everyday miracle of the right person showing up at the right time.

— You detach your emotions from your space and realize you clean more effortlessly and effectively as you gain inner clarity and calm.

Life is always for you, but it won't do it for you. You have to choose.

Drama tornadoes are life's everyday way of giving you the option to spin in circles and busy yourself until you die—or claim responsibility and create an intentional relationship with how you move through the world.

Thresholds of Purpose

Humans are masters of tying ourselves in knots. We've been at it for centuries, and navigating these tensions is not new. Ancient teachings from many traditions point to the freedom on the other side of empowering yourself through suffering.

In one parable of the Buddha, which I mentioned briefly before, he was on the edge of enlightenment when he was attacked by Mara, who personified temptation. Mara rained arrows down upon him to disturb and distract the soon-to-be Buddha. Instead of reacting in anger or defense, the Buddha remained open and peaceful. As the weapons came near him, they transformed into flowers.

One of the best descriptions of karma I've ever heard is the cycle you get trapped in trying to manipulate life to avoid feelings you don't like and experience ones you do. Basically, something happens, and you have an emotional reaction to it, good or bad. The next time something similar happens, you can't see it clearly because you either do or don't want to feel that way again. So you start acting differently—trying to coerce or cajole specific outcomes to avoid or create certain feelings. Eventually, you twist yourself into inner pretzels trying to manipulate life and call it karma instead of realizing your distorted actions are bungling up your energy and experiences in the first place.

In this new paradigm of purpose, suffering is a threshold into greater purpose like all experiences. It is one way you can accept the power of your Dark Fuel and allow it to propel you towards embodying your soul's truth more fully. It's how you embrace the arrows of inner suffering and transform them into flowers of truth.

Consciousness Shifter — Love as a Way of Life

Your true state of Awareness—your soul—knows that you are always okay and that nothing can threaten or diminish your inherent wholeness. It's only the mind that thinks something is going wrong when you feel bad or life throws you curve balls.

Imagine you are in the best mood of your life. Perhaps you just won the lottery or you're about to propose to the love of your life. You feel on top of the world. In that energy, you could deal with a cranky barista, rush hour traffic, or a curt email without taking it personally. You'd just move along extending compassion to everyone you encounter while still feeling joyous and excited yourself.

This is the truth of your soul.

You can make your way through life witnessing and experiencing it all without ever making events or emotions mean that you are anything but whole, loved, and deeply supported just as you are. Each emotion and experience is just a new doorway to float through as you feel more empowered and grounded in your Truth.

The key is… and this is the secret that everyone is searching for… no one is going to force you to walk through that doorway.

No one is even going to force you to recognize that the doorway is an invitation and not evidence of your deepest fears and lack of power.

The meaning you make of the doorway is up to you, as is the attitude you bring and the love you embody.

Remember the Green Doors?

Life is not a linear experience from being who you are now to becoming a perfect version of yourself. It's not an A to Z, where Z is when you are finally good enough to be accepted, loved, and worthy of your life. You're living your life now. It's happening now.

So there must be another way of approaching life that allows you to live fully in this moment while also growing into the next.

In this new paradigm, life is like a spiral of continual growth and expansion.

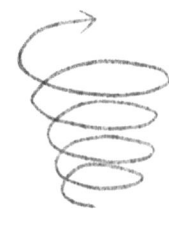

You're always becoming more of who you are, but because you're also already whole, you're in the process of expanding. I like to imagine one of those penny catchers that used to be in shopping malls in the U.S., but instead of the penny swirling around the giant funnel until it falls through the center, you're spiraling up and outwards.

In this model, pain, suffering, and struggles are like the green doors. You might encounter a thousand painful doorways in your lifetime. But instead of bringing you back to Square One, each one ushers you into a better understanding of yourself. They show you where you run, how you hide, and how you react when life gets tough and feelings get unpleasant so you can make new, empowered choices.

Each doorway is the threshold through which your deepest fears become Dark Fuel. Each new room on the other side of the door is a deeper and broader claiming of your soul's truth. It's your Dark Fuel showing up to help you expand into even more joy by healing your fear, hurt, and trauma more fully. This is how perpetual growth and soul expansion work.

Every part of you is perfect, including the pain and hurt you experience. You can turn them into the greatest empowerment of your life.

This is the path of purpose and how suffering—and truth—set you free.

Are You Doomed to Suffer Forever?

Not at all. The doorway metaphor is meant to illustrate the evolution of nuance. As you grow, you become so intimately familiar with the totality of your purpose—including the disempowering side—that you recognize it faster, dance with it more freely, and move through it more quickly.

Many of us secretly hope that living on purpose means never feeling bad, sad, or mad again. Instead, I view "progress" along this inner journey more like the chart below. You're not getting rid of challenging moments because that would be limiting your experience of life. We want fuller lives, not more limited lives.

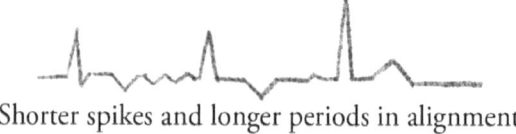

Shorter spikes and longer periods in alignment

Longer spikes & transitions back into alignment

As you live more authentically, you may feel painful moments more intensely because you're feeling versus thinking your emotions. The more I work with my Dark Fuel, the more pure and intense emotions are in the moment. Like a momentary spike on a heart monitor, they're also much shorter because I recognize the emotion sooner and know how to transform it into empowered truth.

Staying with the heart monitor analogy, your hard times no longer have to look like long plateaus that make you panic that something is truly wrong and you'll never recover. When you know what caused the spike, you know how to come back "down" to Truth, plus you have the tools to help yourself shift between.

Mastery doesn't come from having fewer painful experiences. Mastery comes through shortening the length of time you spend believing your fear before you embrace it as Dark Fuel. Once you recognize the spike for what it is, it can usher you into new levels of empowerment.

There are still experiences that ignite my core fear that I am not enough, such as setbacks in my fertility journey or business. Now I see them for the Dark Fuel they are sooner. I don't get as carried away by fear or insecurity—mostly because I have both a personal practice that helps me recognize the tell-tale Dark Fuel thoughts and feelings when they pop up, and a community of loved ones who can help me spot them. By facing what needs to be integrated and seen, I can find a doorway into a more awareness of my wholeness.

In the grand scheme of life, we could all awaken to our natural state of Awareness and view this up and down as a fun game we play with ourselves. We could see it for the *lila* of life—the divine play of experience—and stay rooted in bliss as we relish in the totality of human emotions.

I hope that the green door metaphor will help you do that. I hope it helps you continually remember that there's a bigger picture here. A picture in which you're always growing and expanding and becoming more of who you are.

As you move along your becoming journey, you might encounter ten green doors or ten thousand. It doesn't matter, because it's all for you. The doors are your invitation to remember yourself whole and expand into embodying your soul's Truth more fully by embracing the parts of you that are scared you're not already whole. This is how you walk yourself home.

It's all for you.

Nothing is going wrong.

You have the power to see life differently in the blink of an eye.

Favorite Static Stations

My personal favorite is to throw my identity into total chaos. When I am in the "static" of my Dark Fuel, my mind loves to tell me that I don't know who I am or what I do. It says nothing is interesting or unique about me, and I'm a complete blob in style and tone. My friends laugh because this is so often my go-to habit, it's like regularly meeting up at our favorite coffee shop. Perhaps since I work on helping people feel like life is meaningful, it makes sense that my dark days are about feeling completely meaningless! From a spiritual perspective, it's also seemingly true because—like all of life—we are always changing. Settling into one fixed identity is fleeting.

For me, this habit is another sign that I'm at a green door. It's green because I'm feeling not enough (my soul's Dark Fuel). The static builds until I realize this is another doorway and an opportunity to stop feeling powerless and victimized and instead claim a new level of Truth and wholeness.

> **Static Station Top Hits**
>
> Not unique
> No style
> Boring & Basic
> No idea who you are
> No clue what you're doing
> Lost

By contrast, there are times when I'm struggling with a project or new skill but still feeling relatively neutral. I'm not throwing myself toddler-style into a temper tantrum about how the situation is so hard, life isn't fair, and nothing is ever easy for me (classic static thoughts). Instead, I might feel like I'm not practiced enough in a skill, haven't reached a level of mastery that I would like, or need help from someone else. These moments are still growth in the ever-expanding spiral of becoming. They're building the capacity to stay in Truth longer.

Building the Muscles of Soul Strength

These muscles are important to build because identity will start to fall away as you move through your journey of awakening. You'll begin to shift beyond the safety of the characters you play and the beliefs and perspectives you hold. This is the pathway to wholeness. By opening to more possibilities, you're able to engage more fully and spontaneously with life.

Embodying your purpose is a method of awakening.

Mastering Dark Fuel Alchemy® is the equivalent of decades of meditation and spiritual study. In my opinion, this is the fastest pathway of awakening. Like all pathways, they lead you to the place where you no longer need them because you become embodied in resonant Truth. This is where you are going, using purpose like a walking stick to steady yourself on the path, only to drop it when you feel strong enough.

You can't get it wrong. Life is either inviting you through the doorway into greater Truth or helping you build the capacity to stay in Truth. You are becoming the peace and joy you seek. It's all for you.

Chapter 9 Summary

- The biggest hurdle to living into your purpose is not that you don't know your Truth, but that you don't believe you can live it.
- Renegotiating your understanding of suffering is essential to living in harmony with your soul.
- All experiences are equal in their potential for enlightenment.
- No event in life comes with a built-in meaning.
- The meaning you make determines your experience. You have the power to choose meanings that empower you.
- Invitations show you the path from Dark Fuel to Truth.
- Dark Fuel is a catalyst to transform fear, doubt, and pain into greater power and purpose.
- As you live more authentically, you may feel painful moments more intensely because you're more present and also feeling versus thinking your emotions.
- True humility is owning your gifts so that you can be a better steward of the healing that flows through you for others.
- Your "job" isn't to judge the inspiration flowing through you or its impact; it's to become the best channel for it.
- *Drama tornadoes* are seemingly urgent and fixable problems that keep you stuck spinning in the daily tasks of life.
- You are the only one who can journey the path of your purpose, even if you wish others could give you the answers.
- Mastery is not about having fewer struggles. It's about skillfully transforming Dark Fuel feelings into greater purpose.
- Awakening involves shedding limiting identities and allowing yourself to become who you need to be in each moment in the highest service to yourself and others.

PART III

CONNECTING WITH YOUR SOUL

Your soul's voice may be quiet, but it has the power to guide you through the noise of the world.

In Part III, you'll discover your soul's ideal world and purpose. You'll also be guided on how to use your unique Dark Fuel to propel you into greater purpose, inside and out.

To connect with your soul is to glimpse the infinite within yourself.

10

YOUR UNIQUE SOUL'S WORLD

*"I'm coming home to me. All in an instant.
I'm exhilarated, feeling connected, feeling aligned…
PURPOSEFUL"*

Over the next few chapters, you'll be guided down a pathway to connect with your soul's unique understanding of the world and purpose. This is not a system to create your soul's world, but rather to connect with what's already inherent and true within you. This process will help build a bridge between your conscious mind and your deeper truth so that you can finally gain the clarity and insights you've been craving. My role is to help you build the bridge and apply the process to your life; the depth and magic of what you discover is all yours and continually new in each moment.

> *The soul speaks when the mind believes you are in the realm of the impossible.*

Into the Impossible

Your beautiful brain is about to get a workout. While your mind is a vital part of this process, it's not particularly helpful in the soul's world.

Your soul's reality is beyond this specific world and what you know you want for yourself. It's not "I want to make a million dollars, have a home in Malibu, and drive a Range Rover." It's not even "I just want to be happy and loved and do good work." That's what your mind thinks will make you a good person and make you feel safe, happy, respected, and more.

Soul doesn't care about that. Your soul only cares about your truth.

The soul speaks when the mind believes you are in the realm of the impossible. That means you have to get to a level of thinking when the mind says, *This is ridiculous; I'm out* for the soul to feel safe to express what your true focus is for your life.

Over the past ten years guiding others through this process, I've noticed that a lot of people tune in to their soul's world and then immediately try to drill down to their life:

"What does it mean for my job / relationship / next step?"
"But that's not possible!"
"How would I even DO that??"

This is natural, and it takes you out of the conversation with your soul.

As soon as you link your soul's world to the limitations and restrictions of this reality, you lose the gift of what your soul is sharing with you. This also puts you back in a transactional and disempowered relationship with your truth because you immediately create separation between what your soul knows and what you think you're capable of or is reasonable. It leaves you judging your truth and trying to milk your soul for quick wins in your life without *becoming* the person who lives your soul's truth.

Instead, let yourself think big. Let yourself imagine beyond what you believe is possible and what society would say is realistic or not. Let yourself be guided to discover your soul's truest expression.

Your Internal Operating System

Most of us have had an experience that something happens and it feels off or wrong. We think, *That's not how life has to be. That's not how life is. That's unfair!* This is our shared reality hitting up against your soul's world. It's a sign that your soul holds a unique imprint of how and what the world could be.

This process will help you gain clarity on what your soul knows. This is important because your truth influences everything you do, from your choices and relationships to the opinions you form. Your soul's world impacts every action, thought, and feeling that you have because, at the deepest level, it is what makes you you.

Your soul's world is like the operating system running in the background of your consciousness. Similar to a computer operating system, it does not care if you feel bad or good. To the soul, those are two sides of the same coin and only reflect your judgment and preferences, not truth.

But since you most likely do care and have a preference about how you feel, this process will help you bring awareness to your soul's unique world and purpose. Then you'll be able to both understand who you are and what makes you unique, as well as continually grow in ways that feel meaningful and feel good.

But What If It Doesn't Work?

If you find the following exercises difficult, I suggest reading this entire book all the way through, including the troubleshooting sections, and then coming back to the exercises.

For many people, the first time they're introduced to their soul's world, the mind fights the experience. It either discounts what arises or hyper-focuses on how the world answers pressing questions like "What should my business be about?" or "What's my next career move?" When I'm supporting you in person, I can help continually guide you back into the space of your soul. In this medium, I can only prepare you by sharing the ways I've seen people struggle in the past and offering my best tips on how to make the process successful.

It's hard to break the habit of "milking" insights for instant gains. Many people dip one toe into the soul's world and then try to figure out how to turn that into clarity, money, and success right now. Again, this is normal because we want immediate results and action. Plus, we have a cultural narrative that says if we know our purpose, then joy, contentment, and money should flow endlessly and effortlessly. This process is about becoming the person who lives and embodies your purpose for a lifetime of fulfillment and growth, not making a quick buck. Notice when you may default to using your soul transactionally; we're breaking big patterns here.

You may have to spend more time in the energy of these new concepts and the paradigm shift this process represents. It may take a few tries to start accessing your soul—not because it's not immediately available, but because the mind is powerful and convinced of its perspective and approach.

I had one client do the process three times in a period of a few weeks with radically different results.

1) The first time, she was still convinced that her purpose had something to do with her career, and she didn't understand what the soul's world had to do with her micromanaging bosses. She felt frustrated by the process and like it wasn't helpful.

2) The second time, she started putting her soul's joy first, making little changes to her routine, and creating boundaries.

3) The third time, she realized a deeper truth and decided to move across the country and start a new business; she almost immediately sold out her offer and created a waiting list of clients.

This was within just a few weeks. Trust the process, and keep surrendering to your soul. It works.

I want you to succeed in connecting with your soul. It is your birthright and the deepest truth of who you are. Keep surrendering to the process and trust your soul to guide you in exactly the right way at exactly the right time.

What If You Can't Visualize?

You are not alone! Many people struggle to visualize, and some genuinely cannot. Every brain is different, and I invite you to find your unique way of navigating the sensory world of your soul.

While I was living in New Zealand, I spent some time studying at a Yogic ashram. Their retreat center was located along a mostly deserted beach next to a lush forest. Between the healthy food, miles of empty beach, and jungle-like nature, I felt like I'd hit the jackpot. At least, until our meditation sessions began…

We were guided to visualize symbols, colors, animals, and energy moving as a way of training the mind to focus. After each session, other students would report having seen the most remarkable visions—witnessing their chakras spinning, seeing energy flowing in hyper color, or animal totems and goddesses. I saw pretty much nothing. I could feel my body, and I could feel my breath. That was about it.

It took me years of practice to be able to visualize. Even now, I likely don't "see" the same way other people do. For example, I can imagine that I know a photograph of my mother, but I cannot "see" the photograph or her face in my mind; I just know that I know the image.

Honoring Your Wisdom and Abilities

There are many kinds of wisdom available to us all. These are often called psychic or intuitive abilities. I like to think of them as heightened sensory capabilities because you are picking up on subtler, unseen energies and "translating" them through your senses. These abilities are available to everyone and can be strengthened with practice.

Below is a brief overview of the multiple ways you may understand information through your senses. I share these so that you open to all the ways you may experience your soul's world and honor your unique approach.

Clairvoyance

Clear seeing. Similar to daydreaming, you may see symbols, images, visions, numbers, or other visual cues. You may see scenes playing out like a movie in your mind or have vivid dreams. You might also notice external visual cues like repeated numbers or signs like cardinals or butterflies.

When I was trying to get pregnant, a friend messaged me one morning that she'd woken up from a dream yelling, "Alexis, Baby!" I had just received news the night before that our in vitro fertilization procedure had failed. She encouraged us to keep trying based on the vividness of her dream.

Clairgustance

Clear tasting. Imagine the flavor of a meal transporting you back to a special moment in your life or reminding you of someone you knew. Clairgustance is like that but without the actual food or beverage. Your body creates a taste that gives you a signal or message. This may include tasting non-food-based flavors like blood or metal.

My friend Keisha Dixon shared this example with me from her mentorship practice:

> The first time I became aware of clairgustance, I was facilitating a session with a client, and she was presenting with an 'indecision loop.' I started to taste something sweet with a bitter aftertaste, and my jaw kept clenching against the tartness. I shared this with my client, and she immediately responded, "That sounds like pomelo. I ate it every day when I was in Bali." That opened up

a deeper level of inquiry around her desire and what her trip to Bali represented. Armed with that remembrance, she was able to choose the path that felt most liberating and harmonious to her.

Clairalience

Clear smelling. This might show up as smelling your grandmother's perfume, smoke, or other scents when there is no cause for the smell around you. As I was writing this chapter, I freaked out my husband because I could smell campfire smoke while we were watching TV, even though he couldn't detect anything.

My most memorable experience with this was in a guided meditation. My teacher prompted the group to stop the meditation if they smelled sandalwood, and my tenth or so time practicing, I could smell it as if it was right there. In that case, I wasn't necessarily tuning into energies around me but rather stimulating the parts of the brain that awaken psychic-smelling abilities.

Clairaudience

Clear hearing. Contrary to popular belief, you may not necessarily hear voices or sounds as if they are outside of you. Instead, you may sense names, dates, phrases, or a message like you would "hear" a conversation or song lyrics you're repeating in your mind. This could also show up as your ears getting hot or catching a message in a song on the radio.

Once on a ghost tour of an old mansion, I was overcome with the words "I love you" and also felt hot and nauseated. I could "hear" the voice of a mother wishing her child to know she loves them in my mind.

Claircognizance

Clear knowing. This is when you just know something. You may know something is going to happen, know something about another person, or even know information about past lives. These types of insight feel spontaneous, random, and truly beyond reason.

Back in my government days, I had a flash of claircognizance one afternoon while leaving the office I shared with another woman. As I stood up to go, I received an absolute clear insight that she would move to Germany, marry a German man, and have German babies. She now lives in Berlin with her husband and two children.

Clairsentience

Clear feeling. This is the most common ability. It's like your "gut feeling" on steroids and can overlap with being empathetic. It can also show up as physical sensations or goosebumps.

One evening, I was chatting with a friend on the phone. I started coughing and having lung pain. It turned out my friend had just smoked a cigar, and I could feel his lungs aching.

There are also a few lesser-known abilities:

Clairempathy

Clear emotions. This is often described as feeling how others feel when they're not near you or in connection with you. For example, knowing a loved one is hurting even if they're in a different country because you feel the grief or sadness in your body. This is not dependent on time; you may sense how someone felt in childhood or may feel in the future.

Keisha Dixon again graciously shared her personal example of a mother's connection:

> Two days before my son transitioned, I had a dream that I was searching for him. I called him when I woke up and got his voicemail. When I didn't hear back from him within a few hours, I called his brother and asked, 'Where is your brother?' – it was like my dream had come to life. A few hours later, Chase reached out and asked why I was worried and looking for him. Forty-eight hours later, I was preparing for a client session and suddenly felt an intense sadness that I could not explain or shake.

My breasts felt like they had a fever and were hot to the touch. I canceled the remainder of my day and went to bed. About two hours later, I was informed that Chase had transitioned around the time I felt the fever in my breast.

Clairtangency

Clear touch. Think of it as understanding the energetic story behind certain objects. For example, using your grandmother's cooking spoon and feeling how she felt cooking with it.

I lean heavily on claircognizance, and to a lesser extent clairsentience and clairempathy. That means I know things with unshakable clarity, feel what's true or not true, and feel others' emotions and physical sensations. These skills are one of the main reasons I can help people connect directly with their soul; I know and feel when they are in resonance with their soul's truth.

You may have more experience and comfort with other senses. As you explore your soul's world, use your strong suits to sense into the world. You may want to add additional cues to notice what you taste, smell, or hear as you visit your soul's world.

I tried to use both inclusive and sensory-neutral phrasing throughout this book when possible. As any human, sometimes it's hard for me to recognize what is outside of my own experience. You may find some steps in this process lean towards knowing and feeling because that's what I've practiced with myself and clients and can confirm works. I invite you to adapt the steps to your strengths.

You don't have to visualize to tap into your soul. You are inseparable from your truth, so it's already there. The question is how you will allow yourself to tune into the truth.

Preparing to Tune In

One final reminder—your soul's world is not the world we live in now. That means none of the rules have to apply. People could be walking upside down and communicating without language. There could be eternal peace and happiness. This world is beyond the bounds of what you think is possible. Because when the mind taps out and you enter into the realm of the impossible, the soul says, *Finally! Let me start to show you what I know...*

Over the next few chapters, you'll be guided through three separate explorations. I've broken them up so that you can practice exploring your soul's world multiple times and get curious about different aspects of the world each time. You can do them all in one day or week or spread them out over a few weeks or months. Trust yourself to find the right tempo for you.

Each exploration includes a real-world example to help you understand the process. You'll follow along with a client named Michael as he tunes into his soul's world and discovers his unique purpose too.

Have a journal nearby or the *Wildly Towards Truth Workbook*. Writing by hand is better than typing because it engages more of your brain. I highly recommend jotting down everything you can remember after a visit with your soul because it may be valuable in the future, even if it seems small or insignificant now.

Chapter 10 Summary

- Your soul's world is like the operating system running in the background of your consciousness.
- Your soul's world impacts every action, thought, and feeling that you have because, at the deepest level, it is what makes you you.
- This process helps you build a bridge between your conscious mind and your soul's world so that you can better align your actions with your truth.
- Allow yourself to imagine beyond what seems possible. The soul communicates best when the mind steps aside.
- It may be hard to connect with your soul if you're trying to milk your soul's world for immediate answers to problems in your life. Trust the process and be mindful of treating your soul transactionally. You'll discover the solutions you seek as you embody your soul's truth more fully.
- The more you connect with your soul, the more you will understand your soul's world. Stay patient, curious, and open.
- You don't have to visualize to connect with your soul. Use the sensory abilities that work best for you.
- Keep a journal or jot down everything you can remember after a visit with your soul. Even seemingly small or insignificant details can lead to valuable insights later.
- Writing by hand can help you integrate more fully.

Living into your purpose is allowing for the truth of your soul to become real.

11

SOUL'S IDEAL WORLD EXPLORATION #1

"I feel more me than ever."

Guided Exploration

Get comfortable. This process is about being able to tune into yourself. It's not about getting it right or wrong. You're exploring and being curious.

You might enjoy lying down or leaning back in your favorite chair.

Take a few deep breaths in through the nose and out through the mouth if available. This is important, so don't skip over it. I call these Reset Breaths. They interrupt the normal patterns of thinking and breathing to bring you more fully into this moment right here, right now.

Breathe in through the nose and out through the mouth.

Your only task in this moment is to be and breathe.

Now, I'd like you to imagine that you could paint the world over again. You might visualize you have a magic wand and, in one flick, the entire world is reshaped to reflect exactly what you know is possible and true in your heart.

Or you might feel or sense into what you know is true.

Allow your truth within to begin to unfold until the entire world reflects what you know is possible in your heart.

This isn't about you being the all-knowing ruler or leader…

You're allowing for the truth of what you know to become real. Allowing for your deeper truth to emerge.

Imagine the kind of world you know is possible. The kind of relationships you know are possible. The joy and love you know is possible.

Getting curious about this ideal world…

What do you notice about this world?
What are the first things that stand out?

You may see images.
You may feel certain emotions or sensations in your body.
You may see colors or scenes like a movie.
Allow yourself to be curious about your ideal world.

This is not about your life specifically because this is bigger than your life. It's what's possible for everyone. What you know is possible for everyone.

Explore the emotions and connections in this ideal world:

How do people feel in this ideal world?
How do people treat each other?

Reflecting on relationships:

What do people know about their relationships with each other?
With the world around them?
With Nature?

With themselves?
What do they understand and know about themselves?
How does this inner understanding shape the way they live?

Feel into this deeper truth:

Knowing what they know, feeling how they feel… what does that allow them to do or be?
What possibilities does this open for them?

As you tune in more deeply, allow yourself to sense the details of your soul's ideal world. Open to all kinds of understanding and knowing, including sensations and emotions.

How do people spend their time in this world?
Do they live in big cities, small communities, family units, and/or another way?
How do they communicate? Through words, shared understanding, or another form of connection?
What else do you notice?

Tune into more and more details about your ideal world, letting yourself focus on what feels significant or true.

You don't need to understand how it works. Just notice what stands out to you—whether it's an image, emotion, feeling, or sensation in your body.

Take note of any final details you want to remember.

Thank your soul for sharing and giving you a glimpse of your deeper truth.

Take a nice deep breath in through the nose and out through the mouth.

Make sure that you're fully aware of your body. Bring gentle movement back to the body. If available, wiggle the fingers and toes. Feel the outer edges of the body. Feel yourself sitting in the chair or lying on the floor or the bed.

Become aware of your body in the room.

Take another deep breath in through the nose and out through the mouth.

When you're ready, take some notes about what you experienced.

Do This Right After

Jot down what you noticed. I highly recommend noting everything you can because it may end up being valuable in the future, even if it seems small or insignificant now.

It's okay if you have trouble finding the right words to explain how you felt or what you knew deep down was true. Do your best with the language you have.

Use these questions or the *Wildly Towards Truth Workbook* to help you capture your experience:

> What did you first notice in your soul's world?
> Did images come to mind? Colors? Sounds? Smells?
> How did people feel in your soul's world?
> What did they know about themselves?
> Each other?
> The world?
> How did people treat each other and interact?
> What else do you want to capture about your soul's ideal world?

Stay in the space of your soul for as long as you'd like.

Take It Further

You can try these exercises over the next few days, months, or whenever you feel inspired to explore deeper.

Your soul's vision is the core foundation of your life. It has been playing out either directly or indirectly your entire life. I invite you to spend time getting curious about how you have already been living or trying to live your soul's world. This may include the ways you are living its opposite because frustration and pain also point you towards truth.

Here are three suggested avenues to explore:

1) Ways your soul's world is already being expressed in your life.

    You are already living your vision internally, so it's bound to show up in big and small ways in your life. Perhaps your soul's world inspired you to become a nurse; is the 'why' behind the charity you support; or is the mysterious pull that keeps drawing you to meditation. Give yourself time to see how your soul's world is already playing out in your everyday life.

2) Ways you are trying to bring your soul's world into reality.

    This might include your volunteer activities, focus in school, or chosen career path. It also might include your personal philosophy on how you treat people. For example, perhaps you know everyone's name at the office or make eye contact with the grocery store clerk because your soul knows that everyone is valued and equal. Perhaps you're the friend that always cheers on others or is a safe space for them to share. Look across your entire life, from your political views to what mattered to you as a child, from your community engagement to your values. It all stems from your soul's world.

3) Ways you feel frustrated or disappointed that our shared reality doesn't match up with your truth.

    In addition to expressing your truth and helping to manifest it, you may also feel frustrated life isn't like your soul's world. This might show up as disbelief that your country is still dealing with a certain problem in this modern era. It could be outrage at the state of the environment, or education system, or that you don't know your neighbors. These feelings point you straight back to your deeper truth. You may also want to look to times that you've felt hopeless, shocked, excluded, or betrayed by people or situations in the past. Whether these moments were personal to you or relate more broadly to the state of world affairs, both reflect a distance from your truth and soul's ideal world.

Michael's Example

Let's go through an example together using Michael's ideal world. Michael and I came together to help give words to his deeper truth and also renew his confidence in his path and choices. Michael describes himself as an artist and heart-centric leader.

> In my soul's vision of the world, love is the dominant language. Everyone takes care of each other, and abundance flows throughout. There is a deep sense of belonging. People feel happy to contribute their part in the larger whole, and there is a symbiotic appreciation for what each person does. Creativity is championed, and artists help lead society forward. All people feel expanded and supported by the world to live out their highest experience. Everyone has access to the resources, community, and care they need to evolve and grow. People want to do their best and trust in God and the Universe. They live in harmony with the planet, and Nature is honored.

Based on his soul's world, we can already see some of the ways it's showing up in Michael's life:

He is an artist and loves creative expression.
He frequently collaborates with others in business and art.
He is deeply spiritual, and his faith in God empowers him.
He champions voices in the arts and media.
He shares online about the power of love.

These examples are just from the little bit we know about Michael. Imagine what you might discover knowing all that you know about yourself!

Journaling Prompts

Here are a few journaling prompts to help you go deeper and explore how you are in relationship with your soul's world now:

- Choose one aspect of your soul's world—perhaps a way people in your vision feel about themselves—then use the questions below as inspiration:

  - How do you try to get people to show this feeling to you? Do you ask for it directly? Provoke people into showing / telling you that it (or its opposite) is true?
  - How have you tried to seek validation that you are worthy of that feeling?
  - How do you naturally gift this feeling to others? Do you use specific words, actions, gestures, or other cues?
  - How does this feeling relate to the work you do or the roles you play?
  - Was this feeling present in your life growing up? If not, would it have helped you feel better in yourself?

Repeat this process with a few notable aspects of your soul's world. Look to different areas of your life, like relationships, hobbies, spirituality, self-confidence, body image, friendships, career, schooling, childhood, and so on.

Every element of your soul's world may show up in empowered and disempowered ways, so scan your fears, insecurities, and painful memories too. Sometimes, the biggest way our soul's ideal world is playing out is in its noticeable absence from our lives.

There is no time limit on when you say yes to your soul and cross the threshold into a truer you.

12

SOUL'S IDEAL WORLD EXPLORATION #2

"I woke up this morning with an inner peace, as if I'm being held. I can stop worrying and can live with a calm approach to life."

Guided Exploration

Before you begin, have a journal nearby or the *Wildly Towards Truth Workbook* to capture what you discover.

Once you're comfortable, take a few deep breaths in through the nose and out through the mouth. Let yourself arrive more fully in this moment right here, right now.

Every time you visit your soul's world, it's an opportunity to discover something new about yourself and your truth. Each experience is unique. It may be similar to what you've experienced before, or you may gain a fresh perspective. Whatever unfolds is right in this moment.

Tuning in now.

Imagine you have the power to reshape the world. Perhaps you visualize waving your magic wand and allowing everything that you know in your heart to become real. Perhaps you feel into your truth and allow the possibilities to take form in whatever way feels right.

You're not an all-knowing ruler or leader trying to control the world... instead, you're making space for your truth to come to life.

As you tune into your ideal world, notice what stands out to you in images, feelings, sensations, and ideas.

How do people spend their time?
What motivates them?
If they feel a desire to grow and expand, what drives that desire?
If they feel content and fulfilled, what do they understand about themselves and life that creates those feelings?

Consider how people contribute—whether through work, creative expression, or another way:

Do people work?
Create art?
Is the way people contribute organized and structured or more free-flowing?

Allow these prompts to inspire you to explore what's interesting and meaningful to you. Go in any direction you feel guided.

Do people create together or individually?
If together, do they come together intuitively or intentionally or...?

Now, think about challenges in this world:

Do people experience problems or challenges in this world?
If so, how do they relate to those experiences?
What do they know about the experiences or themselves that help them navigate them?

If needed, do people reach out for support? Is support offered intuitively? Another way?
Can people make mistakes in your ideal world?
If so, how do they view those experiences?
How do other people view someone else's mistakes or growth?
How do others respond?

Reflect on what's possible for people in this world:

What are they able to become, do, or create?
What does this freedom feel like?
How do they interact with and treat children?
What do people understand about the role of children and community that creates this dynamic?
How does this understanding shape their relationships with younger generations?

Take a moment to notice anything else that stands out about your world and how people feel, act, believe, and connect with themselves and each other.

Soak in any final details you want to remember.

Thank your soul for sharing and yourself for taking the time to connect with your truth.

Take a nice deep breath in through the nose and out through the mouth.

Make sure that you're fully aware of your body. Bring gentle movement back to the body. If available, wiggle the fingers and toes. Feel the outer edges of the body. Feel yourself sitting in the chair or lying on the floor or the bed.

Become aware of your body in the room.

Take another deep breath in through the nose and out through the mouth.

When you're ready, take some notes about what you experienced.

Do This Right After

As soon as you can, jot down what you realized in your soul's world. I highly recommend writing down everything you can because it may help you in the future. Do your best to capture your insights in words, even though words aren't always able to express how it felt.

> What beliefs were at the core of how people felt about creativity, work, and contributing?
> How did people navigate challenges and support?
> What emotions and beliefs made it possible for people to feel and act in these ways?
> What else do you want to remember about your soul's ideal world?

Stay in the space of your soul for as long as you'd like.

Take It Further

As you may be starting to notice, your soul's ideal world is playing out in your life whether you consciously realize it or not. You may have just discovered the core truths that drive your beliefs about work, creativity, and your personal contribution, not to mention support and acceptance.

Allow yourself time to explore how these truths have been playing out in your life. Remember, it's equally possible to notice the absence of these truths through frustrating and hurtful experiences. For example, if in your world, everyone is inspired by creative passion, this may show up in your current reality as feeling insecure about your creative gifts or not having enough time or the opportunity to be creative.

Michael's Example

Let's continue with Michael's world as our example:

> In my soul's vision of the world, love is the dominant language. Everyone takes care of each other, and abundance flows throughout. There is a deep sense of belonging. People feel happy to contribute their part in the larger whole, and there is a symbiotic appreciation for what each person does. Creativity is championed, and artists help lead society forward. All people feel expanded and supported by the world to live out their highest experience. Everyone has access to the resources, community, and care they need to evolve and grow. People want to do their best and trust in God and the Universe. They live in harmony with the planet, and Nature is honored.

First, let's pull out some of his core beliefs about how work and life function from his ideal world. Here are a few that I noticed:

Work, contribution, and creativity.

1) Everyone happily contributes.
2) Each individual contribution is part of a larger whole.
3) People are appreciated for their individual contribution.
4) Artists are leaders.

Fulfillment or personal growth.

5) People feel a pull to expand into their highest experience and feel supported in that.
6) People feel a desire to do their best.

Support, mentorship, and guidance.

7) Creativity is supported and encouraged.
8) Everyone has what they need to grow.

Now let's explore how these may be showing up in his life and career.

- ✓ Michael mentors others to discover their inner magic, which reflects his truth that everyone contributes with joy.
- ✓ He is a multi-passionate and multi-talented artist, which reflects his truth that creativity is encouraged.
- ✓ He has won multiple prestigious awards, which reflects his truth that artists are leaders.
- ✓ His faith in God and commitment to being a source of love in the world reflect his truth that everyone is supported in their desire to expand to their highest.

Now it's your turn! Remember, your truth may show up in this reality as ways that you feel stuck, stymied, and frustrated, as well. Those ways are still worth noting because they are still your soul guiding you towards truth.

Journaling Prompts

Below are a few journaling prompts to help you continue your exploration.

- Make a list of the truths that your soul showed you about the following. Feel free to add more depending on what you discovered in your world:

    - Work, contribution, and creativity.
    - Support, mentorship, and guidance.
    - Teamwork, collective activity, and community engagement.
    - Personal growth.
    - Challenges and opportunities.
    - Creative expression.
    - Fulfillment.

- For each item on your list, identify an area of your life where you are actively living, promoting, or experiencing that truth.

  In Michael's example above, he's actively promoting his belief that each individual contribution is part of a larger whole by helping artists and others to share their unique gifts. He's also living his belief that artists are leaders by highlighting innovative artists through his work and by winning awards himself.

- If your current circumstances don't reflect the truths in your soul's world, write down a few specific examples of how and why not.

  For example, in my ideal world, people work together towards shared goals. I was naturally drawn to or created that environment for myself in the government. Now, as a business owner, I spend much of my time alone and working towards my own goals by myself, which runs counter to my truth.

- Choosing one aspect of your current life—work, personal growth, relationships, faith—identify specific changes you could implement or request to better align your daily tasks with your truth.

  For example, my ideal world helped me realize that I work better collaboratively on a team with a shared vision. My soul's world helps me see how important it is for me to brainstorm with others and have a team around me, even if it's just a like-minded friend and my husband.

- If you're feeling bold, take action on one of those changes!

  Switch up your work duties, schedule coffee with a friend, meditate for ten minutes, or make loving eye contact with your partner. It doesn't matter what the action is, only that you're taking a step towards living your truth more intentionally!

Sprinkle in Grace

One last note about these seemingly simple prompts and ideas:

Your soul's world invites you to be radically honest about your life and how you're living it. That can be confronting, disheartening, inspiring, enraging, and liberating—sometimes all of them within the same minute.

Give yourself grace to be realizing what you're realizing now. You may need a few weeks, months, or even years to consider some of these questions. You can't be behind because your soul is pulling you forward in exactly the ways you most need to become who you truly are. Every doorway is an invitation, and there is no time limit on when you say yes and walk across the threshold to a truer you.

Take your time with these questions and prompts.

The energy and attention you invest here will come back to you with interest as you start living your truth more fully.

Actualizing your purpose is about living your truth, not just intellectually knowing it.

13

SOUL'S IDEAL WORLD EXPLORATION #3

"Feeling like my flame just got much, much bigger!"

Guided Exploration

Before you dive into exploration #3, ensure you have a journal nearby or the *Wildly Towards Truth Workbook* to take notes afterwards.

Get comfortable and take a few deep breaths in through the nose and out through the mouth. These Reset Breaths are a soothing way to interrupt the normal patterns of thinking and breathing and bring you right here into this moment right now.

Set an intention to have a fresh experience in your soul's ideal world and allow yourself to explore with an open heart and an open mind.

Take another deep breath in through the nose and out through the mouth.

As you tune into your soul, imagine you have the ability to reshape the world. Not as an all-knowing ruler...

Instead, you're recreating the world exactly as you know it could be—the way you know people could feel, act, and believe.

Get curious about this ideal world:

What do people value in this world?
What do they hold dear within themselves?
Others?
Society?
Are there shared values?
If so, what are they?

These values may reveal themselves to you through images, feelings, or a knowing of what is right and true.

What beliefs or behaviors help people feel safe and secure in this world?
What sensations arise in your body when you think about everyone feeling deeply rooted in their safety and worth?
What is important to people in this world?
Do they champion any causes?
If so, what do they support and advocate?
What emotions, understanding, or ideas are behind these causes?

Bring your awareness to the characteristics or behaviors that are valued in this world:

Are people praised for certain qualities?
Are approval and support assumed?
Another approach altogether?
How do people view differences in ability, background, beliefs, or experiences?
What do they believe about diversity?
How does this shape their understanding of each other?

As you explore more, get curious about the fundamental beliefs people have about themselves and the world:

What do people know or believe that allows them to express themselves fully and authentically?
What do they have the freedom to become, do, or create?
What feelings or beliefs are no longer necessary in your soul's vision of the world?
What aspects of present reality are absent?
What do people in your ideal world know or feel deep down that makes this world possible?
Is there a clear linchpin—a key feeling, belief, or understanding that makes this world possible?
Is there a fundamental truth people carry within themselves that allows this world to flourish?
What must people know or feel in their core to make this vision come alive?

Stay in this ideal world for as long as you desire, tuning into the feelings, beliefs, and understandings that guide how people live, create, and connect in this space.

When you're ready, thank your soul for sharing, and thank yourself for taking the time to connect with your truth.

Take a nice deep breath in through the nose and out through the mouth.

Make sure that you're fully aware of your body. Bring gentle movement back to the body. If available, wiggle the fingers and toes. Feel the outer edges of the body. Feel yourself sitting in the chair or lying on the floor or the bed.

Become aware of your body in the room.

Take another deep breath in through the nose and out through the mouth.

When you're ready, take some notes about what you experienced.

Do This Right After

Write down or voice record everything you discovered. Even if a detail doesn't seem important now, it may gift you an aha! moment later.

> What belief, feeling, or knowing is at the core of your soul's ideal world and makes it possible?
> What do people value in themselves, others, society, and the world?
> What qualities are important or celebrated in people?
> How do people view differences?
> What aspects of this reality are missing in your soul's vision?
> What feelings or beliefs are no longer necessary in your soul's vision of the world?

Know that you can return to the space of your soul any time you'd like. You'll discover more with each visit because you're creating a deeper relationship and conversation with your soul.

Take It Further

One of the fastest ways to feel more aligned with your soul is to clarify your values and bring them more intentionally into your daily life. Your values are what you stand for, the qualities you strive to embody, and how you intend to show up in the world. They influence your choices and behavior, impact your thinking, and shape your character, as well as create the cornerstone of your resilience. Luckily, your soul's vision is filled with clues about what you value and believe in at the deepest level.

A quick internet search will give you hundreds of ways to come up with a list of your values. Personally, I've struggled with many of the methods because:

> A) I care about a lot of things. When I see a big list of value words, I want to choose them all.

B) Sometimes, we choose values as a way to shame and blame ourselves for not being the good-enough humans we think we should be. This is a sneaky way to keep yourself stuck in old, familiar feelings instead of making the courageous decision to embody a more resonant truth. This can look like valuing kindness but then beating yourself up for being hard on your kids (not kind to yourself), or valuing honesty and then continually feeling like you're unworthy of love because you had an affair years ago.

C) I'm not always sure which "me" is doing the choosing, my truth or my fear. I often second-guess myself, wondering if I chose freedom as a value because it's an innate driver of spiritual expansion or because I feel trapped or limited in some aspect of my life at the moment.

I like using the soul's ideal world to mine for values because your world is already honed in on what matters, and it reflects the core truth of who you are, not who you aspire to be.

Michael's Example

Let's revisit Michael's world as our example. I have underlined some of the words that could point to his values:

In my soul's vision of the world, <u>love</u> is the dominant language. Everyone takes care of each other, and <u>abundance</u> flows throughout. There is a deep sense of <u>belonging</u>. People feel happy to <u>contribute</u> their part in the larger whole, and there is a <u>symbiotic appreciation</u> for what each person does. <u>Creativity</u> is championed, and artists help lead society forward. All people feel expanded and <u>supported</u> by the world to live out their highest experience. <u>Everyone has access</u> to the resources, community, and care they need to evolve and grow. People want to do their best and <u>trust</u> in God and the Universe. They live in <u>harmony</u> with the planet, and Nature is honored.

We can pull out a few values from this brief description:

a) Love
b) Abundance
c) Belonging
d) Contribution
e) Symbiotic appreciation
f) Creativity
g) Support
h) Equity
i) Faith
j) Harmony

That's quite a big list, and yours may be even longer. You might also have chosen different words than I did. Trust yourself to highlight what matters most to you.

If your list is long like Michael's, then I suggest a second step. As you consider what each value means to you, jot down a quick sentence to describe each one. Then, review your list and notice if any are similar and can be combined.

For example, Michael may be able to condense his initial list into a few overarching values:

- Support, equity, and abundance may point towards the same feeling of being <u>innately held and cared for in life</u>.

- Contribution and belonging may relate to a sense of being <u>part of a larger whole</u>.

- Faith, creativity, and symbiotic appreciation may go together because everyone can relax into their <u>individual uniqueness</u> instead of competing.

- Perhaps harmony and love fit together as natural extensions of <u>loving yourself, others, and Nature</u>.

It doesn't matter how you combine them or if you get it "right" or whittled down to a perfect list of 3-5 values. What matters is that you spend a few moments thinking about what each value means and makes possible for you.

For example, when I feel connected to myself, others, and Life, I feel much more open, creative, free, and at peace. You can probably sense in this book and process how important it is for me to help you feel connected to your soul, your truth, yourself, as well as the broader human journey and spiritual pulse of life. This value is a driving force for my personal practices, relationships, and career.

But I wouldn't have chosen the word "connected" on a list. Connection is so ingrained into who I am and how I move in the world, I didn't recognize it as distinct or important until I noticed it threaded through my soul's ideal world. That's the power of continually revisiting your soul's world. You discover new layers and nuance every time.

Journaling Prompts

Here are a few journaling prompts to help you explore more:

- What values, truths, tenets, or beliefs are reflected in your soul's world?
- What moments have let you know your soul's world is different than our shared reality?
- Reviewing your own life, what are a few examples of where you're not living in alignment with your world?
- What could you do to be more in touch with your world?

Practices to Intentionally Live Your Soul's Ideal World

Actualizing your purpose is about living your truth, not just intellectually knowing it. I offer these tangible practices to help you start *becoming* you.

- Choose one aspect of your soul's ideal world to practice bringing into your life this week.

    - If you had full permission to live it, what would you do differently?
    - If it was already true, how would you feel differently?

- Choose one value and explore how you could live it more fully right now today. The shift doesn't have to be big—it can be as simple as changing a thought or even smiling more!

- Write a Manifesto of your soul. A manifesto is simply a statement of your beliefs and views. Capture your soul's truth in a Manifesto of You.

Example Manifesto of You

I believe in the strength of my body.

I believe in the wisdom of my soul to guide me to my highest calling.

I believe in helping others.

I believe I am the puzzle piece that makes the world complete. Without me, the world cannot be whole – I am invaluable.

I believe I am beautiful. I believe I radiate. I believe the power of my love can envelope the world and hold us in safety and acceptance.

I believe I can feel fulfilled and that my life matters.

I believe I can...
- Heal wounds gently
- Move beyond fears bravely
- Laugh easily
- Love more fully
- Open up confidently
- Explore boldly
- Contribute harmoniously
- Soften safely
- Connect deeply
- Accept gratefully
- Give graciously
- Live gracefully.

I believe I have the power to create the life I want.

I believe I can only change myself. I can shine my light brightly and illuminate others in the process.

I believe I am love.

I believe I am connected to everyone and everything – I am and we are one vibration, and that vibration is love.

I believe love is the reason, purpose, and meaning of life.

Coming into resonance with your truth is a process of letting go. You're letting go of who you think you are to make space for who you really are.

14

SOUL PURPOSE EXPLORATION #1

"I found it!!! My purpose!!! I know it's a work in progress and it's like peeling back an onion, but I feel closer than ever."

Slipping Through the Eye of the Needle

In this chapter, you'll gain clarity on your unique purpose. This is the emotional essence you are here to embody so fully that it brings your soul's ideal world to life.

Remember, your soul is ruthless in its efforts to live in resonance with your truth. When you view your life through that lens, even the most heart-breaking traumas can be seen with fresh eyes. The Universe is not trying to break you with challenges. Life is trying to pull you forward into your truth.

Imagine the soul is drawing you through the eye of a needle. To make it through, you've got to strip back to your core energetic essence and release all the emotional baggage, habits, and beliefs weighing you down. For example, if you know in your bones that you're meant to feel wildly happy and healthy with the sun kissing your shoulders as you bury your fingers into your garden… but you're angry about unhealthy food choices, feel trapped living in an apartment, and don't believe you'll ever find love or happiness, then you have to release a few layers of beliefs and resistance to bring you into that truth.

Another metaphor that I like is imagining your true self in the future holding a cord that's connected to you today. Your future self is pulling you forward, and the lighter you are, the faster you'll be able to move through the experiences between now and then to merge into your resonant truth.

While living into your purpose is a process of discovery and becoming that may require you to learn new skills, the journey of becoming is a process of letting go. You're already a radiant shining light. The only work is to let the blankets covering your light fall away.

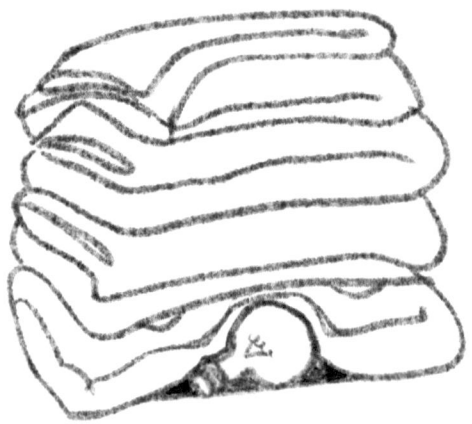

How Your Purpose Fits into the Bigger Picture

Your purpose is the key element to your soul's understanding of the world. It is the force that underlies all feelings, beliefs, and truths in your ideal world and makes the whole vision possible. So to hone in on your purpose, first you start with your soul's world. If you have not done the three explorations in the previous chapter, back up and go start those now.

Once you are familiar with your soul's ideal world, you can get curious about what lies at its core. What makes this world possible? What foundation has to be there for everything you know to be true to unfold?

In my soul's world, the linchpin is that people know they're enough. This deep, inner knowing means that, unlike in our consensus reality, people in my soul's world don't feel like they need to seek validation, confidence, a sense of power, or even resources outside of themselves. This knowing ripples into a pervasive sense of peace in my soul's ideal world.

As you'll soon discover, the cornerstone of your soul's world might be that people know they are all connected or loved or supported. At this stage, it is okay to be vague. We want high-level, big feelings like "people need to know they are accepted to feel creatively expressive."

You are not searching for a purpose like, "I'm meant to be a supermodel," or a teacher or a doctor. Those are ways that you express and explore your soul's bigger purpose. I share that loving reminder again because the old belief that your purpose is your career or role is strong!

Guided Exploration — Your Soul's Truth

Make sure you have a few moments when you won't be disturbed. Have your journal nearby or the *Wildly Towards Truth Workbook* to take notes afterwards.

Get comfortable.

Like an archaeologist uncovering a hidden temple, you're going to visit your soul's ideal world again, this time with a delicate brush to gently reveal the inner sanctum. With the same enthusiasm as the archaeologist might have after years of anticipating this moment, the goal is to enjoy and stay open and curious. You have time to figure out what it all means later. For now, you're uncovering piece after piece and marveling at the wisdom and beauty of your soul.

So get comfortable. You might enjoy lying down or leaning back in your favorite chair. Set an intention to explore with an open heart and an open mind.

Take a few deep breaths in through the nose and out through the mouth. Your Reset Breaths bring you more fully into this moment right here, right now.

Breathe in through the nose and out through the mouth.

Once you feel a sense of calm or a gentle heaviness in the body, begin to tune into your soul's world.

Waving your magic wand and repainting the world to reflect exactly what you know is true in your heart.

Feel into the world you know is possible, and the kind of relationships, joy, and love you know is possible.

Remind yourself of all the beauty and magic of your soul's world.

Feel the bliss of this world in your body. Feel as if you are living it right now in every cell of your being.

With the same delicate care as the archaeologist brushing away dirt to reveal the sacred center, get curious about what lies at the core of your soul's vision:

What do people in your ideal world need to feel deep down to bring this world to life?
What must they know or understand to create this world?

Reflect on the fundamental beliefs people carry about themselves and how the world works.

What do they need to know or trust to live this way?
Is there a clear linchpin you must feel, be, or know to live in this world? The piece that makes the world possible?

Stay in your ideal world until you have a clear sense of how people feel and what belief, knowledge, or feeling makes this world possible.

Take a nice deep breath in through the nose and out through the mouth.

Make sure that you're fully aware of your body. Bring gentle movement back to the body. If available, wiggle the fingers and toes. Feel the outer edges of the body. Feel yourself sitting in the chair or lying on the floor or the bed.

Become aware of your body in the room.

Take another deep breath in through the nose and out through the mouth.

When you're ready, take some notes about what you experienced.

Do This Right After

Write down or voice record everything you discovered. Even if a detail doesn't seem important now, it may gift you insight later.

> What emotion, belief, or knowing lies at the heart of your soul's vision?
> What does that make possible in your ideal world?
> Looking at your life…
> How do you feel acknowledging this truth within you?
>> Does it feel like you knew this on some level already?
>> Does it feel like it makes sense?
>> If not, why not? What does it feel like?
> How have you tried to cultivate this feeling or knowing in yourself throughout your life?
> How are you helping yourself to feel or live it now?
> In what ways are you already championing this truth in your life?
> How has it been revealing itself to you in your values, work, beliefs, how you treat others, or other areas?

Take your time with these questions. Because they touch on the fundamental truth of your soul, they are by nature deep as well as deeply personal.

Trust that what you discover today is the perfect amount for now and that more will be ready for you as you start embodying this work.

Michael's Example

To help explain purpose in this new paradigm, let's revisit Michael's ideal world.

> In my soul's vision of the world, love is the dominant language. Everyone takes care of each other, and abundance flows throughout. There is a deep sense of belonging. People feel happy to contribute their part in the larger whole, and there is a symbiotic appreciation for what each person does. Creativity is championed, and artists help lead society forward. All people feel expanded and supported by the world to live out their highest experience. Everyone has access to the resources, community, and care they need to evolve and grow. People want to do their best and trust in God and the Universe. They live in harmony with the planet, and Nature is honored.

Here is an excerpt from our conversation in which Michael got to the core of his ideal world:

> Alexis: "So imagine that there is a doorway right now between this world that we're living in and the world that you just described, and when we walk through that doorway, the door frame has to zap us with a knowing, a belief, an understanding, a way of feeling, like something that shifts so that we can now live in this world. What is that? What is that deep, deep linchpin, knowing or feeling that makes this possible?"
>
> Michael: "It's knowing that God is with you. These people know that they're in this world, but there's this outside force that's taking care of them that they feel supported by. Because they know it exists and they have faith in it, this force is able

to manifest and express itself through the physical experience that they're experiencing. So they don't feel disconnected from this spiritual power or this consciousness of love that is this experience of energy that exists outside of this world."

Alexis: "If you had to describe it in an emotion, is it a feeling of connection? Is it a feeling of support?"

Michael: "It's just, it feels like love. It just feels like, oh, I'm loved. It means I'm not alone. So then it means I'm together, maybe?"

As the conversation continued, Michael identified the linchpin of his soul's world as a feeling of togetherness and the knowing that God is with you. So his soul's focus—his purpose—is to find deeper and more nuanced ways to embody the feeling of togetherness and knowing that God is with him.

Your purpose is an invitation for you to claim your deepest truth no matter what is happening in your life.

For Michael, his purpose applies even when he feels like he's missing out on work opportunities or going through a breakup. It applies when the person he likes doesn't like him back or when his art is criticized or overlooked by others. It also applies when he's feeling deeply loved and connected with friends and when he's feeling left out and misunderstood.

You might notice that Michael's linchpin is more conceptual. As you'll learn in "Troubleshooting - you've narrowed it down to a concept," that's okay as long as you can feel the truth of it in your body. At the moment, these might be the best words to describe what you're feeling. As long as they feel right and resonant to you, then I defer to you: you know you best.

This process isn't always a slam dunk for everyone. If you are struggling to hone in on the linchpin of your soul's ideal world, you're not alone. In the sections that follow, I share five common ways people get stuck and a few ideas that may help.

Troubleshooting — You Have Multiple Options for the Linchpin

First, you may have multiple options for the linchpin.

This is common. Trying to get the root of the root can sometimes lead us into a riddle like, "Which came first: the chicken or the egg?" I suggest you keep excavating to see if there is another emotion or knowing underneath.

For example, Lee identified feeling loved and held as the core of her soul's ideal world. As a next step, she might get curious:

- Can you feel loved in this world without knowing that you are held?
- And vice versa, can you feel held without knowing that you are loved?
- Which word or idea feels more expansive or heart-opening in the body?
- Which lights you up or fills you with a sense of calm and ease?

Lee ended up choosing loved as her linchpin because that knowing felt more solid in her body.

You could try the same type of questioning with loved and valued, connected and All One, or enough and whole. There is no objectively right answer because it depends on what's true for you. The words matter far less than how the truth feels in your body.

Troubleshooting — Safety is Your Linchpin

In general, I recommend assuming that safety is a given in your ideal world. If you narrowed it down to safety, try choosing a different belief, feeling, or understanding that's possible once you feel safe.

The hurdle of safety is the leap from our shared human reality into the realm of the soul, no matter what your soul's vision entails. The soul feels inherently safe because it doesn't fear being destroyed like the human mind does. The question at the heart of the soul is what truth unfolds once you've made that leap into the safety of the soul.

Troubleshooting — You've Narrowed It Down to a Concept

In this process, you're trying to put words to something that is beyond the realm of language. That's not a challenge unique to you; it's a universal experience. The soul speaks in emotion, imagery, and metaphor, while the mind thinks in concepts, language, and ideas. Ideas are how we categorize and rationalize our shared reality. Inspiration and imagination are how we catalyze ourselves to create new realities.

Here are a few examples of more conceptual linchpins:

We are all One.
Love is the truth.
I AM.
Inherent sense of self.
I am okay.
Responsible for own emotions.

These are real examples of the feelings, beliefs, and knowing clients have described at the core of their souls' visions. I have no problem with these statements because I was live with each of these people and know that these phrases capture how they felt in their bodies at the time. These words point towards a feeling that they can practice and embody. Over time, the feeling may identify itself in new words that are more succinct and tangible.

Since I'm not with you live to guide you through this process and make sure you're feeling and not thinking, I invite you to do your best. It takes a lot of self-awareness to guide yourself through the soul's world and experience it while simultaneously reading the map. You're doing beautifully.

If your linchpin sounds like one of the above, get curious about which feeling the concept represents for you. This may take practice. You're looking for a physical sensation and reaction in the body when you hold this knowing or belief in your mind. It often feels like softness, lightness, solidness, or a feeling of being very present and open.

The sensation may be hard to capture in one word. You're not trying to find the perfect language because all language falls short here. Instead, you're trying to approximate the best word for the way you feel when you hold the core truth of your soul's ideal world in your mind.

For example, using the conceptual linchpins above:

We are all One may be the sensation of connected.
Love is the truth could be faith.
I AM may be wholeness.
Inherent sense of self could be worthy.
I am okay could be happy.
Responsible for own emotions may be empowered.

Your body is the stage upon which life plays out and your soul's world expresses itself as your purpose. The more you get into the very real and physical experience of sensations, the more you literally begin to embody your purpose. Keep practicing, and don't worry if the words change as you become more adept with the practice.

Troubleshooting — You Can't Settle into Your Soul's Vision

The fourth reason you may feel stuck is because you don't feel steady in your ideal world.

Allowing yourself to surrender to your soul's world is the first step in clarifying its linchpin and your purpose. Often, people jump in and out of the world because the well-trained "rational" mind says this ideal world is impossible, idealistic, and pie-in-the-sky thinking. This is a defense mechanism, or what I call a coping skill and trauma response.

When I'm guiding a client through the process, it can show up like this:

> Client describing their ideal world: "People live in such a symbiotic way with nature. They recognize how interwoven we are with all of life. They honor nature like it's blood in their own veins."
>
> Me: "It sounds like they feel inherently part of all of life. How does that play out in their relationship with food and animals?"
>
> Client: "Better than now when we poison everything with pesticides and destroy the environment with toxic chemicals and plastics!"

Do you notice how the tone changed? How the client shifted from describing a possibility to expressing frustration? They bounced out of their soul's world and back into our consensus reality, in which they feel powerless to change an important issue.

If you feel this bouncing in and out of your soul's world, it's possible that it hasn't been safe for you to indulge in feeling free, expansive, safe, open, and loving—all feelings your ideal world most likely inspires within you. It's also possible that you've had to rely on being "realistic" as a way to handle being disappointed and let down by people in your past. Or perhaps you just pride yourself on being logical and grounded in the here and now.

Whatever the deeper reason, this process invites you to go beyond your rational mind into the realm of your heart's knowing. That may be uncomfortable, if not entirely new to you. The more you practice, the easier it will be.

I recommend interrupting your mind when it starts to pull back from this new and expansive way of feeling. You might say to yourself something like, "I know this is new, but I want to try it out," or "This is just an experiment, so humor me." I guide clients back to elements of their world that they've already shared with me, repeat what they've discovered, and we start exploring again. Keep practicing visiting your world until you can hold it long enough to be curious about how it works and why.

Troubleshooting — You're Thinking More Than Feeling

The dance of the soul's world is that it's an undefinable knowing that we're trying to translate into language. The soul is gifting you feelings, visuals, sounds, and insights that have specific relevance to you. It's your job to extract the meaning from these clues and translate them into actionable thoughts and words.

Often, we're so practiced at the actionable words part that we struggle to sit in the space of witnessing, absorbing, or feeling. The linchpin to your soul's world isn't something your mind can figure out through deduction or reasoning. It's an intuitive insight—an aha! moment imbued with a deep knowing that it's right and true.

If you're having trouble feeling into the linchpin, spend more time feeling into your world.

> How would you feel if you were part of this world?
> What would it be like to be treated that way?
> How would your posture change?
> Your outlook and mindset?
> How would it feel in your body to open to trusting, loving, and connecting in the ways you know is possible?

Practice in the safety of your home, perhaps when you're falling asleep or waking up when the analytical mind is less active.

This is a powerful practice. Your entire life can transform just by mastering feeling comfortable and intimate with your feelings.

Take It Further

Getting to the core of your soul's world is a big deal. As much as you can, allow what you've realized to percolate on the back burner of your mind. It's natural to want to rush into action; humans are really good at doing things. Your purpose is about embodying this feeling or knowing—it's about being.

I invite you to sit with what you've discovered. Feel into it. Notice how even a gentle awareness starts to show you ways you can experience and embody your purpose more fully.

If you must must jump into action, use the practice below to create a big-picture approach to embodying your truth.

Brainstorming Inspired Action

Grab your journal or *Wildly Towards Truth Workbook* and get curious:

> What new intentions for yourself and your life would help you better live your soul's truth?
> What tools and skills would support you in becoming the person who lives your vision?
> What inspired actions would help you embody your soul's truth more fully?

You're looking for high-level categories or buckets of activities. General is better because general allows you to focus on the outcome without getting lost in the details. In strategic-planning speak, you're identifying strategies to help you better embody your purpose, not specific goals or actions to achieve those strategies.

Michael's Example — Inspired Action

Let's go through an example using Michael's world.

> In my soul's vision of the world, love is the dominant language. Everyone takes care of each other, and abundance flows throughout. There is a deep sense of belonging. People feel happy to contribute their part in the larger whole, and there is a symbiotic appreciation for what each person does. Creativity is championed, and artists help lead society forward. All people feel expanded and supported by the world to live out their highest

experience. Everyone has access to the resources, community, and care they need to evolve and grow. People want to do their best and trust in God and the Universe. They live in harmony with the planet, and Nature is honored.

The linchpin that makes this soul's world possible is the feeling of togetherness and the knowing that God is with you. That means Michael's main gift to the world, as well as his inherent truth, is a feeling of togetherness.

Now that he knows his truth, Michael can identify a few big-picture areas in his life to focus on living it more. Using a three-year timeframe to help him think more broadly, here is what he might brainstorm:

> Over the next three years, I will take inspired action to move closer to embodying my mission and manifesting my soul's ideal world.
>
> These specific strategies will help me:
>
> - Build a community of like-minded artists committed to leading in love.
> - Cultivate an inner sense of trust in myself, my community, and God.
> - Disconnect from places, activities, and people that do not help me feel supported and appreciated.
> - Move beyond old habits of abandoning myself, including in relationships.
> - Expand my circle of support and care.

These strategies are powerful because they act as intentions and focal points while also allowing for life to unfold naturally. Your soul knows far better than your mind exactly which experiences and emotions will help you embrace your truth effectively. When we try to micromanage that process, we cut ourselves off from our natural path of growth.

Your Turn

Your list might look very different. Your intentions might center around loving yourself more, creating more comfort and safety in your body, or trusting your instincts more, for example. The tools and skills that might help you could include supporting your nervous system, calming your mind, or better expressing your emotions. Actions you might take could include advocating for yourself at work, creating healthier routines, and joining a club or community that excites you.

As much as you can, stay general. When you start thinking about your new daily workout or scheduling your day differently, you've dropped to the level of actions. That's not helpful right now because actions get old and stale. The last outcome you want is to quit moving towards embodying your purpose because you unwittingly connected it with 6 a.m. running sessions. Early morning exercise is just one way that you might create healthier routines that help you feel good about yourself. There are thousands of other ways that might be a better fit if you allow yourself to be inspired and for life to surprise you. Focus on who you're becoming, and let life guide you towards the best and most impactful route.

What If You Feel Sad or Grieve Once You Realize Your Purpose?

You may feel grief rise up over the next few days or weeks. This is normal. When you touch into your truth, it brings to light all the ways and times you felt separate from your soul's truth. Be gentle with yourself. No matter how exciting it feels, your soul's essence is a tender revealing.

It helps me to make sure I'm hydrated, eating slightly healthier and lighter foods, and walking outside in nature. I also like naps and light stretching to help my body integrate.

You may also want to seek out professional support for your mental and emotional health.

Like the metaphor of being squeezed through the eye of a needle, coming into resonance with your truth is a process of letting go and getting lighter. While the end result seems freeing, the daily reality of that transformation is a blend of grieving, remembering, seeing with a new perspective, making empowered meanings, changing relationships, and feeling. You're letting go of who you think you are to make space for who you really are. Part of that is grieving the ways you've felt less than and hurt. It's natural, and your truth is worth the healing journey.

Should You Share Your New Discoveries?

You may feel excited to share your newfound purpose with others. Unless the person you share with is also reading this book and going through the process, they might not understand what you're sharing or the depth of truth this represents for you. I recommend being mindful of who you share your process with for three main reasons:

1) Most people believe purpose is related to your career choice, so talking about embodying an energy or knowing may not make much sense to others. They may ask questions that burst your proverbial bubble, like, "So what are you going to do with this?" "What does that mean about how you'll make money?" Or "Are you quitting your job now?" You may find it hard or disorienting to try to explain the gap between how purpose is currently used in culture and the spiritual awakening this process represents. You may also feel pressure to have immediate and tangible answers to their questions—questions that I'm intentionally inviting you to delay asking so that you can open to the gifts of your soul more fully.

2) I've witnessed well-meaning loved ones try to be supportive by responding, "I've always seen your gifts. Your soul's truth makes total sense!" This can feel both validating and belittling to your

realizations. Your world may feel brand new while they're responding like it's routine, as always.

3) People may be curious about their own soul's vision and linchpin. Like most of us, they want answers to how they can feel fulfilled, happy, and like they're meaningfully contributing to the world. I speak from experience that it can be disheartening to share this process excitedly with someone, only for them to disregard it a week later. This process takes time and commitment to unwind the inner knots around purpose and powerfully decide to embrace a new way of being. Without that commitment, the simple answers may not be that impactful.

True transformation doesn't come from knowing the words for your soul's truth; it comes from embodying it. The journey you're on through these pages is reshaping how you navigate your relationship to the world. It's shifting your experience with personal responsibility, power, and self-trust. Allow people to embark on that journey when and if it's right for them and travel only as far down the path as they desire.

Touching into your soul is a tender process of trust-building. Gift yourself the time and space to develop your relationship. The choice to share will always be there.

Practices To Embody Your Soul's Purpose

The following are a few ideas to practice being in your purpose:

- Daily "feeling-i-zation."

    - Practice feeling the emotion or knowing of your soul's truth daily for a minimum of one full minute.

        "Feeling-i-zation" is a made-up word to describe a body-based version of visualizing. The goal is to calibrate your body and nervous system to your ultimate truth. Please note this will stir up all the ways you're currently not embodying your truth (i.e., your Dark Fuel feelings).

Many people visualize by creating pictures in their mind of what they want to have and experience. They may say affirmations like "I am wealthy. I am a sought-after expert. I enjoy free time with my loving family." They may even have vision boards by their bed or desk with images of their desires.

This is not that.

This is about feeling in your body as if it were already true now. It will most likely feel light, open, expanded, and more. It may also feel uncomfortable at first.

- Remind yourself of your soul's truth A LOT.

  - Change your phone screen to that feeling or knowing. You can do this by opening the notes on your phone, typing the word(s), taking a screenshot, and then adding that screenshot to the home screen.
  - Write it on sticky notes and place them on your mirror, refrigerator, or computer screen—wherever you are likely to see them.
  - Find other fun ways to keep your truth top of mind.

  This helps remind you that everything in your life is revolving around your soul's truth. It's like the invisible force spinning the globe of your life. Everything is about embodying your truth more fully.

  * I do NOT recommend getting a tattoo of your truth until you've worked with the process for a few years, because the word(s) can change as you build a more nuanced your relationship with your soul *

- Start looking at life through the lens of your truth.

  Your soul is continually guiding you to be more fully you. This is the path of purpose. Practice embracing this belief and get curious if and how your perspective on your life changes.

You might ask yourself questions like the following. I'll use "connection" as the example truth. Feel free to play around with these questions until they spark an awareness in you.

- If you knew you were 100% connected to yourself / the other person / all of Life in this moment…
    - How would you feel?
    - What thoughts would you have?
    - What actions would you take? How might your actions change?
- If you embraced your true knowing of connection right now…
    - What might be possible?
    - How would this experience change?
    - How would your perspective on the experience change?
- How can you be more connected in this moment?
- What do you need to do to feel more connected right now?
- How can you create more connection with yourself / others / Source?
- How is this experience showing you where you're not believing in or embodying connection?
- What thoughts, beliefs, or actions can you let go of to allow for more inherent connection?

Your past is the perfect series of events to help you become the living embodiment of your soul's wisdom.

15

SOUL PURPOSE EXPLORATION #2

---

*"I am truly shifting. I am stepping in to ME.
I am starting to be who I am, really I AM."*

The Flip Side

Your purpose is a totality experienced through duality. You are a whole, complete being, and that wholeness carries within it paradoxes that feel like opposites.

On one hand, you have the expansive, limitless sensation of your truth that you explored in the previous chapter. On the other hand, you have the constrictive, bottomless pit sensation of your fear. Like two sticks rubbing together to make fire, it is the interplay of your truth and fear that creates the alchemical reaction of growth I call Dark Fuel Alchemy®. This magic is how you live a meaningful life of purpose.

> *Like two sticks rubbing together to make fire, it is the interplay of your truth and fear that creates the alchemical reaction of growth. This magic is how you live a meaningful life of purpose.*

In the following section, you'll be guided to hone in on your deepest fear. This is the emotion or belief that kicks you out of the expansive, safe space of your soul and brings you to your proverbial knees. It lies at the core of your bad feelings and also subconsciously influences your behavior in two main ways:

1) You go to great lengths to avoid feeling it, including pushing people away, disengaging from intimacy, quitting projects without really trying, and more.

2) You recognize the feeling in many parts of your life and use its continual presence to validate your fears that it's true. This is a coping strategy to justify your choices. For example, you may find it easier to believe you're unworthy of love and stay in unfulfilling relationships that validate this belief rather than learn how to value yourself.

It's not fun to feel this fear or belief. It might feel like your stomach drops or you have tightness in your chest. It might feel like your mind goes blank, and you're exhausted all of a sudden.

Feeling it is still worth it.

Gaining clarity on the big, scary feeling that's driving your decisions can change your life. It can propel you from feeling stuck—and doomed to experience the same disappointments and frustrations over and over—to feeling like you can finally see a path forward and take charge of your life. In other words, it can give you power.

Anytime you directly look at your core fear, it has the potential to bring up a lot of difficult memories and emotions. You may also have trauma that deserves to be tended to with care and professional support. Before you dive too deeply into your Dark Fuel, first make sure to gather a support team, as well as tools to help yourself feel safe, loved, and nourished.

Guided Exploration — Your Dark Fuel

A friendly reminder that this entire process is about being able to tune into yourself. It's not about getting it right or wrong. There is no right or wrong when it comes to connecting with your soul because it's your soul and your life, and you're the only one who can feel what's true for you.

To prepare, take a few breaths in through your nose and out through your mouth.

I love these Reset Breaths because they help you bring your attention back to your body in this moment, right now.

Breathing in through the nose and out the mouth.

Notice if you can feel the belly moving with the breath, expanding on the inhale, and gently softening on the exhale.

When you are ready, bring in the feeling of your essential truth.

This is the linchpin belief or emotion at the core of your soul's world.

Amp up that feeling or knowing in your body until you can feel your energy lifting. You may feel calm, hopeful, and simultaneously grounded and spacious in your body. Keep expanding that feeling or knowing until you feel it in every ounce of your being.

Imagine experiencing it so fully, you feel like it's humming and radiating through you. The body knows how to feel this, so invite the mind to call in the emotion or belief right now.

Now, holding this magnificent feeling, get curious:

What is the felt opposite of this feeling for you personally?

You're seeking what feels like the opposite for you. It doesn't have to make logical sense or be an opposite in the dictionary.

It may feel heavy, tight, or like the floor just dropped beneath you. That's normal and okay.

Try to match a word to the sensation you're feeling.

Once you feel an answer, get curious:

Have you personally felt this emotion or belief before?
Bringing to mind some of the most painful experiences of your life—does this belief or emotion capture the core of how you were feeling?
In those moments, if you had truly known your soul's core truth, would it have helped you feel better or navigate the tough time more easily?

When you feel ready, thank your soul for sharing and yourself for taking the time to connect with your truth.

Breathe in through the nose and out through the mouth.

Bring your attention back to your body. Bring gentle movement back to the body. If available, wiggle the fingers and toes. Stretch and move the body in a way that feels good.

Then, take a few notes on what you experienced.

Do This Right After

Write down or voice record your insights. Capture anything that arose for you, even if it doesn't feel related.

Use these questions or the *Wildly Towards Truth Workbook* to help you record your experience:

What is the opposite feeling of your soul's truth?
What word(s) best fits that feeling right now?

Do any specific memories, images, or thoughts come up with the feeling?
What sensations do you notice in your body with this feeling?

Looking at your life…

How do you feel acknowledging this fear within you?
> Does it feel like you knew this on some level already?
> Does it make sense?
> If not, why not? What does it feel like instead?

When have you personally experienced this emotion?
> How might those experiences have been different if you'd known your soul's truth?

How do you see this feeling playing out in your life right now?
> How has it been revealing itself in your relationships, creativity, career, self-esteem, etc?

What beliefs do you hold that stem from this feeling and your experiences with it?

What actions do you take to avoid feeling it?

How do you see this emotion playing out in other people?
> For example, college kids wondering what to do with their lives, stay-at-home moms feeling alone and unsupported, or retirees craving more joy and passion.

Be patient with yourself and take your time with these questions. The heart of this process is understanding this disempowering feeling so that you can recognize and alchemize it into greater truth and power. The word may change over time, especially if you repeat these steps a few times. That's because you're building a closer relationship with your emotions, soul, and truth.

If you don't feel clear just yet, that's okay. Take a break. Take a walk. Drink some water. You've gone your whole life without having words for this; a couple more days or weeks is fine. Keep visiting your soul's world and embodying your truth. It will get easier and easier.

Michael's Example

Let's revisit Michael's world to find his Dark Fuel:

> In my soul's vision of the world, love is the dominant language. Everyone takes care of each other, and abundance flows throughout. There is a deep sense of belonging. People feel happy to contribute their part in the larger whole, and there is a symbiotic appreciation for what each person does. Creativity is championed, and artists help lead society forward. All people feel expanded and supported by the world to live out their highest experience. Everyone has access to the resources, community, and care they need to evolve and grow. People want to do their best and trust in God and the Universe. They live in harmony with the planet, and Nature is honored.

Below is an excerpt from my conversation with Michael, beginning where we left off in Chapter 14. He had just identified his linchpin as a feeling of togetherness and the knowing that God is with you:

> Alexis: "Tune into that feeling that God is with you. For you personally, not in the ideal world, but for you, Michael, right here—what is the opposite of that feeling that God is with you?"
>
> Michael: "Abandoned."
>
> Alexis: "Again, not in the ideal world, but you, Michael, have you experienced times in your life where you felt abandoned?"
>
> Michael: "Mm-hmm."
>
> Alexis: "If you thought about some of those painful moments in your life, could they be described as times when you felt abandoned?"
>
> Michael: "Yeah."

Alexis: "In those moments, if you deeply, deeply knew that you were loved and God was with you, would it have helped?"

Michael: "100%. Yeah."

Alexis: "Awesome. Let's take a nice deep breath in through the nose out through the mouth. Beautiful."

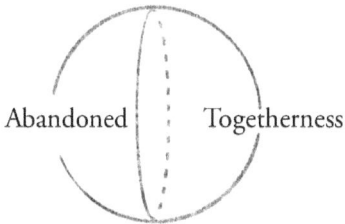

The linchpin of Michael's world is a feeling of togetherness and the knowing that God is with you. Togetherness is his essential Truth.

For Michael, the opposite experience of his truth is the feeling of abandoned. So his soul's "purpose globe" would be togetherness in the empowered Truth hemisphere and abandoned in the disempowered hemisphere.

His purpose is to find deeper and more nuanced ways to embody the feeling of togetherness and knowing that God is with him. This is his soul's focus for his life and the intention behind all of his experiences. That includes the good- and bad-feeling moments and everything in between.

The easiest way for Michael to start consciously living in alignment with his purpose is to:

- Start noticing all the ways he feels abandoned, abandons himself, abandons his faith and knowing, and more.
- Challenge himself to bring his soul's truth into those moments and feelings.

For example, the next time he's stood up by a date and feels like he's never going to find love, he might notice how he's abandoning himself by assuming the other person determines his future and worth as a partner.

Or he might notice that he feels hurt and tenderly attend to his emotions because a snub feels like being abandoned for him.

He might also become curious about how he would experience the situation if he truly knew God was with him. Perhaps he might feel relieved that the person excused themselves from his life because they clearly weren't a good match. He might even have more confidence knowing that God has his back and he's not alone in figuring out every aspect of romance himself.

These are just examples of how Michael might use the empowered and disempowered sides of his soul's globe to live into his purpose more fully. The interplay between the two creates the pathway for his inner growth and expansion. Embracing this concept allows him to work with every experience in life—no matter if it seems "good" or "bad"—to become a living embodiment of his purpose.

Troubleshooting Your Dark Fuel — Finding the Right Fear

I call this step in the process "gut-checking your truth," and we do it for two main reasons:

1) If the fear doesn't feel deeply personal, then it's not the right fear.

    This system rests on the belief that all of life is *for* you. Every single experience is an opportunity to become more fully you. This includes the painful times, too.

    We all have lots of fears. We're afraid of dying, being alone, being hurt, being embarrassed, and so on. What we're looking for in this step is the special flavor of fear that cuts you to your core.

    This is the fear or belief that was imprinted when you were a little kid; maybe you were hiding in your closet while your adults argued, or sitting on the sidelines while the other kids played, or crying as your first relationship ended. The pain of these experiences is the same pain you feel later in life getting overlooked for a promotion, worrying your kids will grow up to hate you, or wondering if you'll ever fulfill your potential and destiny.

The seed of this one terrifying fear sprouts a thousand branches in your life.

2) If the fear doesn't feel deeply personal, then the feeling of your soul's truth may not be quite right.

Because you hone in on this fear by embodying the feeling of your soul's truth, you have to feel clear in your truth first. If you can't feel the fear—or if it doesn't feel relevant to you—then you might not have focused on the best linchpin for your soul's world.

This can happen if the mind sneaks in and starts trying to control the process. Or if the energy of your truth is a little shaky because you're not used to holding that expanded feeling. Or it might happen if you are on your way down a path that feels right, and you're just not quite to the point when you can identify your truth clearly.

This step is another way of "gut-checking" your soul's world and linchpin to make sure that you're on the right track and tapping into what's most real and meaningful for you.

Troubleshooting Your Dark Fuel — You Can't Feel an Answer

For many people, Dark Fuel is the easiest step in the whole process because pain is a familiar experience. That doesn't mean it will feel easy and obvious to you.

The clarity you discover in this step builds on clarity you had previously. If you struggled to identify the linchpin to your soul's world, then it will be difficult to feel into its opposite. Spend more time in your ideal world until you can feel the essential truth at its core.

Similarly, if your linchpin is a bit more conceptual, you may struggle to feel its opposite. I suggest revisiting "Troubleshooting - you've narrowed it down to a concept" in the previous chapter. Remember, it's okay if the words express more of a concept. The important part is that the words capture how you feel when you tune into your soul's truth. Practicing feeling into your soul's ideal world and truth.

If living your purpose was a logic puzzle, then the mind would have figured it out by now. Life is experiential, which means it's happening in the soft aliveness of your human body. Allow yourself the time it takes to get comfortable feeling in your body. It is the fastest path to the inner peace and freedom you want.

Troubleshooting Your Dark Fuel — You're Not Sure You Did it Right

You may be unsure if you did the part about your own life and painful experiences right.

Identifying your deep fear is a special moment in this process. It is when you transition from the infinite possibility of your soul to the very tangible reality of your human life. It can feel like hitting a wall driving sixty miles an hour, even as it offers a new pathway to understanding and forgiving your past.

You know you did it "right" when:

1) You've felt that way before, including during many of the painful moments of your life.

    Using Michael's example, he had a few very painful memories of his dad leaving, being bullied at school, and going through a hard breakup. Tuning into each of these, he realized how the fear of being abandoned made each experience worse. He also felt alone, which is contrary to his deep knowing that God is with him. Feeling alone is a key sign for him that he is feeling abandoned.

2) If you truly, truly believed your soul's truth and lived it with every cell in your body, you would have felt better in those painful moments.

For Michael, if he truly lived his truth of togetherness and knowing God is with him, then these situations would not have been so painful. They may have still hurt because a full range of emotional experiences is normal, but they might not have confirmed his deepest fears that he is destined to be alone and abandoned.

This is important because once that intense fear is activated, it can overpower your ability to soothe yourself in the moment, as well as influence your future choices. So instead of having a good cry, reaching out to a friend, and keeping an open heart during a breakup, because he knows he's deserving of love and will find a good partner, Michael may feel utterly hopeless, isolate himself, and hold back in his next relationship, because he assumes he'll be abandoned again. Ironically, the feeling of being abandoned can cause him to abandon himself and his truth. That's how powerful the Dark Fuel emotion can be.

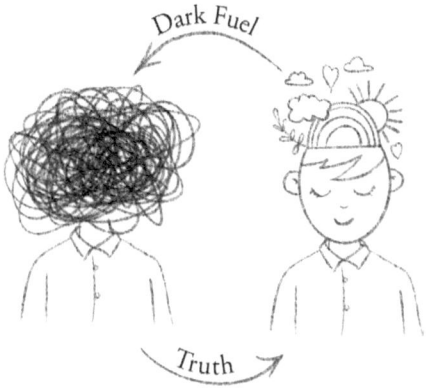

Remember, we're talking about the energy of the soul here. The soul doesn't struggle or suffer in the ways you do as a human. It lives in the ideal world of your truth. Imagine it as if you are carrying around two realities at all times—the tangible, collective consensus reality your mind lives in and the ideal reality your soul inhabits.

The doorway between these realities is the totality of the emotion captured by your Truth, which also includes your Dark Fuel emotion. Like the symbol of the yin and the yang, no emotion is whole without its opposite experience.

When you feel your Truth —> you move into your soul's ideal world.
When you embody your Dark Fuel emotion —> you move into consensus reality.

The goal is not to permanently live in either reality; rather, it's to create a synchronous flow between them so you know how to transform the worst into the best and infuse the best into the worst.

3) If you tried, you could brainstorm at least a few ways your life starts to make sense through the lens of this painful feeling.

Let me explain that more fully in the next section.

All roads lead to living your truth.

Absolution & the Moment I Live For

The beauty of this process is that it offers you the opportunity to understand your past as the perfect series of events for becoming the living embodiment of your soul's wisdom.

In other words, nothing has gone wrong. You're the right person at the right place at the right time.

If Michael hadn't felt abandoned by his father, he might not have focused on building community. If he hadn't felt alone and bullied in school, he might not have become an advocate for artists. If he hadn't felt the heartache of a breakup, he might not have pursued personal development and created a better relationship with himself.

All roads lead to living your truth. That is the power of Dark Fuel Alchemy®.

At every turn, Michael has been invited by his soul to embrace togetherness and his knowing that God is with him. It's like stepping outside to look at the night sky. Sometimes, you have to stare into the void for a long time before you see specks of light.

The Dark Fuel step in the process helps you zoom out on your life and see it from the evolutionary perspective of your soul. All of a sudden, every painful experience you've had may make sense in the context of inviting you to embrace your truth. In this moment, you can instantly drop all the internalized hurt you carry and see yourself as immensely powerful and whole. I've experienced clients sobbing in relief and laughing with the lightness of no longer having to carry the weight of the past. It is a moment of absolution and true freedom—and what's possible for you if you commit to your soul's truth.

You have had a lifetime of big and little hurts. You may have lived through horrific experiences and carry with you the pain of trauma no one should ever have to endure. Yet your soul is unscathed.

Your soul knows that no struggle is in vain and no experience a mistake. It is all an opportunity for you to claim power—the power of your soul's truth and purpose. You can make it all for you. This is how you set yourself free.

Take It Further

My husband is originally from India. When we met, I was already cooking and eating Indian food frequently thanks to my Yogic roots. He gave me a helpful piece of advice to improve my Indian cooking that I still follow today: "Let it sit for a day. The flavors get better when they have time to meld."

The same goes for your Dark Fuel.

Gift yourself some time. Take a hike. Drink lots of water. Take it easy on your insides with healthy foods.

Let your insights integrate.

This process is not rocket science. Hopefully, it's not confusing or even surprising. Yet it is deep.

Many of us have spent a lifetime believing our deepest fear is true. In my case, that I'm not enough and never will be. In Michael's case, that he's abandoned by everyone, including God. Because of that, we've trained ourselves to be hyper-alert to people, events, and even thoughts that make us feel that way. We can sniff out even the smallest hint of this feeling in the most mundane moments.

Just this morning, I tripped into not-enoughness. My husband asked how writing this book was going and what my writing plans were for the day. Instead of hearing a friendly question from my spouse, who was trying to be supportive, I heard, "Nothing you do is ever enough, you're not contributing enough, and you probably won't in the future either, because your book is going to be a failure." Ten minutes and many tears later, I realized that my inner fears distorted his otherwise common and unthreatening question. I could not be present for his conversation because of the power and intensity of my Dark Fuel emotions.

Integration suggestion

Over the next few days, notice how your core fear or belief is showing up for you.

I am willing to bet that it's popping up multiple times each day, whether you realize it or not. It may be the backdrop to your conversations and interactions, like my example above. Or the motivation behind why you go to the gym, wear your hair the way you do, or keep texting that person who is clearly not invested in you.

Just like your truth is infused into everything you do, so is your Dark Fuel. You embody the fullness of them both.

You're becoming an emissary for your truth

It might not be fun to see how much you're thinking, feeling, and acting from fear each day, but you can't make a different choice until you do. Even a soft awareness can begin to reveal a new pathway towards more authentic freedom and joy.

You are not powerless to your fear. Your power comes from transforming it into purpose. You are becoming a better emissary for your soul's truth.

Journaling Prompts

Next are a few questions to support you when you'd like to explore more. There's no rush to dive into these now. You can wait until it feels exciting or at least intriguing. Your soul is guiding you through the exact right experiences you need at the exact right time to embrace the truth of who you are.

Before you begin, ensure you have support, as well as any tools and practices you need to navigate difficult emotions.

When you feel safe and supported, bring to mind a scenario playing out in your life right now:

> How is your fear or belief influencing your thoughts in this situation? Actions? Responses?
> What beliefs is this situation reinforcing?
> How would this situation change if you saw it as part of your soul's journey and as Dark Fuel for you to alchemize into power?
> What truth does your soul know about this situation?
> What are you being invited to claim, realize, choose, or embody through this experience?
> If you fully embodied your soul's truth, would you feel differently about this situation? Think differently? Respond differently?
> What changes do you notice in your body when you feel your Truth?

What reminders can you set for yourself to pause in the moment and get curious if & how your core pain is playing out?
What daily habits or skills would help increase your awareness?
How do you feel about your past knowing that it's all been inviting you to claim your power and purpose more fully?
What would be possible if you allowed it to all be for you?[4]

Practices to Embody Your Soul's Purpose Using Dark Fuel

Here are a few ideas to practice being in your purpose. These build on the exercises in Chapter 14, because your truth and fear are the empowered and disempowered sides of the same coin:

- Daily "feeling-i-zation."

    In the previous chapter, you practiced feeling the emotion or knowing of your soul's Truth daily for a minimum of one full minute.

    As described in Chapter 14, "feeling-i-zation" is a made-up word to describe a body-based version of visualizing. The goal is to calibrate your body and nervous system to your truth.

    Because this practice stirs up all the ways you're currently not embodying your Truth (i.e., your Dark Fuel), you can use it to practice the art of Dark Fuel Alchemy®. For this inquiry, you'll explore looking at a challenging area of your life through the lens of your Truth. Just

---

[4] A loving reminder that allowing all of life to be for you is not that same as you causing every experience. As I shared in Chapter 5, you can take responsibility for making lemonade from the lemons life gives you without having been the one who grew the lemon tree and dropped all the fruit on your doorstep. Working with life is not believing that the lemons are on your doorstep to sour your life, prove that's all your worthy of receiving, or make you squirm in pain when they rub into your open wounds. Instead, it's knowing that you can feel more and more powerful with every lemon you squeeze, as you create a soul-reviving nectar that restores you to your wholeness.

like how tinted glasses change the colors you can see, or how your mood influences how you interpret someone's tone of voice, looking at a challenging aspect of your life from your Truth can radically change your perspective.

A) Start by feeling into your essential Truth. If you need to, revisit your soul's world until you can fully feel your Truth throughout your whole body and energy.

B) Then bring to mind an area of your life that feels a little heavy. Perhaps you're feeling confused, unhappy, or stuck.

C) Give this area a word. For example, "Mom", "work", "illness", or "skating." It can be a specific name or activity that encapsulates the issue for you.

D) Notice any differences in how you feel focusing on your Truth versus this challenging area of your life. You might notice changes in your posture, tension, or mood. You may realize that you're holding your breath versus letting it flow, that your thoughts are racing or more calm, or that you feel more tired or alert.

E) Now return to feeling just your Truth. Make sure you can feel it through your whole body, mind, and energy. If you can't feel it, imagine that you can.

F) Keeping a sense of openness in the body, gently bring to mind the challenging aspect of your life. You might repeat the word silently or just be aware that this area of your life exists. Hold it loosely, like you might hold a coffee mug while talking to a friend. You know that it's there, but it's not your focus.

G) Get curious:

What does your Truth know about this situation?
What wisdom or gifts does it have for you?
How would your perspective or actions change if you embraced this Truth fully?
What might you do differently?

After the practice, jot down what you realized. It can be hard to remember your Truth when you're caught up in fear. Having notes is like leaving breadcrumbs for yourself to follow the trail back home.

If you didn't feel or notice any changes, keep experimenting. This practice is built on being able to access the emotional muscle memory of your soul's world, so the more you practice feeling into your Truth, the easier it becomes.

It also can take time to hold two different energies at once. You may be an expert at getting swept up in the strong emotions and thoughts of your frustrations, yet relatively new at witnessing aspects of your life without immersing yourself in them. Be patient. You are honing new skills, and everyone struggles on the path to mastery.

- Remind yourself of your soul's purpose spectrum A LOT.
  - Change your phone screen to your Truth and Dark Fuel words.

    You can do this by opening the notes on your phone, typing the words, taking a screenshot, and then adding that screenshot to the home screen.

    You can have them both on your screen or experiment with just one. Notice if one helps you more than the other. Perhaps seeing your Dark Fuel word reminds you to zoom out on the daily dramas of life and see them as invitations more than as evidence of your fears. Or perhaps seeing your soul's Truth reminds you to pause and find your way into that feeling, even in the bleakest situations. Maybe you prefer to see them both together as a reminder that your power lies in alchemizing your struggles into truth.

  - Write them on sticky notes and place them on your mirror, refrigerator, or computer screen—wherever you are likely to see them.
  - Find other fun ways to keep top of mind both your truth and the tough feelings that invite you to embody it more.

    This helps remind you that everything in your life is revolving around your soul's truth. Everything is supporting you to embody it more fully.

* Again, I do NOT recommend getting a tattoo of your truth or Dark Fuel until you've worked with the process for a few years, because the word(s) can change as you build your relationship with your soul. *

Mastering your life starts with mastering your inner cues.

- Get clear on your Dark Fuel symptoms.

    Each of us has signs and symptoms that clue us in to when we're feeling disempowered. The faster you recognize these symptoms, the faster you can invite yourself into greater purpose.

    Just like you may know your child's hunger or tiredness cues, these signs are your personal "tell" that you're caught up in your fear instead of using it as Dark Fuel. The symptom may have nothing to do with the area of your life in which you're feeling disempowered; they don't need to be related. They're just showing you that you don't feel resourced and steady in your truth.

    − Make a list of your signs and symptoms. You may want to keep it on your phone so you can refer to and add to it on the go.

        For example, here are some from my personal disempowered playbook:

    1) Criticizing people or decisions, no matter how insignificant and unrelated to my life.

        Decorative shutters are such a waste of money.
        Our alley is the only one with trash in it; why are our neighbors so terrible?
        Who needs a lifted truck with double wheels in a city? The drivers are so selfish to care only about how cool they feel instead of the planet.

    2) Feeling stressed.

> *The house is messy, and it's stressing me out.*
> *I can't talk about that today; I'm already at the end of my rope.*

3) Feeling like you're doing more than others and/or discounting support.

   > *Why am I the only one doing all the cleaning, dishes, laundry, child/pet care, etc?*
   > *I give so much, and it's like no one even cares or supports me.*

4) Feeling tired.

   > *I can't even think; it's like my brain is all fuzzy.*
   > *I just wish I could go back to bed.*

5) Feeling like nothing you do is enough or you are not enough.

   > *I'm never going to get there.*
   > *It's pointless.*
   > *I'm broken beyond repair.*

These are just a few examples of how your thoughts and mood might show you that you're feeling disempowered. You might also have physical clues beyond tiredness like tension, headaches, stomach aches, anxious feelings, neck pain, shallow breathing, and more.

Mastering your life starts with mastering your inner cues.

- Start looking at life's challenges through the lens of Dark Fuel Alchemy®.

  Your soul is continually guiding you to be more fully you. That's the whole process of purpose. Whenever something happens—you get a bad review at work, your partner picks a fight, you feel frustrated with your health—this is in invitation to dive into the depths of that feeling and surface on the other side in Truth.

  The next time you notice your personal symptoms of feeling disempowered, things like feeling confused, down, hopeless, irritated, snippy, righteous, or annoyed, get curious about how these might be doorways into more power.

Here are some example questions you might ask yourself. I use "connection" and "abandoned" as the truth and fear. Feel free to play around with these questions until they spark an awareness in you:

- Where are you feeling abandoned?
- Who is abandoning you or something/one you care about?
- How are you abandoning yourself in this situation? Your values? Your beliefs? Your commitments to yourself? Your dreams?
- If it were, what is this experience trying help you claim, realize, or embody?
- How is this experience showing you where you're looking for evidence of being abandoned? Showing you where you're not believing in and / or embodying connection?
- If you knew 100% that you are connected in this moment, what would change?
- How would it feel in your body to hold that truth of connection in this situation?
- How can you be more connected in this moment?
- What do you need to do or think to feel more connected right now?
- How can you create more connection with yourself / others / Source?
- What thoughts, beliefs, or actions are creating an experience of feeling abandoned? Are you willing to let these go and feel more connected?

This type of self-reflection is what sets you on the trail of mastery and the alchemical path of purpose.

Your purpose is a tuning fork—bringing your life into resonance with your truth.

16

YOUR SOUL PURPOSE STATEMENT

"I can attest to the shift: IT IS LIFE CHANGING!!"

You've named the emotional linchpin of your soul's vision—your Truth. You've identified how it challenges you—your Dark Fuel. You've felt how one opens you, and the other dims you. Now you'll capture your insights in a short statement that can help you continually expand into your purpose.

Your Soul Purpose Statement is like a tuning fork that helps you come into harmony with your essence. It anchors you in your center and reminds you of your deeper purpose, especially when you feel lost or confused.

The Anti-Climax

While this may seem like the culmination of the book, the embodiment practices in the previous chapters are far more impactful for becoming who you are and living your Truth.

Creating your Soul Purpose Statement is like putting a gold star on your chore chart at the end of the week. It's exciting—and it's the daily actions that create the results you desire.

Consider your statement like an armband with your favorite phrase or a locket holding a loved one's memento. It hints at your essence; it doesn't hold the entirety of it. Only you can live your purpose.

The statement gives your mind something to focus on when it feels out of control and unsteady. It offers a centering thread when you crave a clear identity. Still, hold it lightly. You are always evolving, and your statement is a guidepost, not a fixed destination.

What Your Statement Will and Won't Do

Your purpose statement is a grounding force. It helps remind you of your Truth and the pathway to embodying it, especially when you feel caught in drama tornadoes or overwhelmed by coping skills and trauma responses.

Because purpose is something you live and express, not something you achieve, your statement won't tell you:

- What job you should have.
- What to say to people who only see purpose as action.
- What to do, study, or create.

It also won't help you live your purpose unless you actively engage with it. Your statement is an arrow, not the answer. It is an invitation to embody your soul's empowered energy more fully.

As a messenger for your soul, your purpose statement will:

- ✓ Remind you of who you are.
- ✓ Capture the gift you bring to the world just by being you.
- ✓ Point you toward truth when you're feeling lost.
- ✓ Invite you to keep expanding into purpose.

Use your statement as a touchstone. Post it on your fridge, make it your phone wallpaper, embroider it on a pillow, and let it gently call you back to the daily practice of becoming who you truly are.

Your Statement's 3 Parts

Your Soul Purpose Statement includes three parts:

1. Your Truth - the feeling or knowing you are here to embody.
2. Your Dark Fuel - the disempowered beliefs and emotions that make your Truth feel out of reach.
3. Your Invitation - the reminder that you are always on purpose and your Dark Fuel isn't a mistake—it's a doorway back into Truth.

All three parts matter because your purpose is to embody the totality of your soul's essence. In the fog of Dark Fuel emotions, it's easy to forget that you are still "on purpose"—or even that there is no "off purpose." Dark Fuel feelings highlight where you can embody Truth more fully, no matter how hard or uncomfortable it is.

Step three can be as simple as choosing a few of the Dark Fuel signs and symptoms you identified in Chapter 15. These become invitations to feel more empowered in your purpose. They help remind you that you are the key to living your purpose, not your external circumstances.

Here's my soul purpose statement as an example:

> My purpose is to embody enoughness. My Dark Fuel is feeling not enough. Whenever I find myself feeling insecure, second-guessing, trying to prove myself, or judging others, I remember

to embrace my wholeness and stretch into the truth that I am enough.

Habits like insecurity, second-guessing, or judgment are my canary in the coal mine. They let me know it is time to breathe new life into my Truth.

Michael's Example

In Michael's ideal world, the linchpin is the feeling of togetherness and knowing that God is with him. The emotional opposite for him is feeling abandoned.

Using the Soul Purpose Statement framework, Michael's statement is:

> My purpose is to find deeper and more nuanced ways to embody the feeling of togetherness and knowing that God is with me. My Dark Fuel is feeling abandoned. When I notice I feel alone, worried, or unloved, I remember God is with me.

This statement can help Michael catch himself in moments when he feels unloved or alone and reframe them as invitations into deeper connection. It can also help him open his heart more fully and live with greater freedom and trust, knowing that he's never truly alone.

Your Turn

Complete the three lines below using your Truth, Dark Fuel, and moments of invitation:

1. My purpose is to…
2. My Dark Fuel is…
3. When I notice I feel…, it reminds me to…

Take a breath and honor this moment. You've done something extraordinary—you've given voice to your soul and created a simple map, both back to yourself and forward into Truth. This is sacred work.

Don't worry if it doesn't feel 100 percent "right." You're aiming for honesty, not perfection. Choose words that reflect how you feel now and capture the most obvious signs of when you feel disempowered.

Your Soul Purpose Statement is not a finish line. It is a living guide you can return to, reshape, and deepen into as you grow and become more fluent in your soul's energy.

Example Purpose Statements

Here are a few purpose statements from past clients. Each includes the three parts—Truth, Dark Fuel, and Invitation—along with a brief summary of what drew them to this process to help you understand how their statement supports their journey into greater purpose.

You may notice shared themes or even similar words. The same word can carry a vastly different meaning depending on the person and their focus. Creating your statement isn't about finding the perfect words or phrasing; it's about finding language that resonates with you.

Wendy

Wendy was in her early 30s and wondering if she'd ever find a job that felt nourishing instead of draining. A gifted fundraiser, she struggled with over-giving and setting boundaries. After changing jobs to escape an overbearing boss, she found herself even more micro-managed in the next role.

1. My Truth is to embody kindness.
2. The Dark Fuel side of my purpose is selfishness.
3. When I notice I feel selfish or think others are being selfish, it reminds me to offer myself deeper and truer kindness.

> My purpose is to embody kindness. The Dark Fuel side of my purpose is selfishness. As I expand into my purpose, I gift myself truer and deeper kindness. I'm reminded to recenter in kindness when it feels selfish to put myself first, I feel others are being selfish, and/or when I believe I am being selfish.

Her statement captures the linchpin of her soul's vision, its felt opposite, and how she can use experiences of selfishness to more fully claim her purpose and bring her soul's vision to life.

Glen

A serial entrepreneur and successful business owner, Glen was considering his next business move. He was also just beginning to explore the hurt he carried from his childhood and being adopted into a performance-driven home.

1. My Truth is feeling connected.
2. My Dark Fuel is selfishness.
3. My moments of invitation are judging myself, worrying or feeling judged by others, and experiencing selfishness in the world.

> My purpose is to embody the feeling of connected. The Dark Fuel side of my purpose (my core wound and biggest fear) is selfishness. Every time I notice I'm judging myself for being selfish, worrying, or feeling judged by others, or experiencing selfishness in the world, it is an invitation for me to reconnect with myself, my truth, and my heart, including the truth that we are all connected.

As his facilitator, I didn't love the "core wound" wording (see Chapter 8). Yet, this was important language for Glen at the time.

Dark Fuel Alchemy® is not about being spiritually realized or perfect. It's about being honest about what's true for you in the moment, accepting everything you think and feel, and inviting yourself one tiny hair closer to Truth. Everything is available to you in that process, including words, tools, and frameworks that help you gain insight and wisdom in one moment, even if they aren't helpful in the next.

Miriam

When I met Miriam, she was feeling frustrated that her creative and business projects weren't taking root. She was a dynamic speaker, engaging leader, and respected activist. She had the credentials and talent, yet still felt stuck.

1. My Truth is to embody wholeness.
2. My Dark Fuel is feeling unsettled.
3. My moments of invitation are avoiding feeling whole by not accepting, listening to, or trusting myself.

> My purpose is to embody wholeness. The Dark Fuel side of my purpose is feeling unsettled. The more I become aware of the subtle ways I avoid feeling whole, the more I can find deeper and more nuanced ways to accept, listen to, and trust myself, as well as serve as a model of how to connect with yourself for others.

Miriam now helps others feel more playful, confident, and at home in themselves. Her soul purpose statement captures how she embodies this herself and expands into greater Truth when she forgets.

Harris

A retired executive, Harris was unsure how to maintain a sense of self and purpose without his former job title. He wanted to start his own consulting business and hone in on his unique contribution.

1. My Truth is to embody connection.
2. My Dark Fuel is feeling disconnected.
3. My moments of invitation are feeling alone and unable to contribute.

My purpose is to embody connection—to myself, others, and the greater mission. The Dark Fuel side of my purpose is feeling disconnected, alone, and unable to contribute, which point me towards the deeper and more nuanced aspects of feeling connected.

Retirement felt disorienting and scary for Harris. It also invited him to own his value and recognize his inherent contribution beyond his job. This allowed him to explore his deeper beliefs that everyone matters in our broader connected whole.

Troubleshooting Your Statement

You may struggle to find words for your invitation statement. This can happen if your Truth or Dark Fuel are more conceptual. The following examples are from two clients whose linchpins and/or Dark Fuel were more of a knowing than a feeling.

Life is unfolding in this moment in your body. Your purpose is playing out in your sensations and way of being. The more you practice connecting with your soul's world, the easier it will be to feel your Truth in your daily life.

Georgia

Georgia was a creative entrepreneur who wanted to define her purpose in a way that aligned with her business goals. She was just beginning to develop more fluency with her emotions.

1. My Truth is that it's going to be okay.
2. My Dark Fuel is feeling isolated.
3. My moments of invitation are feeling isolated, disempowered, like life is working against me, and like I'll be shunned if I truly shine.

My purpose is to embody the faith that "it's going to be okay." The Dark Fuel side of my purpose is feeling isolated. When I feel isolated and alone, it reminds me to recenter in my trust that I will be okay. When I am rooted in this faith, I know I have the ability to create my reality the way that I desire.

If the linchpin of your soul's vision is a phrase or knowing like "it's going to be okay," keep practicing feeling into your Truth until you can sense an emotion connected to your knowing. For Georgia, the phrase "it's going to be okay" became a felt experience of faith and trust, which helped her know what to do when the familiar feeling of isolation arose.

Haley

A former attorney turned stay-at-home mom, Haley was struggling with how to channel her energy now that she wasn't working. She assumed that starting a business was the next step. She felt called to do something new and meaningful—but didn't know what that was.

1. My Truth is the joy of knowing life is a miracle.
2. My Dark Fuel is believing life is random.
3. My moments of invitation are feeling unmoored, unsafe, and out of control.

> My Truth is the joy of knowing life is a miracle. The Dark Fuel side of my purpose is believing life is random. Every time I notice I feel unmoored, unsafe, and out of control, it reminds me to recenter in the miracle of life and open to life with more joy and trust. I am living in the miracle.

Since "random" is not an emotion, and neither is "knowing life is a miracle," Haley had to spend time in her soul's ideal world to discover that joy is the emotion attached to the concept of knowing life is a miracle. She also realized several feelings arise when she believes life is random. This helped her identify how her Dark Fuel feelings showed up and use them to reconnect with the joy that stems from believing life is a miracle.

Your purpose isn't something you chase. It's something you remember. Something you choose to return to—again and again—with love, openness, and, hopefully, compassion for yourself.

Let your Soul Purpose Statement be a guidepost when you feel lost, a mirror when you forget who you are, and a reminder that even your most painful feelings are part of the path home.

Now that you've named it, you can consciously live it—gently and earnestly.

PART IV

BECOMING YOU

---

*The journey of becoming you is not about the destination
but surrendering to the fullness of your life already unfolding in
every step.*

In Part IV, you'll gain clarity on the next steps for living in authentic presence, plus what lies beyond this process in your journey of liberation and awakening.

*Your truth is not a destination;
it is a way you move through life.*

17

LIVING YOUR TRUTH

---

*"I feel so much lighter lately.
It is like a ton of blankets were released at one time."*

Cost Of Admission into Purpose

Your purpose is you. You're already living it right now. Yet, you may not feel like you're basking in your soul's bliss or however you hope purpose will help you feel. That's not a reflection of truth but of how engaged you are in living it.

Purpose is not an end state. Like all of life, it is ever-changing and expanding. So while you may want a definitive answer that grants you eternal happiness, purpose is more like a well-worn trail map guiding you home to deeper truths within. You are walking the path of purpose as you open to greater purpose.

As you continue in your journey, you're invited to lighten your inner load by releasing what's not essential:

- Your past, including and especially the disempowered meaning you've made of past experiences.
- Your beliefs, particularly those about who you are, who you have to be, and who you can be.
- Your habits, especially the coping skills and trauma responses that arise from your Dark Fuel fear, hurt, and worry.
- Your identities, including the ones that make you feel good and important.
- Your roles and characters, particularly if they feel like burdens or requirements.

There is a you beyond who you think you are and have to be. This is the truth you're seeking. This is the you who lives at peace and on purpose.

Consciousness Shifter — Do You Have to Change Everything?

The invitation into truth isn't about losing yourself. It's about finding your real self beyond the pretenses you've relied on to move through the world.

For example, you are not a "hard-charging boss." You choose to show up with a certain demeanor in certain contexts. Perhaps because you want to, or think you have to in order to succeed in that role, or believe it's the most beneficial approach for the moment. The reason is less important than realizing you're making a choice.

Similarly, you are not the "funny one." Humor is one way you express your truth. Perhaps as a coping skill and trauma response, perhaps because you love bringing joy to others. You aren't bound to sacrifice your wholeness in service to being funny. It's a choice.

Living into your purpose doesn't require you to limit your choices for how you express yourself. It gives you more options. Instead of feeling like you have to be a certain way, you can choose what feels best and most fitting for the moment. Sometimes that may be what's best for you. Sometimes, that may be what's in the best service to another person or situation.

Purpose gifts you a pathway to embrace your authentic presence, beyond the expectations, judgments, or assumptions that have shaped how you've shown up before. Choice is power. Recognizing your power leads you to liberation.

Doors won't open until you're the version of yourself capable of passing through them.

But You Still Have to Change, Right?

Life is full of paradoxes. This is one of them: you are already whole, and yet you can become more. You are already perfect as you are, and yet you can feel more joy and ease.

Because life is you and you are life, you are in an intricate dance with yourself. You are always leading and following, and more importantly, right in time. The question isn't whether opportunities are available, but perhaps, are you the person who can dance with those opportunities right now?

In other words, the doors you're seeking won't open until you're the version of yourself that's capable of passing through them. You don't have to spend time wishing for possibilities. Instead, spend time becoming the version of you who lives in possibility.

Is This Manifestation?

You may have heard similar language about manifestation. "Fake it 'til you make it" and other axioms aimed at helping you create the life you desire. At their essence, these point to the same universal truth: who you are shapes what you experience.

The key is to focus on letting go of false layers of identity without adding more. You're not faking truth. You don't have to "put on" calmness. You may need to practice new ways of being because calm or confident are new experiences for you. But you're not adding more veneers to your truth.

Character work is powerful. What I mean by that is playing with different ways of thinking, being, and behaving is an incredible opportunity to realize that what you do is not who you are. You can take on and off the masks of roles you play. You can step into and out of a character depending on the needs of the moment. Yet, you exist beyond any role or character.

There are inherent aspects of you that grow stronger and more pure in their essence as you pull back the blankets covering your light. These truths are captured in your soul's ideal world and highlighted through your Dark Fuel. As you identify more with your light instead of the blankets of social conditioning and characters you've assumed were your personality, you have the freedom to be you and become a clearer reflection of your truth.

Your Ego Doesn't Need Transcending

You may believe that you have to transcend your ego to live into your spiritual potential. This language is frequently misinterpreted to mean disavowing "lesser" human qualities in favor of more refined ones. For example, transcending greed and jealousy in favor of generosity and compassion.

Spiritual teachers have used this language for centuries to guide seekers towards a deeper understanding of truth and the pathway to a more liberated life. All language falls short of capturing ineffable truths of the soul because the soul is experiential and language is descriptive. In this case, the phrasing may still be the best fit, but the interpretation of the meaning has changed.

I translate ego like your personality. In practice, it's your individual outlook and perspective. It's what allows you to label things as your opinion, your experience, and your feelings. Ego is your understanding of your existence as a unique emanation of life. There's no way around it, and you can't get rid of it. Even your understanding of consciousness, Oneness, and the soul is through the lens of this singular human experience. Your ego is as much a part of being human as breathing, eating, and excreting.

> *Truth requires you to relinquish all of who you think you are to cultivate a relationship of authentic presence.*

If we follow the dictionary definition of transcending, it means going beyond the limits of ego or surpassing it. In that sense, yes, to live into your purpose, you are invited to stretch past who you think you are. Truth requires you to relinquish all of who you think you are to cultivate a relationship of authentic presence. This is how you wield the full power of being you in the moment.

When we debase our understanding of ego to something bad to be matured beyond, we bifurcate our experience into what's holy and what's human. We default to duality instead of expanding ourselves into a broader understanding of wholeness.

Transcending the ego isn't about going beyond any part of your humanness. It's about shifting your perspective to the stage instead of the actors. It's about changing your vantage point to witnessing your daily life from above the clouds instead of staying caught below in the whims of the weather. In short, it's about growing bigger than the problems you're currently facing rather than trying to never have those problems again. Awakening invites you to expand your awareness and ability to hold more of life's paradoxes, not limit yourself to the meaning you've previously assigned to your experiences.

Becoming a Vessel for Your Soul

The path of purpose is a path of becoming. This isn't because the soul needs to be refined; your truth is inherent. The journey is for your tender animal body to soothe itself into trusting your Truth more than fear.

Your mind, body, and emotions are the containers that carry you towards—or delay—your liberation. They deserve your loving attention if you want to live more fully into your purpose.

Dark Fuel Alchemy® offers you a roadmap for approaching all three. As you challenge yourself to work *with* life, the mind is invited to confront disempowering thoughts and beliefs. Beliefs that keep you trapped feeling victimized, powerless, and separate from both others and the goodness you desire. These beliefs aren't bad. They serve to point you towards Truth and are important in the journey to live into your purpose.

As you embody the empowering sensations of your soul's world, you invite the intricate wiring of your mind, body, and emotions to establish a new baseline. Instead of being rooted in fear, worry, and insecurity, your soul beckons you to build a new foundation in faith, trust, and love. Your system reflects how you embody beliefs at any moment in time. It shows you how you've turned assumed meaning about experiences in your past into your ongoing reality. Dark Fuel Alchemy® shakes you and your assumptions to the core. It shines a spotlight on the ways you both impact and respond to the world around you and challenges you to question your role in your reality.

As you strengthen your capacity to embody your soul's Truth, you gradually heal yourself into wholeness. You no longer need your old coping skills and trauma responses to navigate the world, and instead develop new skills grounded in authentic presence. The stronger and more steady you become in yourself, the more capable you are of living your soul's Truth. The spiral of expansion continues.

Joy is the third muscle you build and strengthen on the path of becoming and living into your purpose. Like truth, joy is your inherent nature. It's not something you need to strive for or add extra special events to your day to feel. Instead, it's experienced by peeling away the fears and habits of self-protection that surround and dim your joy. Your capacity for joy increases as you show up for your emotions and cultivate inner safety.

In turn, joy triggers an overflow of emotions you may associate with purpose, including gratitude, compassion, and devotion. Joy allows you to shift out of self-preservation and into self-assured service. It is the cup from which your gifts runneth over and pour into others.

Armed with the knowledge of your soul's ideal world and purpose (both Truth and Dark Fuel), your daily focus to live into your purpose is to:

A) Work with life.
B) Bring healing and safety to your body, mind, and emotions.
C) Expand in joy.

These are the developmental tasks of becoming more fully you, responsive to the needs of the moment (aka, in service), and present.

Chapter 17 Summary

- Purpose is like a trail map guiding you towards deeper truth within.
- To live into your purpose, you're invited to release old identities, beliefs, and habits rooted in fear and embrace the authentic you.
- When you are present in the moment, you are freer to act in alignment with your soul and in the highest service to all.
- Life is paradoxical: You are already whole and always expanding into becoming more.
- The doors you're seeking open when you're the version of yourself capable of passing through them.
- What you do is not who you are. Your actions are an expression of your truth.
- Exploring characters and identities can help you discover an inherent you beyond the roles you play.
- You are like a radiant light dimmed by blankets of expectations and social conditioning.
- Joy is an inherent part of your being. Gratitude, compassion, and service flow effortlessly when you're present in your Truth.
- Ego is a part of being human. You can stretch into new perspectives of yourself without shaming or disowning your human experience.
- Your body, mind, and emotions are the vehicles carrying you towards liberation. Dark Fuel Alchemy® gives you a roadmap to travel with all three, so that you can build trust in your truth, heal past fears, and replace survival mechanisms with authentic presence and safety.

Everything is of you and for you on your one-person journey of spiritual liberation.

18

TRUSTING YOUR INNER IMPULSE

*"I exploded out of the closet as my authentic self.
My soul mate showed up; my inner wisdom was right. I feel like
the pieces clicked in. I can trust myself. I can be fully here on the
planet. It's like a rebirth. I'm coming back into the world.
There is so much love everywhere I go."*

Yielding in the Dance of Life

When you flow with life, you move to an inner current. Like water being beckoned by gravity, your presence allows you to respond to the subtle suggestions of life. The more at home you are in yourself and your Truth, the easier it is to yield to the moment.

Life is already whispering to you. You have inner impulses every day that guide you to snooze just a bit longer, take a different route home, or crack a joke at just the right time. You may have also noticed signals that something feels off or wrong with your health, work, relationships, lifestyle, or other area of your life. Your deeper knowing is guiding you using the tools it has—emotion, intuition, pain, pleasure, and all the variations therein.

As you learn to trust these signals, your sensitivity to them heightens. You may no longer need highly charged experiences or life-altering catastrophes to be reminded to align more fully with your Truth. Instead, you may begin to meld with the moment in an intimate dance, effortlessly responding to life's smallest cues.

Living your purpose is less about what you do and more about how you navigate the experience of living and being you. When you know how to decipher your inner signals, then your mind, body, and emotions become a tight-knit group of friends, helping you become your most authentic self.

Tripping Yourself Up Externalizing... Again!

Even the terms Life or mind, body, and emotions make it seem like something is happening outside of you. Language brings us into a duality that doesn't exist in experience. Notice if the way you think about your struggles and solutions awakens old coping skills and trauma responses that make you feel like you have to act right or be perfect to get the outcomes you desire.

You may believe or have expressed phrases like "Source has my best interest at heart." This is still externalizing. Not to a person or circumstance, but rather to Life, the Universe, or God. Depending on your proclivity, it can set you up for feeling championed or victimized, uplifted or belittled, as well as all the meanings you assign to those feelings. Notice how and when language circles you back into habits of feeling secondary, less powerful, or infantilized.

Cultivating a relationship with life is not about externally finding solutions to your problems, but rather working with the events in your life to recognize when you're not honoring your soul. Everything is of you and for you on your one-person journey of spiritual liberation.

Signs You're in Your Dark Fuel Hemisphere

There are as many ways to find yourself on your inner map as there are people and situations in the world. While I can share my experience, it's your relationship with your own experience that matters most.

Below are a few signs and signals I've noticed in myself and others that indicate you're on the disempowered side of your purpose. This list is not exhaustive. Hopefully, it sparks your curiosity about the ways your purpose is inviting you into greater Truth.

- Feeling stressed.
- Racing thoughts and overthinking.
- Repeating the same thoughts and scenarios over and over in your mind.
- Having unhelpful and unloving thoughts.
- Holding your breath.
- Breathing quickly or shallowly.
- Sweating.
- Feeling exhausted.
- Wanting to cry.
- Feeling angry, emotional, hopeless, or enraged.
- Feeling numb.
- Spinning thoughts and inner stories about what someone else did or should have done.
- Changes to your voice, often becoming higher because of increased throat tension.
- Clenching your jaw, belly, or pelvic floor muscles.
- Tensing your shoulders.
- Feeling achy and sore.
- Looking for excuses, reasons, or ways out of situations, like hoping friends will cancel plans.
- Feeling overwhelmed or at the end of your rope.
- Being indecisive or feeling stuck without a solution.
- People-pleasing.

- Being overly agreeable.
- Not honoring your boundaries.
- Disconnecting from your body or feeling spacey.
- Being hyper-attuned to your environment, including other people's emotions and body language.
- Feeling lost or like you don't know who you are.
- Prioritizing others' needs over your own.
- Biting your tongue or not expressing feelings, even when it matters to you.

These symptoms aren't a life sentence. They are signposts pointing you directly toward your higher Truth.[5] Your role is to recognize them, feel the fear or hurt at their core, and then practice embodying your empowering truth to expand in your purpose.

This is how your suffering can become salvation, and how your hurt can become Dark Fuel.

Signs You're in Your Truth Hemisphere

Unlike the disempowering sensations of your Dark Fuel hemisphere, you may not have as much experience recognizing or embodying your Truth feelings. Because of that, the signs below may feel out of reach or aspirational.

---

5   This list may look like a description of how you might feel or act if your nervous system is dysregulated. There are many overlaps between feeling dysregulated and being in the disempowered hemisphere of your purpose. I draw a distinction between them, because Dark Fuel is inherent to life regardless of your nervous system state. You can cultivate a regulated nervous system and still feel sad, frustrated, alienated, angry, and the like, without being dysregulated. These emotions invite you into greater Truth and purpose without ever having to rock the boat of your nervous system's regulation. This is how you attune to more subtle energies and work with every aspect of your life, even as you feel more grounded, steady, and joyful.

Be mindful as you review the following list and notice if any shame-based thoughts arise. Thoughts like you're not healed, perfect, or good enough for these feelings. These feelings are also signs from the soul, pointing you to your current location on your inner purpose map so that you can find your way to more empowered feelings instead.

- Feeling calm.
- Feeling soft in your body.
- Having tender or nurturing thoughts towards yourself and others.
- Seeing old patterns from a new perspective, such as not wanting to push yourself to complete your to-do list when you're tired.
- Slowing down your movements, thoughts, and responses.
- Sensing more vibrance and beauty in your surroundings because your senses are more receptive.
- Desiring to enjoy the moment and sometimes literally stopping to smell the roses.
- Laughing and smiling more.
- Taking things less personally.
- Staying focused on what matters or seeing drama tornadoes without getting involved.
- Feeling more patient with how events and situations unfold. Not needing to rush or control the outcome to feel safe.
- Waiting to act until it feels right or easy. This may feel like being in the flow, guided, or following the path of least resistance.
- Overflowing with generosity while also nourishing and honoring yourself, aka giving without depleting yourself.
- Allowing others to be as they are without making their choices mean anything about you.
- Sleeping better.
- Tending to your feelings and well-being first before reacting to provocations.
- Prioritizing others and their needs and desires without diminishing yourself.
- Feeling lighthearted and playful.

- Gravitating away from things that don't feel good without a justification or story about why.
- Noticing simpler and possibly fewer thoughts.
- Having more uplifting thoughts.
- Making more nourishing choices in relationships, health, work, your schedule, exercise, etc.
- Perceiving more choices and options versus feeling stuck or victimized.
- Witnessing the ways you play into old dynamics and feeling a lack of desire to put additional energy into them.
- Feeling more clear about what is loving and healthy in the moment.

These are just some of the changes I've experienced and witnessed in others. These feelings support and feed into each other, like a snowball gaining in size as it rolls down a hill. The more you open to your Truth, the better you feel. The better you feel, the easier it is to open to more Truth.

The earliest shifts may be the most obvious and specific to you. For example, I started having a spontaneous response of "ouch!" when my mind or someone else would say harsh or critical words to me. I felt an immense desire to care for my hurt and be present with how I felt in the moment. That was a noticeable change for me. Before, I would feel almost frozen as I tried to figure out if the comment was accurate, and then spiral into self-pity about why people treated me poorly or how I'm doomed to be disrespected and belittled.

The signs may be tiny, but in your journey of awakening, each step is massive.

What If Truth Feels Confusing?

Truth can be disorienting. Often, it can feel like nothing, especially if you're used to feeling a lot of emotions or physical sensations.

For example, I typically experience a lot of physical pain. Jaw pain, teeth clenching, belly clenching, tongue strain, neck pain, hip and knee pain, not to mention the ache of my muscles and connective tissues… I've been given medical explanations, and I also choose to play with these sensations in my spiritual practice. As I guide myself into finer inner alignment, sometimes the pain disappears completely. That feels miraculous and wonderful and also really scary.

In my self-inquiry, I've realized that my understanding of what it means to be "me" includes continual physical feedback, particularly unpleasant sensory feedback. So when those sensations disappear, I feel ungrounded, confused, and like "I" don't exist anymore. I feel like a floating ball of awareness peering out of two eyes connected to a weightless body, and it's disorienting, to say the least. That doesn't mean it's bad or unwelcome; it's just different, and my mind responds to the difference with confusion and fear.

How will I know if I'm tired?
What if I push too hard because I can't feel anything and then get hurt?
What if I exhaust myself?

My inner dynamic was designed to limit and protect myself out of fear that I might feel more pain or tiredness. Embracing a new way of being challenges me at the deepest levels to redefine what I think it means to be me. It invites me to unhook from identities I'm holding, even if those identities are objectively limiting and don't seem like ones I'd want to hold.

Liberation is an unknown. It sounds alluring, yet it can spark deep fear and confusion. Dark Fuel Alchemy® helps you navigate a new understanding of yourself with greater ease.

Pulling Out the Rug from Under You

Just because something is familiar doesn't mean that it's true. The more you practice embodying how your soul's ideal world feels, the easier it will be to stay in those feelings longer.

Imagine you're standing on a well-worn rug. This rug represents who you've been, who you think you are, how you interact in your relationships, and so on. Next to you is a beautiful, brand-new rug. Most self-development advice tells you to focus on the rug under you. Examine it for "toxic" people, declutter it, or feel more grateful that you have a rug to stand on, period. It doesn't matter how much you pull on, examine, or explore the well-worn rug beneath you—if you want to move over to the new rug, you have to stop standing on the old one.

The Dark Fuel Alchemy® process helps you place one foot on the new rug and slowly build your strength to shift your body weight onto it fully. Eventually, the old rug will fall away, and you won't even have to think about it. This is you getting bigger than your struggles. It's becoming the version of you who has the capacity to live into your purpose more fully.

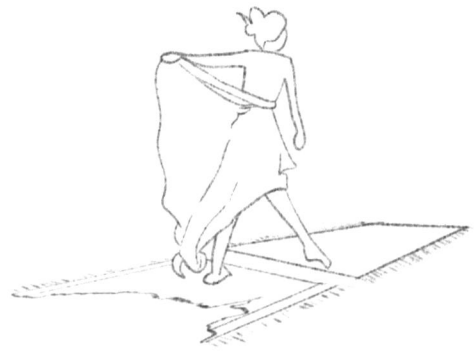

Traversing the Neutral Zone

When you're in the process of shifting to your new rug, you may go through a period in which you have one foot on each rug but don't feel firmly rooted on either. In that in-between space, you may not be sure how to feel or respond. You no longer automatically default to your old ways, yet you're not sure what new options there are.

I call this the *neutral zone*.

The neutral zone can be very disorienting, mostly because it feels so empty and open. It's as if your mind goes to search for feelings or thoughts, and it can't find the door into your old habits—and the room with your new responses is empty. You may wonder if this is enlightenment or freak out that nothing feels the same, or both.

Many clients share their worries that—all of a sudden—they don't feel love or care in the same way. They feel disconnected and passionless, as if they can't be bothered to engage in their life with the same intensity. When our old ways of feeling are intertwined with coping skills and trauma responses, then emotions without baggage can feel like… well, nothing.

On the other side of the neutral zone, I've found that emotions return with a new sense of clarity and purity. When you're firmly on the new rug, you have a larger capacity to feel safe in intense sensation. You can embody pure emotion without attaching needs, worries, or demands to it or feeling compelled to fix it. It's like watching a storm pass by from the comfort of your porch and enjoying the experience instead of panicking about whether you'll survive the squall.

On the new rug, you breathe, feel fully, and let the experience be what it is.

Consciousness Shifter — Letting Go of Control

Control comes from trying to change the rug you're standing on instead of changing where you're standing. It's okay to need strategies to feel like you'll be safe, loved, and happy in the world. All of us rely on some habits or beliefs to shape our choices in life.

Asking yourself to release the grip of control is dangerous when you don't yet have the tools to feel safe being more open. It's asking you to pull the rug out from under yourself without giving you anything else to stand on. It's shame masquerading as self-improvement while keeping you stuck feeling disempowered. No wonder it feels so difficult.

When you're in your Dark Fuel hemisphere and feeling all the painful emotions, thoughts, and sensations, it makes sense to search for active ways out. You want to feel better, safer, and more confident, clear, and happy. Humans love taking action, so you may dive into organizing your house, looking for a new job, changing your diet, signing up for dating apps—anything to take charge and change the situation.

But you can't control, manage, or do your way out of what's meant to be Dark Fuel.

The action in your Dark Fuel hemisphere is to feel. You challenge yourself to bring in your empowered Truth feeling or knowing and apply it like a healing balm to where you're hurting. You find your way into your embodied Truth, no matter how hard or uncomfortable it is. This is how you continually expand into your purpose.

Your power lies in choosing to shift your embodied state of being towards greater Truth. It's not about letting go of control, per se. It's letting go of pretending that you can fix the circumstances or manipulate the outcome or find the safety, happiness, and peace you want outside of yourself. Instead, you're "controlling," aka claiming, the one thing you have sway over—how you feel and who you're being.

From your soul's perspective, there is no control to exert or release. You're in harmony with life, so there's nothing to resist or fear. When you're more grounded on your new rug and feel empowered in your purpose, you stop caring as much about having control. It becomes more interesting to relinquish false identities and discover who you are on the other side of the parts of you that used to grip in fear. Letting go becomes a game because you have a new sense of yourself beyond who you thought you had to be and the roles you had to play before. It starts to feel better and better to strip back the habits, beliefs, and expectations keeping you from living in ease.

Dark Fuel Alchemy® helps you stay focused on the bigger journey of your soul's purpose. The invitation is to notice your Dark Fuel signs and signals (your old rug), bring in your core Truth feeling or knowing (your new rug), and practice embodying your Truth longer and longer (building the capacity to stay on your new rug). Everything else is most likely a drama tornado disguising itself as a new and urgent way to fix or heal yourself.

Practicing Surrender

I used to teach in-person Yoga and meditation classes. Teaching was hard and rewarding, and also deep practice for living into my soul's Truth. Every class, I would challenge myself to say whatever came to my mind, even if I didn't understand why it needed to be said or think that it was relevant.

During one particular class, I felt inspired to share about forgiving your mind for the brutal way we punish ourselves and our bodies for not living up to our own ideas of perfection. At least five students started quietly crying as they pressed their hands to their hearts or bellies. After class, my Mom, who had participated, asked why I had decided to share those words since they seemed unrelated to the rest of the class. I told her about my promise to myself to speak what came to me and how it had impacted the other students.

Class became my place to practice stretching beyond the boundaries of how I thought I should act, speak, and behave. It was a space to begin trusting myself and my inner impulses. I learned to tune into the subtle tension in my body when I was holding back and also the relaxed calm I felt when I followed my inner guidance.

I highly recommend finding safe spaces to experiment and practice new ways of being. This is one of the reasons I offer group programs and try to cultivate community through my work. It gives like-minded people a place to be seen and celebrated as they open to their Truth. Whether you practice in an online forum, through volunteer efforts, at your job, or with a supportive community, intentionally choose an area of your life to practice trusting your inner impulses.

Freeing Yourself Up for Your Future

The easy part is having dreams and desires about who and how you could be. The hard part is letting go of past dreams to make room for who you're becoming in the future. The soul is calling you to relinquish anything you no longer need to live into your truth and purpose—including who you thought your purpose was calling you to be.

Remember Angela, the aspiring dancer?

Angela didn't want to be a Broadway star, so she tripped herself up at every turn, including turning to alcoholism and alienating herself from family and friends. Now that she's clean and reconnected to her community, she can see how denying her desires led her to "fail" at what she thought she wanted.

This is an important distinction: she didn't fail because she couldn't succeed; she "failed" because she didn't want it.

I've been through the same realization myself, wondering why I didn't make that final promotion in the government. I told myself it was because I wasn't clever or relevant enough. In truth, I didn't go further because it's not my path. Full stop. I'm not meant to be writing policy papers; I'm meant to be writing this right here, right now, for you.

If you're trapped in a quiet lie, telling yourself that you want something you never really wanted, this is your invitation to let go of the idea and what you think people expect of you. Let the dream die. You have to clear out your old dream closet to make space for new, better-fitting dreams. As you do, you build more trust with yourself, which you need for the leaps of faith your soul requires.

What If You Don't Know What Your Dream Is?

In many ways, your dream is you. It's who and what you are meant to be—and you can never be separated from that. Your dream is as much who you are as the air you breathe and the blood you circulate.

As you grow into your purpose, your purpose guides you into deeper becoming through your experiences. Your dreams unfold as you become the person who lives them. Your path feels fated in a way because the only option is for you to expand and heed the signals of your soul. The trail of your expansion leads in a certain direction, and you either find the courage to follow it or the resolve to stay stuck. Both take strength.

The more I surrender to my purpose, the less choice I feel, although I feel more powerful in that choice. It's clear to me that, in the past, I have entertained different options as a way to avoid being present and doing the inner work of living into my purpose. In other words, I used possible career paths to stay disempowered instead of recognizing the confusion, fear, and doubt as Dark Fuel pointing me towards Truth.

I tormented myself for years debating if I should pursue comedy, writing, coaching, running a Yoga studio, becoming a minister, or getting a "real" job. It meant that I tentatively tried all of it without committing myself fully to any of it. I could envision a future in all of them, yet I didn't want to limit myself by choosing just one. Now I realize the questioning was a drama tornado itself.

The soul doesn't ask you to choose a job title or contain yourself to just one expression in the world. Only the mind does that. Wondering, worrying, and feeling like I had to decide were all signs of being in the disempowered hemisphere of my purpose—for me, not feeling enough. Instead of seeing them as the drama tornadoes they were, I bought into the confusion wholeheartedly. I believed I was uniquely struggling to find my path. As soon as I recognized the habit, I embraced the fears, and they propelled me straight into more authentic Truth and purpose.

Your truth sets you free to get out of your head and just be.

Chapter 18 Summary

- Your body, mind, and emotions are giving you continual feedback about where you are on your inner purpose "map." They are a tight-knit group of friends helping you become your most authentic self.
- The more sensitive you are to your inner impulses, the more quickly and easily you may respond to the soul's cues.
- Even using words like soul, mind, body, Source, or God may bring you into dualistic thinking.
- Understanding your Dark Fuel signs and symptoms can help you use them as doorways into greater purpose.
- Your current sense of self may include Dark Fuel symptoms, which can make it harder to believe those symptoms are arrows pointing you towards Truth and not truth themselves.
- Each step you take in the direction of Truth is a massive leap in your purpose.
- The "Neutral Zone" is a transitional space in which you've released old habits but not yet fully embodied new ones.
- The more you practice embodying the feelings of your soul's world, the easier it will be to stay in those feelings longer.
- You have to stop standing on the rug of old identities to shift into new possibilities.
- It can be helpful to find safe spaces to practice expressing yourself to build trust with yourself and your soul.
- You may need to let old dreams go to make space for what's true and alive for you now.
- In the journey of your soul's purpose, the invitation is to notice your Dark Fuel signs and signals (your old rug), bring in your core Truth feeling or knowing (your new rug), and practice embodying your Truth longer and longer (building the capacity to stay on your new rug).

*Purpose brings you home to yourself so that
you can share yourself with the world.*

19

A CALL TO POWER

"I would not be where I am today and as TRULY happy and at peace with myself and my past life experiences… and excited about my future if I hadn't done this."

Expanding Beyond You

The path of living your purpose is about building a stronger sense of self so that you can use all of your gifts in service beyond yourself. In other words, the process gives you a deep sense of self so that you can finally get over yourself. Not because you're bad or wrong or need to transcend yourself, but rather because we're all One, and we're here to show up for each other. It's all about you and not really about you at all.

When you're disconnected from your Truth, you end up focusing on yourself. You spend your energy trying to fix, heal, or solve the frustrations of feeling misaligned and off track. You don't show up and contribute fully because you're still questioning how to contribute. You rob the world of your radiance and gifts because you're too busy sorting out your own life.

Purpose brings you home to yourself so that you can share yourself with the world. Your contribution is inherent to your existence. The more you center in your beingness, the more your actions flow in the current of your purpose.

A Collective Calling

You are an invaluable piece of a larger puzzle. The collective is not whole without you, and you are also not whole without it. Your soul is calling you forward as it heeds a bigger call; while you can make out the sound of a violin playing, your soul is hearing a whole symphony.

You cannot contribute to the song without first being able to play your instrument and part.

It's easy to think that pursuing purpose is selfish. It's easy to fall into shaming and blaming yourself for dedicating your life to your own living. This is a tried-and-true tactic to stay small and suffering. Yet, there is no other option than expanding into your fullness if you wish for a truly healthy society. You cannot contribute to the song without first being able to play your instrument and part.

Your power rests in you, and yet is not for you. You are the most extraordinary gift you could offer the world, and it is your duty to do so free of expectations or judgments. Dark Fuel Alchemy® is not a path of navel-gazing for the goal of self-improvement. It is a journey of embodying your power for the goal of communal liberation.

Your freedom frees us all.

Mindful Awakening

Any tool is a doorway to liberation if you engage with it intentionally. Mindfulness is perhaps the most helpful tool to begin working with your Dark Fuel. It helps you remember to view your experiences through the lens of Dark Fuel Alchemy® rather than getting caught up in the convincing winds of drama tornadoes.

You transform through the tension between the duality of your empowered and disempowered "purpose hemispheres," not from settling into one or the other extremes. This allows you to feel more balanced and whole and live with more ease and clarity. You work with the truth of every moment to expand into your own Truth. Mindfulness can help you notice where you are on your "purpose globe" and remember to allow every moment to bring you closer home.

Life is unfolding for you. Allow each moment to transform you into your fullness.

Consciousness Shifter — Fierce Surrender

You already are the person you want to become. Living into your purpose isn't about changing you. It's not about perfecting or altering yourself or being more disciplined. It's about allowing you.

You soothe yourself into your Truth. You soften into the ease of allowing yourself to be fully, wholly you. From truth, all life expands.

Even your expansion is inevitable, yet still optional. You're not forced to evolve no matter how powerful your soul is. You choose to evolve—not for your future self or the blessings increased consciousness might endow—but to enjoy your life now. The present moment is enough. You are enough. Recognizing this choice sets you free. It's what unhooks you from the patterns of striving to succeed within the game of life and allows you to take in the journey and enjoy the ride.

> *Fierceness is a commitment to your soul—to bring love to everything you do and to be love at the core of who you are.*

Dark Fuel Alchemy® invites you to master the skill of being you. It gives you a roadmap to surrender into your potential while simultaneously embodying your sovereignty. It is how you find yourself to lose yourself. This journey requires fierce conviction.

Being fierce does not mean being aggressive. Fierceness is a commitment to your soul—to bring love to everything you do and to be love at the core of who you are. Fierceness is what moves you forward and evolves your spirit. It is required to truly live your calling.

Fiercely stand in your truth. Fiercely call yourself into your power. It is the only way.

A Glimpse into The Future

Dark Fuel Alchemy® is the fastest and most effective path to awakening available today. The process provides you with the structure you need to start living into your purpose and embracing your wholeness so that you can contribute freely to our collective liberation. It helps you reconcile your soul's immense power with your personal desires and dreams so that you can move forward as a unified whole in body, mind, and soul.

Yet, this too is must fall away.

All structure eventually dismantles itself because the goal is never the structure, but to live in authentic presence.

Dark Fuel Alchemy® is guiding you home to yourself. It's helping you frame the mind so that you can have an authentic soul experience.

That is who you truly are.

Allow yourself to engage with life. Allow this process to build an unshakable knowing in yourself. Allow it to awaken your truth and build your capacity to stay there for longer and longer.

Then, when it's time, allow it to slip away like footprints in the sand disappearing in the tide.

Follow only your inner knowing of what is true, sacred, and alive in this moment.

Chapter 19 Summary

- Living into your purpose is a journey of embodying your power for the goal of communal liberation.
- Your alignment matters. You contribute to our collective song better when you're able to play your instrument and part.
- Mindfulness helps you recognize and navigate Dark Fuel so you can align with your purpose more intentionally.
- Fierce conviction is what moves you forward and evolves your spirit. Fierceness is a commitment to your soul—to bring love to everything you do and to be love at the core of who you are.
- Dark Fuel Alchemy® helps you frame the mind so that you can have an authentic soul experience.
- Ultimately, even Dark Fuel Alchemy® falls away because the goal was never the structure but to live in authentic presence.
- Follow only your inner knowing of what is true, sacred, and alive in this moment.

FULLY YOUR OWN

Life, a storm of movement and change.

Nothing to hold onto.
Nothing to grip as you get pulled into the relentless flow of activity and distraction.

Your purpose appears.
Like a staff carved from a thick branch.

Strong.
Steady.
Receptive yet unyielding.

You drive it deep into the ground.
The storms swirl. You stand rooted.

Clear in your purpose
Fierce in your presence

Powerfully you.

Head first, you brave any storm.
Steady, enduring.

One day, you uncurl your fingers from the staff of your purpose,
It falls to the ground.

You stand rooted.

Clear in your purpose
Fierce in your presence

Powerfully you.

GLOSSARY

Throughout the book, I share several unique terms or known terms with new and possibly unique meanings. The glossary is intended to help you quickly revisit and refresh your understanding.

Consciousness shifter

A tool, practice, or moment of insight that shifts your perspective, helping you move closer to your Truth and embody your purpose. Consciousness shifters are opportunities to grow beyond limiting beliefs and habits.

Coping skills and trauma responses

Behavioral and emotional patterns developed to navigate fear, pain, or hardship. These responses, while initially protective, may become barriers to living authentically when they perpetuate old fears or disempowering beliefs. Transformation involves recognizing and evolving beyond these responses.

Dark Fuel

The fears, struggles, and challenges that, when embraced and transformed, become powerful catalysts for growth and alignment with your Truth. Dark Fuel represents the disempowered ways you think and feel that, when worked with intentionally, propel you into greater purpose and liberation.

Dark Fuel Alchemy®

A transformative process to live into your purpose by recognizing, embracing, and transforming disempowering experiences, beliefs, and emotions into fuel for living your Truth. This method helps you embody your soul's ideal world and navigate life's challenges with resilience and authenticity.

It is a simple, teachable process to master being you, awaken to your potential, experience greater freedom, and shift your consciousness towards lasting peace.

Disempowered hemisphere

The state of being misaligned with your Truth, characterized by fear, stress, or emotional turbulence. This hemisphere signals areas of growth and invites you to reconnect with your Truth through intentional self-awareness and transformation.

Drama tornadoes

Patterns of overthinking, emotional overwhelm, or external distractions that pull you away from your Truth and purpose. Drama Tornadoes often disguise themselves as seemingly urgent and fixable problems. They are the reasons we use to stay stuck in the endless daily tasks of life, thinking that if we could just get that off our plate…, then we'll have time for the big stuff like inner work. They are opportunities to recognize when you're misaligned and return to inner clarity. They subside when you decide to create an intentional relationship with how you move through the world.

Embodied truth

The practice of living in alignment with your soul's Truth in body, mind, and emotions. It is not just a conceptual understanding but a full integration of your Truth into how you show up in the world.

Emotional whiplash

A description of how it feels when your old habits of feeling and thinking come flooding back after feeling so open and free in your soul's world. This is normal and happens to almost everyone to some degree. It can be especially intense after the first time you visit your soul's ideal world. The more you practice tuning into your soul's world, the easier it will be to toggle between it and the heavier feelings of your daily life.

Empowered hemisphere

The state of alignment with your Truth, where you experience calm, clarity, and an expansive sense of possibility. In this hemisphere, you embody your soul's ideal world and move through life with feelings of purpose and ease.

Existential depression

A profound sense of disconnection or questioning that arises when you feel out of alignment with your Truth. It reflects a deep longing for meaning and can act as a gateway to reconnecting with your authentic self and purpose. It's the unnerving feeling when you don't want to die, but you're not sure living matters if you can't be happy and fulfill the potential you feel inside you.

Feeling-i-zation

A made-up word to describe a body-based version of visualizing. As a practice, it aims to calibrate your body and nervous system to your ultimate truth.

Fierce surrender

The commitment to release control and embrace your soul's Truth with conviction and courage. Fierce surrender is not passive but a powerful act of stepping fully into your purpose and authentic presence.

Inner compass

The intuitive guidance within you that aligns you with your purpose and Truth. It helps you navigate life's decisions by pointing towards what feels most authentic and empowering, even in moments of uncertainty. You may call this by many names; I call it soul.

Liberation

The state of freedom that arises when you shed false identities and live in alignment with your soul's Truth.

Neutral zone

The transitional space between releasing old patterns and stepping into a new way of being. This in-between state can feel disorienting but is a vital part of the process of growth and transformation, allowing you to build strength in your Truth.

Purpose

The evolving journey of aligning with your soul's Truth and living authentically. Purpose is not a static goal or destination but a dynamic process of becoming more fully yourself. It serves as a guiding path, rooted in your unique essence, that expands as you grow.

Reset Breaths

A simple way to come back to yourself when your mind feels busy or your energy feels scattered. Reset Breaths gently shift your awareness from thinking to feeling, and from doing to being. To practice, inhale through your nose and exhale through your mouth. Repeat three to five times, letting your body settle as you breathe. These breaths support you in feeling more grounded, spacious, and calm.

Soul's ideal world

Your ultimate truth, the movie of reality running in your head, and how you know life could be for the planet and everything and everyone one it. It is the internal landscape of your deepest truths, where you embody your highest potential and source your purpose. It is the vision of what's possible when people live fully in authenticity and joy, unencumbered by fear or false beliefs.

Truth

The core of who you are on a soul level, beyond roles, expectations, or external validation. Truth is not tied to fleeting emotions or beliefs; it is a state of being deeply aligned with your soul's inherent nature. It emerges as you release false identities and embody your authentic self.

ACKNOWLEDGMENTS

This book is a testament to the ideas it shares. It took ten years from the first outline to what you're reading now. While the heart of Dark Fuel Alchemy® remains unchanged, I had to grow into the person capable of distilling it into words. Many people have helped shape this journey along the way, and I am deeply grateful.

Mike Iamele, my confidant and philosophical sounding board—without your encouragement, insights, and uncanny ability to make my scattered thoughts feel profound and coherent, these pages wouldn't exist. Thank you for helping me sort through myself so I can be in greater service to others.

Linda Lowen, my coach, editor, friend, and role model—your belief in me buoyed me through years of doubt and confusion. Thank you for watering my vision and shining your sun on my dreams. I'm proud to finally be one of your success stories.

The Live Your Truth ladies of 2021-2022—my soul-sisters and cheerleaders. Watching you embrace this process and soar has been my continual inspiration to dig deeper and capture the magic you brought to life.

My clients—many of whom have grown alongside me for years. Thank you for trusting in me, believing in yourselves, and so generously sharing your stories. Your souls' worlds fill my days with beauty and my heart with hope.

The Waggers—Jane, Jess, and Kelley—your feedback on an early draft challenged me to make the work more accessible and more impactful. The book—and I—are better for it.

Swami Santoshananda and Keisha Dixon—thank you for your generous contributions to this book, for being game to try every new practice and meditation, and for always greeting me with a radical yes.

My family—thank you for giving me the space to explore, even when my path didn't always make sense from the outside. I am endlessly grateful for the foundation of love that has allowed me to go as deep as I have, knowing I always have a home to return to.

Sarvesh, my husband—you believed in me when I doubted, encouraged me when I procrastinated, and supported me as I slowly became the woman who could write this book. You are the greatest gift of my life and my daily inspiration to live more fully into my truth. I love you.

Finally, to the relentless pull within me—to go inwards, meditate, and write. You make having a social life difficult, but I will willingly strip it all away to go wildly towards truth.

ABOUT ALEXIS

Alexis is an inner peace activist on a mission to create global peace, one soul at a time. A former award-winning strategist in the U.S. Government, Alexis has advised U.S. Ambassadors, foreign dignitaries, the White House, and members of Congress.

After her first career left her feeling spiritually unfulfilled, Alexis set out to uncover deeper meaning and purpose in life. Now, she combines her background in strategic visioning with over a decade of yoga and meditation teaching to help others live authentically with joy and purpose.

Her first book, *Everyday Joy: Stop living for the weekend and start loving your everyday life*, is a 90-day journal to kick-start your life.

Alexis holds degrees from the University of Chicago and Georgetown University and received a Certificate from the Yale Executive Education Program in Business Strategy and Planning. She currently lives in Dallas, Texas, with her husband and two rescue dogs. Discover more of her books, meditations, and courses at www.alexispierce.com

www.ingramcontent.com/pod-product-compliance
Lightning Source LLC
Chambersburg PA
CBHW060550080526
44585CB00013B/507